IN THE WHEEL
OF LIFE

VOLUME III

CENTRUM Publishers

In the Wheel of Life

of Life

Volume III

Wanda Pratnicka

Translation: **Monika Piątek, Marlena Romanczuk**
Copy-Editing: **Kirsten Volkert**
Cover: **Łukasz Rutkowski**

Printed in Poland on acid-free paper

Library of Congress Cataloging-in-Publication Data is available

CENTRUM Publishers
P.O. Box 257
81-963 Gdynia / Poland
Phone: + 48 58 522 9497
Fax: +48 58 550 6812
E-mail: office@WydawnictwoCentrum.pl
Web: www.WydawnictwoCentrum.pl

ISBN 10: 83-60280-89-4
ISBN 13: 978-83-60280-89-8

CONTENTS

INTRODUCTION

Many people are not conscious of Truth. They think their present life is the only one they have. Since they are convinced that they live only once I also approached the subject of the soul as if this was a fact.

This is why I assumed in the first volume that a soul finds itself in the world only one time. I dissembled the question of reincarnation, since each incarnation proceeds in a similar way during every descent to earth. A soul appears on Earth whenever it wants to, regardless of whether it is its first time. It could stay in Heaven where only Love and Perfection reign, but it feels a desire to experience life, which it will do for any price. It could be that a soul doesn't realize that it can't experience the desire it feels from the place in which it resides. The reason for this is that the desire has a completely different vibration than the vibration it dwelled in until that time. There is no higher vibration than the vibration of Love and Perfection; all other desires, are of a lower vibration level. This is why a new desire pulls a soul, throws it out, or moves from a place of vibration of Love and Perfection to a place of a vibration corresponding with this desire. It is nothing but a desire that pulls a soul to Earth.

In order to live in the new, different world, a soul must adapt to it properly. As a diver going deep into water must wear a proper outfit, a soul must wear proper bodies.

The whole process works independently. Whenever a soul thinks about its desire, its subtle bodies start to form. First its the mental body, then the astral body (also known as the emotional), and then the etheric and physical. In that form, completely dressed, a soul enters the physical plane.

It is not a punishment, as religions teach us. The reason is a desire to experience something else. This desire comes from lower vibrations and this is why a soul moves from one reality to another.

It is not a pleasant experience. The sensations of a soul thrown into the world that already exists can be compared to the sensations of someone thrown into a deep, cold abyss. The soul is shocked just like the person thrown into the water. The shock continues till the moment it adapts to its new conditions.

A soul is fully conscious of God and of *Who It is in Essence* in Paradise. It knows that there is no way it could be separated from Him. It is non-viable. God is All-present and He is all in all, which means that a human soul cannot be separated from Him. It is completely impossible.

Nevertheless, most souls presently residing on Earth forgot about Him completely and feel separated from Him. In most cases, it is caused by the fact that we begin our existence in conditions that are already organized somehow. And although we remember where we came from at the beginning of our lives, this memory of the Divine life quickly escapes our minds. We don't see other ways of existing while we're children so we begin to live the way others tell us to.

A reader of the first volume of „In the Wheel of Life" understands things from the perspective of a single incarnation and doesn't have the answers to the following questions: How could God, being pure Love, put us people in such extreme conditions? Why do so many people fear Him and believe him to be threatening, vindictive, and unjust?

In order to explain these big questions of apparent injustice, I've approached the soul differently in the second volume. I described human life on earth, but from the perspective of many incarnations. I guided you, dear reader, from a single life here on Earth and through death and the entire existence following it into the next physical incarnation.

I think that it made you realize that something like death or non-being doesn't exist. What we commonly call death is not the end of life but only a passing from one state to another. We are immortal and we live eternally, and this knowledge completely changes our perception of Life.

You can finally let go because of this knowledge. You now know that life is nothing but an endless process of learning; you go through numerous experiences and learn from your mistakes. They give you deep, true knowledge that comes from practice. You wouldn't learn much by observing other people's experiences. Observation itself, without experience, wouldn't imprint itself permanently on your subconscious. It would give you only a shallow, superficial image of Life and not deep, solid knowledge. The key to learning is experience. Only experience eternally imprinted in the subconscious enables us to use what we learned in practice.

Additionally, you must go through all experiences in order to learn all knowledge and not just fragments. This is why your soul learns some lessons for such a long time. The art of growing is about learning and overcoming invalid aspects of ourselves. A soul learns until it perfectly masters a subject and then it chooses something else to learn from the beginning.

When we become masters of something, we still come back to Earth in order to use this domain in a different way. We don't moil in the wrong aspects that we've already learned. For example, we live in a family of alcoholics yet we don't submit to the disease ourselves. This is why two children brought up in the same environment can have totally different experiences. One must learn to control addiction while the other one has already worked this lesson through and it is easy for him to abstain. The other one must also learn to control what is negative, though, in order to live in this world and not to become moiled or corrupted.

From the perspective of a single incarnation, life can seem unjust, but this injustice disperses like a fog from the perspective of many incarnations. You cannot condemn anyone for what you did yourself once or will do in future. I hope that by learning the truth, you will change your opinion on the „negative" behavior of other people. It can save you a lot of stress, time, and energy. If you don't understand it and use it daily, you will attract what you condemn as your own experiences.

I deeply hope that you won't blame God or bad luck for your difficult or unsuccessful life and that you understand that everything that happens to you is your choice. Although this knowledge encumbers you with responsibility for everything you do, think, and feel, it gives you the tools to change yourself. This will bring fruits in the form of a better life. If you take responsibility for your life, you can escape the confines of an oppressive reality. If it doesn't happen in this incarnation, it will happen in the next.

In the third volume, I would like to show you Life from a different perspective. In order for you to understand in-depth what I mean, I will show you the lives of people that remember *Who They Are In Essence*. On this ground you will recognize a huge difference between the life of a person that remembers *Who They Are In Essence* and someone who does not.

Dear reader, know that nothing can change your experience as dramatically as remembering *Who You Are In Essence*. You will understand why societies of civilizations lost long ago lived on higher levels of consciousness than we do now. You will understand why humanity, in spite of its huge technological progress, has fallen into a valley of darkness and ignorance so deep that it has brought this once wonderful planet to the edge of destruction. The planet can still be saved but it needs an enormous devotion and readiness on the part of each man living on it.

What I discuss below is nothing else but lessons in the School of Earth. These are distant times and scientists are unable to deal with them. You have experienced everything I write about, though. You don't remember it consciously but it is all stored in the eternal bank of your memory since whatever you experienced is never forgotten. This truth is written down in the depth of your Being. When you are ready to confront it, you will see it so you can fully understand its message.

And so, deep inside you know everything that I discuss here; it just slipped your conscious mind. The more you remember about *Who You Are in Essence*, the more you gain from this knowledge. You don't need to search for it because it is stored within you, deep in your heart. When you reach it you will remember the beauty and wisdom of your own soul and when you submit to your Higher Self, it will guide you further.

Understanding what I want to tell you is difficult because

words or concepts that I can use are of this world, the world of perception limited by delusion, time, and space. I don't want you to automatically accept everything I write below as truth, but I want you to organize a system that will help you distinguish what is Truth and what is not.

Dear reader, I want you to know that there is no use in meaninglessly considering things if you don't reach deep within you, to the place where this Truth dwells. You cannot get to know It intellectually, through reasoning. One must contemplate it as long as it needs to get to know it from the inside. This is when you experience enlightenment, illumination, deep understanding, insight, or whatever it can be called. You will experience a condition you won't be able to put into words since there is no word describing what you will feel deep inside.

You may compare it to an experience of: „Aha! Now I understand" when you fall into deep pensiveness for a long time. If someone asked you what you had experienced, you wouldn't be able to put it into words. You inherited a deep understanding and there is no way that you could describe it to another man. Words are just symbols, symbols of symbols even. They are so different from the reality you presently experience that you cannot use any of them. None are adequate enough.

Reaching this far and distant past, I wanted to find the first civilization that gave birth to all others. I didn't want to reconstruct history by any means nor put everything in chronological order. I just wanted to show how a civilization that was permanently connected to God, its Source, functioned, and achieved.

While trying to reach this first civilization I discovered that each of the previous civilizations was formed in exactly the same way and functioned on the same Pure Spiritual principles. Its inhabitants could differ in terms of their looks, skin color, hair, eyes, and height, but their spiritual attitude was the same at the beginning. There is no sense in wondering if it was „this" civilization or some „other." There were so many of them in the span of centuries that the version presented by me could well be a mixture of them all.

All the great civilizations on Earth were founded by a Great, Cosmic, and Transcendental Being. Dear reader, these Beings are so beyond our present understanding that it is impossible to put into words the Power, Majesty of Love, Wisdom, and Powers of the Great Ones.

Every so often, God sends these Great Transcendental Beings to Earth not to teach people the Spiritual Life Laws but to serve as a reminder. If they remember them, they won't forget *Who They Are in Essence* either.

Before humanity obeyed these Truths, there was a time of great progress and prosperity. It encompassed the entire population and not just individuals.

If you had an opportunity to look into one of those great civilizations, you would be surprised to see that there were great changes in every one of them. It would be difficult to believe that it was the same civilization if you compared its beginning, middle, and end. Everything became worse over time.

It is interesting that each of these civilizations developed in the same way. It first resided at a very high spiritual level and gradually descended to the very bottom. It would break down then, become lost in one way or another, and leave no material trace behind. Sometimes, in quite rare cases, it would leave something of value for following generations.

I hope that you come to constructive conclusions while reading this text and you will want to change your life. Otherwise, you will let yourself fall like you have in the past. It is much easier to follow someone's steps than to make a path of your own. It is the same with mistakes. You cannot learn from someone else's mistakes but you can try to avoid them.

While reading the text below, dear reader, you will have an opportunity to glide with your imagination into those distant times and experience what you read about once more, first hand. Who knows? Maybe you'll be able to remember your prior lives quite clearly.

You were incarnated so many times before that you learned how to live well. I will let you wonder about what you did with your life. I am just passing on the information. You must decide for yourself what you will do with this knowledge and how you will use it in your present life.

I hope that when you remind yourself how you lived then and what you did with your life, you will understand where you make the same mistakes in your present understanding of life. Obviously, you can do nothing while reading this text and think that it is all nonsense. The choice is yours, as usual.

Be aware of the fact that there are still people in your present environment who will scoff at what I am writing here and laugh at it. They may just deny my words. Don't worry about it because they will receive a spiritual lesson in the future. A punishment for doubting, and it is a natural consequence of doubt, is never sent by God but the doubtful human mind. The greatest enemy of our times is doubt because it doesn't let us ascend higher.

If you decide to glide along with me into those distant times, you may not realize what you read about at first. This knowledge will be stored somewhere in your subconscious. While absorbed, it will penetrate your consciousness in time and you will eventually remember the Truth. You will understand how you could start to express your life. You will realize where the mistake is, where the difficulties you experience come from, and why you constantly stumble over the same „stones." You will come to understanding why you are sad, miserable, and unable to fulfill your dreams.

You can find this knowledge in the Akashic Records if you are able to get to It. Only a few have access to this knowledge and they receive it directly from Great Wonderful Teachers that we commonly call Masters.

Not all of my readers might have heard of the Masters. I explain to them that these are Transcendental Beings so far beyond our present understanding that it is not possible to put the Majesty of Love, Wisdom, and Powers of The Great Ones into words. They were people once, like us, but they rose above human limitations through their own effort and understanding. It is Them, since time immemorial, who carry the Light of Wisdom and spiritual knowledge to all those who crave it. They teach us that the main purpose of life is to worship God and properly use the Divine spark that each man carries deep within his heart.

MOTHER EARTH

Dear reader, before I start describing the ancient civilization, I would like to share lost knowledge about the planet you live on. You will understand while reading how coherent it is and how much we all need it. The future of our lives on Earth together depends on our knowledge or ignorance. People are slowly destroying themselves and the planet because of their ignorance.

It would probably be different if everybody realized that our World, our Earth, is not a dead solid made of rocks, soil, and water but a living organism! Yes, you didn't mishear me. Our planet is a living, feeling, and continuously growing being. Just like a human organism consists of an infinite number of intelligent, independent cells, the Earth's organism is made of the beating hearts of humanity. Each creature is like a cell of its body.

The Earth is a wonderful, unique Being that consists of

every single life inhabiting It, even the smallest one. Its value is life that is on It.

A man has his physical body and subtle bodies, as I mentioned in the two previous volumes. It is similar with Earth. Besides the tangible, physical external world you see around, the Earth has its own intangible, subtle, internal range. It consists of thoughts, feelings, and powers, similar to a human's. If you looked into it you would see the world of light, life, and beauty that, though invisible, has an enormous power. An external world, both human and earthly, is a mirror reflection of an inner world.

Both the Earth and every being inhabiting it has a particular vibration. Each vibration spreads over the entire Earth and makes a fragment of all other organisms. In this way, dear reader, you touch every being on this planet, even those you don't contact physically.

Your ideas, perceptions, attitudes, fears, hopes, and future are influenced by the vibrations manifesting and disappearing.

As a man, the Earth also has a soul. Each soul influences all other souls, including the Earth's soul, through vibrations created every day. The Earth' spirituality affects people and the Earth itself is affected by spirituality and the integral vision of all souls that inhabit it.

You may think, like most people do, that you are an independent, autonomous individual and that you are different from your neighbor, a totally free being on a Great Plan of Existence. If you think so, you don't realize how wrong you are. You don't know that it is impossible to remove a single body from this Great Plan of Existence for It to manifest further. Each living individual is necessary to Its fulfilment.

This is why, when the body of a being dies, its living vibration fades and this loss affects every organism living on Earth. If you know a soul that incarnates, its vibration will affect you increasingly, and when it leaves its physicality, it will fade together with the strength of a being that comes or goes. If you knew a particular soul in its past incarnation but you don't know it in present incarnation, its vibrations reach you anyway.

Just like every soul participates in its own growing process, the Earth does the same. And as positive, pure, bright, and caring thoughts and actions keep you close to your soul, it is the same concerning the Earth. You, just like all other souls on Earth, are equally responsible for the Earth's future as for your own future. What saves you from destruction will save the Earth, too. If every man inhabiting the Earth realized that Mother Earth lived the same way that he did, he wouldn't act as idly as he has until now.

The Earth lives in an amazing way but the average man is aware of its physical level only. The Earth, however, consciously exists on a great number of subtle levels at the same time.

It is similar with a man. What is most powerful within him is also invisible to the physical eye. It constitutes his spiritual power, manifesting in the process of thinking. Many people don't realize what I am writing about because they don't live in the Mind's Unity with God. Accomplishing this unity is necessary to collect all the truths that are necessary to life. First of all, one knows beyond all doubt that all that Is, is United. The same divine laws govern what is visible to the physical eye and what a human eye is not able to see.

The entire Earth is alive and so is the entire Universe. Cosmic space is a seat of innumerable life forms. People don't even suspect the existence of most of them and this is because their definition of life is extremely shallow.

Besides, the predominant majority of people are not able to perceive energy in vibration zones of higher frequencies. They cannot see the majesty and power of the Universe and they don't see the spheres that could be helpful to them. Only a handful of conscious people and a few clairvoyants truly understand what I am talking about. Every day, the number of people who can see, feel, and know about it increases. The day will come when these states become accessible to all of humanity again.

It is not new knowledge to you. You were made the Earth's guardian long ago. It was the task you were sent here to fulfill. You came as the one who guarded the Earth and cared for It while existing as the fruit of God's love, joy, and beauty. In return for this, your planet generously endowed you with much good. Don't waste what you were so proud of once.

You may not realize it but you have this knowledge and an unlimited ability to understand yourself and the Earth which you call your home deep inside you. What's more is that you also have the knowledge of invisible or imperceptible dimensions that are only a thought apart from you. Can't you access this knowledge? Well, first you would have to accept your own ignorance since this is the reason for your numerous mistakes and slipups along your journey through Earth and space.

Therefore, you should be willing to admit, in front of yourself, of course, that you are a limited creature at the moment and demand from your Higher Self that higher forms of this almost imperceptible life become revealed to you. It is necessary to stop you and others from destroying the Earth and life inhabiting cosmic space as a result of unfortunate ignorance and blindness.

For the time being, observe how natural forces operate. Everything is solid and stable in the mineral kingdom. In the kingdoms of animals and plants, everything is fluid and submits to continuous changes in the process of creating and recreating. The atmosphere has heat, light, and energy. As you pass from visible to invisible, from rawness to perfection, from low potential to high, you will see that each successive zone or domain is more and more perfect and spiritual. While reaching the invisible domain, you will discover energy in its purest, most volatile state.

You will recognize with surprise that everything on Earth is made of the same primal, universal substance that gives birth to everything. You can call this omnipresent, omniscient, all-penetrating substance God, Highest Intelligence, or whatever you wish, but It remains the same thinking Energy, thinking Substance, the same thinking Power. This is what gave birth to the entire expansive Universe. Everything that exists came from its Powerful Essence.

It is a thought that is a creating force. Human thought is a spiritual power of God's Mind that operates through His work. Things you see around you, although made with human hand, must have appeared earlier in the form of thoughts in God's Mind. It is similar with a man.

It is from God's substance that new forms are being created. As something new shows up, the older or useless forms break apart with time—they decay and disappear in order for the new things to be created. Although it seems that they differ so much, each is shaped from one and the same substance.

Creation is continuous. The resources of this universal, primal matter are unlimited, just like God. The elements constructing the visible structure of nature reside in atmosphere, waiting for them to become organized into a form. The atmosphere is a condensed and tangible form of a primal substance of God's Spirit.

All existence comes from this one, living, and intelligent

substance, the One Mind. The first is always what we call spiritual and it is only then that a transformation follows into what we call physical.

Dear reader, you are a tiny particle of the Universe. Everything is a part of this astonishing whole; your body is nature and your soul is God. Each living being is held by His Almighty Intelligence. This is why your consciousness must understand and experience Enlightenment through what your tiny intellect owes to a Great Life of the Universe.

Do you realize that the Earth is a unique planet enabling people to experience perfect love and wisdom? Here, every man can get to know God through experience and grow in the same way while striving higher and higher in his constant pursuit to increase his power and acquire wisdom.

Your life on the Earth has existed since the moment It was created. Geologists talk of billions of years although they have only an approximate idea of Its age. You, as a spiritual being, have lived always. Always. You are light and energy before anything else, and not a physical body, because God is light and energy.

At spiritual level, your identity is a large, concentrated energy mass. At this level, you are always young and eternal. You cannot be described in any way since you were made together with dawn and you have existed as long as the world has existed. And presently? You crossed the bridge from the unlimited zone to your own body just for a moment.

You live on the Earth because it is the only place offering such a wonderful opportunity. You can present your perfection by using reasoning and thoughts. Life challenges you in many ways so you can learn and grow through it. The challenges that you overcome are not punishment but lessons. They serve you to realize that your mind is a creator, architect, and constructor of absolutely everything that exists in the physical world.

You come to the Earth just to learn. The Earth's evolution is a part of your cognitive process and you are a part of a cognitive process of the Earth. Each man must learn the same lessons. Everybody else helps in your individual spiritual growth and you help in the spiritual growth of other people. All of humanity makes one big family.

Not only humanity is engaged in your learning process. Great Hosts of Beings of Light also participate in it actively. It is Them that advise people and help them through Their own emanations. In this way, the Beings of Light help particular people spread Their own Light so that Wisdom and Power can become the driving force for all of humanity, not just those who have already acquired Light or true Mastery. There is nothing unusual or extraordinary in doing so because in all the activity that Light comes from, those who are less advanced in growth are taught by those who are more advanced.

As you can see, dear reader, in the School of Life (which I wrote about in the second volume), everything happens like in an ordinary earthly school. A teacher teaches his pupils so they can become teachers themselves in the future and teach others, and so on.

Even Those we know and reckon to be Masters have Those that are far more advanced in growth than Themselves and who are Their Great Teachers, Instructors, or whatever you would like to call this Great Activity of Teaching. And those who are even Greater in our opinion have Others that are still Wiser. This expands through infinity to God Himself.

Beings of Light only help the inhabitants of Earth that haven't developed the gift of Hearty Loving or the ability to admire and eagerly follow Him in the material form. People need examples of love, its ideal model, in order to grow according to it. Many have engaged in the mission of teaching love and wisdom so the one who knows less could learn from the one who knows more.

As you can see, dear reader, the level of your soul's growth doesn't really matter because everyone has the opportunity to master themselves. I am writing about it because it is important for you to know and understand it so that you can use such Help when you get it. Don't waste your time searching the Master, however. He will come to you when you are ready to become a pupil. In any other case you will try in vain.

When you come to the Earth, you choose to learn things the same way you choose your favorite course of studies. Although your soul chooses the subject (fulfilling its desire), the time and length of its stay on Earth depends on your progress in the School of Life.

You are an individual part of the Universal Mind. All people are equal and no man is bigger or smaller than the other. Your so-called individuality is just the way you create your relationship to the whole. You exist in relation to the whole and other people. It is this relation that creates your environment and not the other way round.

Every difference you see between people comes from the level of consciousness that they manifest in their life. You cannot see equality among people only because single men don't want to be equally self-conscious.

Most people don't know *Who They Are in Essence*. Although they ultimately pursue the same goal, the level of their engagement differs. This is where differences in virtue, inclination, wealth, rights, faculties, talents, intelligence and so on come from.

I will put it in other words. If you feel the greatness of

God inside you, you easily connect to His wondrous Source and appreciate It. This makes you automatically reject the fear, anger, pain, pride, and greed that dominate on Earth. If you don't feel the greatness of God, you don't benefit from His Source and you unwittingly sink into all the negative states that abound in the atmosphere.

When you have an access to Light, you are conscious of Truth. When you lack Light, your consciousness is very limited. Do you now understand how people can be so different? Why do some people prosper despite inaction while others work their fingers to the bone and have nothing to show for it? Everything is a matter of consciousness.

If your consciousness is limited, you live without realizing it. This is why you so easily fall into negative emotions and cannot break free from them. You cannot understand that negativity is generated consciously and strengthened by bad leaders, politicians, clergymen, and especially the media.

The people that program you to be afraid instead of pursuing good things, promote violence, and fill your subconscious with terrible visions are the people that cause you to forget *Who You Are In Essence* and Who has created your life force.

You can now see, dear reader, that all the problems of the physical world are nothing more than the workings of the external mind. It happens because most people live in a state of absolute unconsciousness and ignorance. It is only when a man lets himself be unconscious that he submits to the laws established by humanity and the external self.

These laws make people use each other and torment each other. Individuals try to manipulate others to meet their needs. This happens because external, human laws operate instead of God's laws. Everything that is of God is simple, clear, and legible, while what is human is extremely complicated.

Try to avoid negative influence at all costs, especially those coming from television, radio, games, and literature, because they continuously work and weaken your innately loving character. It is because of this influence that these quickly spreading and demoralizing thoughts cling to the Earth like black mold or a spider web. When you give up and submit to pressing negativity, you will have to experience it yourself. It will be extremely difficult for you to break through and return to the Light.

No matter what you're going through, immediately give yourself over to your Divine Self, your inner teacher, the Guide, the One Who Knows, the Holy Spirit. This will decide whether what you hear is true or false.

Your Spiritual Understanding and Intuition cause you to remain in the Light. When your heart and mind are open to a living God, you can influence the course of events in your life and protect both yourself and your loved ones from negativity.

When you lack the connection with your Inner Being, your Divine Self, don't be surprised that you cannot see life inside the Earth or cosmic space. It does exist there, however. You cannot see it since it resides in another dimension. In other words, it functions on different frequencies than the ones you exist with currently. You don't see that because long ago (for the reasons I will describe below) you closed yourself off to this knowledge. This is why you can see only the external Earth body.

This is also why your external senses suggest to you that the Earth is just a flat mass of rocks covered with soil. The Earth is actually a living being. You would still think that way and perceive it the same. However, you learned at school that it was not flat and that it didn't stay in one place as your senses suggested, but that it runs through space (with a velocity of over a hundred of thousands kilometers per hour!) while revolving around the Sun.

Nothing is more certain to your limited external senses than the journey of the Sun through the sky. You can watch it and your eyes tell you it's true. Every morning you see the Sun rising and setting in the evening. It doesn't matter whether it disappears somewhere behind houses, woods, hills, or the sea. You know that a complete darkness follows.

And although your senses deny this knowledge, you are forced to believe that the Sun never rises nor sets, it always shines. Discover that yourself. When you take a fast airplane and follow the Sun to the west, you will be surprised at how long the day lasts.

You are forced to believe that there are various phenomena in the world, although your senses tell you otherwise. The fact that you don't feel a thing doesn't mean though that this thing doesn't exist. Accept the fact that appearances can be deceiving. The Earth is not a dead matter, flat and motionless. The sky is not a dome and the Sun doesn't move. The stars are not tiny dots of light but matter that we once believed to be matter that was solid and can submit to constant changes. And not only matter. Even what you call light is an ever-changing energy form. Light, just like everything else, is only an impression received by your mind that creates it on the basis of the movement of some waves. When the number of waves increases, the light changes its color, and each change of color is caused by vibrations of various lengths and durations.

When you say that a flower is yellow, grass is green, and the sky is blue, know that these colors exist in your mind only; they are *impressions* formed because you perceive the vibrations of light waves. And so, grass is green not because its vibration is green. Grass absorbs all other vibrations except for green and our senses get the impression of it being green.

You understand now, dear reader that you cannot rely on your external senses while evaluating reality. You cannot logically understand what you experience. Understand that your logical mind has its own place, function, and purpose that it doesn't determine your identity.

If you persist in believing that your senses are authority, you don't have a choice but to think that it is the Sun that is moving, the world is flat, and stars are tiny light dots and not large suns.

There are more and more people that can see and feel that the Earth lives and feels just like every other living being. Planets are alive just like we are. We as tiny creatures and they as huge ones are made of the same Substance. Everything is created from the Light and Wisdom of God.

Close your eyes and open your heart and you will feel them. The Earth hides the layers of physical, spiritual, intellectual, and emotional energy within It. The layer of feelings, though invisible for many people, is visible to some and lays just below its shell.

Both you and the Earth, dear reader, have the same energetic fields. I wrote about this in the first volume. The Earth, just like all the delicate and fossilized life forms living on it, is made of life-giving energy.

If every living person wanted to benefit from those continuously bating energy streams in order to strengthen God's essence within, our Earth would naturally change into a Heavenly Kingdom, the same it had been in the very beginning.

In the Kingdom of God there is no hunger or suffering caused by evil. God is never absent. In His Kingdom, strange benefits, benefactors, and non-profit organizations are unnecessary because everything exists in a state of eternal abundance.

This is the true sense of the prayer: „Your Kingdom Come, Thy will be done." Although you don't fully realize these words, you know deep inside what they mean. If you need benefactors it means only that you don't dwell in God's Kingdom and you don't realize His Presence.

The Earth is not an inanimate chunk of matter, it is a wondrous and unique Being. Each man and creature is like a single cell of Its body. It constantly grows and learns just like every other creature in the Universe. This is why the way you treat It and care for it affects the Earth's attitude towards you.

Do you realize that the Earth once shined with etheric light of such an unusual beauty that it was regarded as the jewel of this part of the Universe? It is hard to believe it now but it was so, which you will learn about in the following part of this book.

A question arises: what happened to this once wondrous Earth? The answer is quite simple. People ceased to love themselves, each other, and Earth and they started to perceive it as a cold, unfeeling chunk of matter. Since then they've begun to saturate it with so much panic, violence, and indifference, that it finally transformed to a thick, dark, muzzy ocean of ugliness.

And the Earth perfectly reflects only what It gets from the people it nurses on its body as the most loving mother. Do you feel bad there? Think about the ways in which you don't care for yourself and the Earth as your home. Think about how you treat yourself and other people. How do you care for plants and animals? Do you respect the world of minerals? They serve the Earth, strengthening its physical structure. How do you satisfy your own and Mother Earth's mental, emotional, and spiritual needs? When you listen to yourself deep within, you will know why you feel bad on the Earth and don't see the purpose of your life.

The world you live in reflects your thoughts, that's all. Do you feel out of balance here? It is no surprise if this is the state of your mind and your feelings connected to it. Someone else, living close to you, can feel totally different.

Are you satisfied with what you see? Everything is all right with your life if you are. If you aren't, maybe you should behave with more love, respect, and understanding towards Mother Earth and every living creature on its surface.

It concerns the world of minerals, plants, animals, people, yourself, and all higher vital life forces inhabiting space and all visible and invisible energies the Universe teems with. I mean all life, substance, and intelligence because the Universe is All-love and it bonds all in one system, one whole. The Universe is a single individual, too. Just like the human body contains an innumerable quantity of single, independent, intelligent cells, it is the same with the Universe. A man is a microcosm while the Universe is the macrocosm. Our Universe, however, is only a part of a bigger Universe, which is a part of another one, and God is the whole.

Your consciousness must understand and become enlightened so that it becomes clear to it what it owes the Bigger Life of the Universe and to Life constantly bestowing you with its Blessings.

As you will discover in a moment, you once knew how to live in love and how to give love back or to spread it to all life.

You first gave your love to God, your Creator. Then you loved yourself, your wonderful soul and the beautiful light it created long ago. If you loved truly like you had loved before, you would still draw strength from the higher Spirit, your own Divine Self, and you would simply love all that Is.

You loved not only Mother Earth but all forms of life

placed on It, both visible and invisible to the physical eyes. You got Its great love in return. You felt how the Earth cradled you in Its arms with the biggest motherly love and care and how it cuddled you to sleep at night.

The loved other planets and stars, your brothers and sisters in Heaven, inhabiting numerous planes of God's creation, in the same way. You understood that these Great Beings enable you to grow. You realized how many of Them guarded the Earth and cared for people. Although you may not understand it and appreciate it today, you were fully aware of it then. Just like you feed your pets and water your plants, those Great ones feed all people and care for them. Don't you believe it? Think: is it you that creates rain or dew and cares for all animals, plants, and minerals? No, it God acting through Them.

And so, when you look up to clear evening sky, notice that every pulsing spot is an improbably large number of various life forms and that there is an innumerable quantity of such spots in the Universe. Accept (like you did before) that the Milky Way is a home to many wonderful beings, forces, energies, and vibrations that dwell here and that deeply affect our planet spiritually.

Your life totally depends on what is bigger than you. Without This Bigger Life you wouldn't exist for even a moment. Its service is sending Light and Blessings over our physical conditions. Not only you but every particle of Life has a great debt to pay to the Universe, Greater Life, Nature Forces, and Element's Forces.

The Earth is your home for the duration of your stay. We are all tightly connected to each other. Shouldn't you, having this new knowledge, ask yourself why so many people harm each other? Why do they destroy the Earth and others and take advantage of them? Why are they so heartless and short-sighted?

Well, it is because they cannot love anymore and they don't have access to those wonderful energies.

If you are one of those people who unthinkingly destroy the planet in order to take advantage of it, think about how your life will look when you incarnate here next time. Won't you become one of those children that struggle to survive?

We now allow cutting forests, but what shall we breathe with in future if we destroy all sources of oxygen production? What shall we eat if we now poison or modify our food and water? Shall we be able to live in the open, empty, destroyed space, which it will certainly turn into if we continue like this?

We act so idly because we want to earn money and we fear for the well-being of future generations. But it will be us, not anybody else that will be living in these terrible conditions. We expose ourselves and our loved ones to disaster through our carelessness, idleness, and neglect.

People behave the way they do because they don't realize that they are going to live on this planet many times. Know, however, that you and your loved ones won't have the possibility to escape the conditions you create with your present deeds.

You may say to yourself: „I am not as bad as others. I work, pay taxes, give money to the church, and do good. I am not responsible for what is happening on the Earth nor for the government of the country I live in." You are deceiving yourself, however. Where does all evil around you come from? The world surrounding you is your mirror, and all your feelings, thoughts, emotions, and acts are reflected in it.

It is not just your actions that harm yourself and others. You are killed all the time by what you neglect, what you don't see and correct. As Albert Einstein said: „The world is a dangerous place not because of people that do bad things but because of those who look at it and do nothing".

Dear reader, understand this and see how you are responsible. It all depends on your state of mind because you react to reality according to what you feel and how you perceive it, and this is how it is going to manifest for you in the future.

And so, don't try to defend yourself by saying that you're not the only one who hurts the Earth and that almost everybody does this. It's true but you don't have any choice but to change yourself first, hoping that others will follow. Such change doesn't have to be noticeable at once and it doesn't have to show on a physical plane but it is going to be a catalyst for changes on the spiritual plane. What is spiritual happens first and what is physical follows.

Don't try to calm your conscience by persuading yourself that humanity has been tormenting the Earth for such a long time and that It can bear it anyway and survive. The question of sustainability arises. As you will see in a moment, humanity has destroyed itself and the Earth many times before because people weren't able to predict the outcome.

The Earth is a living being and it can become irritated just like you can. It can wish to get rid of all the people that irritate It in exactly the same way that an animal shake away fleas.

This is why the Earth quakes, volcanoes erupt, tornadoes or hurricanes break, clouds burst, and floods or other cataclysms strike. This is how the Earth removes violence and negative feelings from its surface. This is the Earth's makeshift defense mechanism against harmful human activity but it is capable of much worse if it is provoked.

The Earth has been destroyed more than once and it happened every time because it didn't have a vision of a better future. It had to be destroyed in order to be able to reconstruct itself. It is similar with yourself. In order to keep your attention away from negative things, you must occasionally get shocked.

Otherwise you would completely lose yourself. Every accident, failure, and disease is an attempt to wake you up and communicate to you that something went wrong—you went astray and didn't follow the right goal.

YOUR INFLUENCE ON THE EARTH

First of all, you let yourself to have negative emotions. The reason for this is your logical mind. If you use it too often, you overestimate and overexploit it. You don't pay attention to reality but rather only to what your senses tell you. This evokes an enormous stress that affects your whole body. You submit to the judgment of your senses because you cannot see the whole. You just see one material side of existence, though it constitutes a tiny part of the enormous whole that One is.

A conflict occurs then. Your senses tell you something and Reality tells you something else. When Reality differs from what you feel with your external senses, negative emotions arise within you. You express them by attacking, judging, criticizing, and condemning others.

However, know that what you express never fades. It grows, becomes stronger, and returns to you. This is the Law of a Circle. When something returns to you, it bounces off you by the principle of ricochet, with doubled force and virulence.

In order to prevent catastrophe and the explosion of such a „time bomb," Mother Nature helps us people by defusing it through small failures, accidents, and collisions.

These negative emotions usually concern the population of people, not individuals. They unite then and grow in strength. When they concern a great number of people, an accumulation of negativity forms and a catastrophe follows.

Balance is necessary in the world. This is why, after crossing a threshold of dark negative force, whirlpools start to form. They form because good and bad as two opposite states naturally push each other away. When it starts to boil with an excess of negativity, an explosion follows.

Nature bursts with all the excess of negativity and various cataclysms follow. Violent storms, tempests, powerful hurricanes, floods, volcano eruptions, and earthquakes are nothing but nature's answer to our behavior and negative emotions connected to it.

These conditions can concern only a part of humanity and show in only some regions. We then deal with destruction on a micro scale. When a problem concerns more people and they are spread over the world, waves of energy are formed. Collecting everything in their path, they grow and affect everyone with increasing force. For example, a powerful volcanic eruption affects people around the world and can change the climate for years thereafter. When you experience the effects of such a disharmony, it is difficult for you to recognize your own work. You often get angry, protest, and defend yourself by saying: „This is unfair. What have I done to deserve such a punishment? I have been a good man all my life and the world is so cruel to me. God is blind and lets all of this happen."

Know, however, that your understanding of events, people, and difficulties, and especially this painful experience, is contorted. You say this because you don't realize that you live in delusion and that you're blinded. If you knew the Great Universal Laws, you wouldn't blame God; you would take responsibility for this. You would know that those Great Laws operate similarly to the laws of physics, chemistry, or mathematics. They are, in a sense, ruthless to those who don't know these principles, but friendly and helpful to those who understand the way they operate.

It you lived according to these Laws and applied them to your life, nothing wrong would ever happen to you. Each Law is established for both your own good as an individual and the good of the whole World.

Dear reader, understand that everything must be in God's Ideal Order in order to maintain Harmony. Otherwise, the entire universe would break apart or there would be many collisions of celestial bodies. Everything works like the proverbial Swiss watch.

The Great Plan of All Existence is Perfect. It is infinitely more reasonable, attentive, and keen than human eyes. It assumes ideal harmony with no greater aberrations. This concerns all that is, including the Earth and man.

You may think that the condition of the world is close to a zenith or an escalation of numerous disasters that were not present in the past. There have long been storms of hatred, anger, revenge, and many other outbursts of negative feelings within people that would increase in time. When these outbursts are sent into space by people, they don't disappear or become neutralized.

They have been only minimally strengthened. Most often, such emanations existed in the same state they were sent in. It is completely different in the present. Each emotion is en-

larged to a size it has never been before. The media tries to pro-
voke them, which escalates tension.

Don't be afraid of it, however. Everything that happens
in your world is your mirror. Each person has his own mirror.
The mirror of your husband or neighbor doesn't have to be
yours.

People on Earth experience disasters of thoughts and
feelings, which are manifested as anger with themselves, places,
things, and the world's injustice. They consciously or unconsciously emanate the vibration of revenge.

The Great Ocean Of Universal Substance of the Universe
registers these traits. They are received by the four elements of
nature and stored within. When they reach a level of saturation,
they return these traits to people (single individuals as its
source) in the form of natural catastrophes. They can manifest in
different forms as small accidents or turbulences of a different
kind, such as storms, tempests, cataclysms, and so on.

This is how the Law of the Circle operates. What you
send always comes back to you. If something happens in some
part of the world this just means that these people got back what
they had sent before.

What may seem evil to you at the moment looks this way
because you got to know this only partially. If you had access to
the full knowledge, you would understand that there is no evil;
evil is always the germ of good. There may be some confusion
in your life now since you don't realize Goodness. Having access to Truth, however, you will cease to believe in evil, poverty, disease, misery, etc.

The disease consciousness or misery consciousness are
false because they form in the process of making shallow judgments. We will judge shallowly as long as we remain in the
condition of dissociated consciousness. We cannot be aware of

both Life and disease or misery at the same time. We will lose the consciousness of misery while acquiring the full consciousness of Life.

You must understand that many people must get shocked from time to time because they would lose themselves completely otherwise. This is one way of keeping their attention away from the things that can destroy them.

God knows nothing about disease or misery, so they are not God's revenge as some people think because they have nothing to do with God. They are just the Nature's way of cleansing and shaking off human impurities, conflicted thoughts, and distorted feelings so that It can return again to the virginal condition of God's Flawlessness.

The earthly atmosphere cannot be polluted by negativity coming from you or other people for too long. Each negative emotion is a veil that the Light cannot break though. No negativity can be destroyed or dissolved by any means other than making it burn within you and fizzle out completely.

You experience a temporal loss during this process but you also learn not to make the same mistake twice. Some people learn it the first time while the others need repetitions. Know that nothing is accidental neither in your life nor in your body.

Sometimes you get hurt and suffer indirectly. When a disaster falls and many souls lose their bodies in a sudden accident, we can all feel it. Even when a disaster happened at the other side of the globe, you feel bad and can even fall into depression. It just depends on the intensity of your fear and your degree of guilt.

The burden you feel when this happens is caused by the suffering souls that have lost their direction because of a sudden shock. It always happens regardless of whether those souls remain in the physical bodies or not.

A return to balance or complete health doesn't always mean complete health. A return to perfection concerns a soul being liberated from long-hidden fears or negative thoughts about itself and others. This kind of spiritual healing can follow even after a physical body dies.

You can see for yourself that it is not God sending destruction to Earth, it is human destroying the Earth himself. Do you understand how it works? It is simple. When you are calm, balanced, and full of love, wonderful nature surrounds you. When you boil and burst with emotions, the same happens to the nature around you.

It happened many times in the past that entire civilizations disappeared from the Earth's surface in an instant. Do you want it to happen now? What shall you do if our planet wants to remove violence and negative feelings from its surface that have gathered there throughout the years? Wouldn't it be better if you got rid of them yourself and cleansed yourself now? It is difficult but not impossible. I am not writing this to frighten you by any means, dear reader, but to turn your attention to the Truth. When you understand the seriousness of your situation, you will be able to efficiently change it for good. You will understand how important it is while reading this book.

The source of happiness is simplicity. Any exaggeration in thoughts, feelings, and deeds deprives you of happiness since the excess darkens your fundamental values. Excess in one domain must cause lack in another.

Balance and harmony are disregarded in the contemporary world. Everything is done in excess. People are too fat or too thin. Some eat too much while others deprive themselves of food altogether. Some are excessively stingy while others are too spendthrift. They smoke or drink too much, enjoy themselves into decay, and say nonsense. Many people worry too much. They proclaim their black and white views. They act according to the principle of „all or nothing." But this is not the way of Nature.

There is balance in Nature. Animals decay insignificantly. Plants regenerate. Sources of food once used resurge. A flower brings joy, a fruit feeds, a root or a germ is kept to give new life.

Humanity lost its knowledge of how important balance is and what's worse is that it doesn't care at all. People are most often guided by greed and ambition and they submit to fear. Doing so will cause them to destroy themselves just like they did in the early history of the Earth.

Over the centuries, humanity has destroyed and imposed limitations of the Universal Substance, which is God. It is confirmed not only by the condition of the Earth itself but also by the physical body humanity uses today.

Dear reader, have you ever considered what happens to nature when people breed animals for meat in terrible conditions and kill them, cut down trees in mass quantities, or torment living things? When a human decides to do something like that, all of nature knows who they are dealing with.

Nature is not as helpless as it may seem to you. When it is pushed to the edge, it confronts a human with the elements of earth, air, fire, bacteria, and microbes to defeat those that don't want to live in harmony with it. Have you ever thought about why so many people get ill today or why the climate in some regions changes so violently? I think you know the answer to this question.

However, know that it is neither the Earth's destiny nor your own to destroy. On the contrary, your destiny is continuous growth. When you don't cooperate, you stand at a crossroads. Either a glory or a fall awaits you. Long ago God gave ultimatum to people: don't threaten yourself or anyone else.

Human life has existed on Earth since it was created. I will tell you about the time you came to the Earth in a little bit. You will get a chance to remind yourself about how long ago, in a distant time, you were chosen out of a great number of volunteers to care for the Earth and everything that lived on it, together with others. It was a heartfelt gift filled with love that you and the others like you offered to the Earth. You gave it to It with devotion and engagement.

The Earth returned your favor and while you were here it covered itself with a wonderful beauty and miraculous landscapes. It wanted to tranquilize your heart and cheer up your mind so you could learn your lessons in peace. Don't think that what you see here is your merit or anybody else's.

Know that each square inch of the Earth' surface was created by the spiritual kingdom of the Earth. Don't you believe it? Is it you who influences a plant's growth or do you just collect Its precious gifts?

The Earth draws the energy from the Sun and feeds all life existing here. Do you always remember that? Don't you believe that everything that exists in the world has Life? Check it for yourself. Take a little plant into your hand and cultivate it. Talk to it, send it positive thoughts, and you shall see that it will grow to an unusual size and beauty. You may understand that plants are living beings and that you should treat them with love and respect.

It is true that the Earth became your home for the time of your incarnation. Remember, though, that you are just Its guest. It treats you like it is supposed to treat a guest walking the Earthly Road. It prepared a wonderful feast for you and asks you to try everything that is there.

Everything you get from the Earth is a gift of Its Love. Until Love flows through you, you live in harmony with Mother Earth. You are happy and well. If you close yourself to the Earth's flow, disharmony comes to your life in all of its domains.

INTRODUCTION TO LOST CIVILIZATION

Dear reader, while writing these words I don't turn to your logical mind but to your memory bank so you can remind yourself that you once participated in this. You live eternally as a soul and you are a collection of characters of all kinds, the sum of all experiences the Earthly School can offer.

You live eternally but you return to the Earth from time to time since this is your desire. You come back to fulfil your task with the help of the spiritual power of your Divine Self.

A task is different for everybody since each man has acquired a different level of growth. One part of the task, however, is common to all people: regaining the memory lost. How can you do that?

You would have to realize and remember always that your Divine, Great, Spiritual Self existed many times before in incarnations preceding your present life. You passed through an unimaginable quantity of experiences and you carry a wonderful treasury inside. You may not realize this fact or that you have the ability to benefit from it whenever you wish.

Dear reader, an enormous Truth is at your disposal. It could be an amazing support to you in your everyday life if only you wanted to benefit from It. Don't you have access to It? You are deceiving yourself. Who, if not your Divine Self, makes you feel a zest for life, growth, and learning? It has been calling you all the time but you can hardly hear anyone. You are so very busy with what you reckon to be your life that you are not able to hear It.

You not only carry the abilities acquired earlier, your Higher Spiritual Self is also ready to help you solve the problems caused by your present life in the world of matter. Don't think of yourself as of a weak and helpless being, because this is not what you are. You are as great today as you were at the beginning of your existence.

Nevertheless, if you decide to see yourself as a lame duck, loser, or weak thing, this just means that you use your free will in the wrong way and that you persist in belittling the rays of Love and Wisdom that God sends you continuously through your Divine Self.

You feel so miserable because you don't use the gifts of Love and you don't realize that everything you meet on your path is Its gift. Love sends you abundance but you can benefit from Its gifts only when you live in the Mind's Unity with God. When you live in a state of dissociated consciousness, you cannot benefit from these large resources of Abundance.

You may not have access to all your knowledge at present because much of what you acquired in other incarnations is closed or hidden from your consciousness. You are forced to operate on the basis of limited information. Know, however, that nobody deprived you of this knowledge; it was you who closed yourself off to it. You will learn how it happened in the following part of the book.

In order to understand what I am going to write below, an open mind is necessary. You won't realize anything with a closed mind. You will not only misunderstand what I want to say in this book, you will generally learn nothing. A mind that is closed rejects everything that is different and that collides with its former beliefs, without realizing that its former beliefs are totally wrong.

When you identify only with your physical body, you forget the most important thing—you are the soul that lives forever. Remember the Earthly School from the second volume. You come to the Earth to learn through experience and when you learn your lesson, you leave. Sometimes you leave this world to rest from learning and when you gain new strength, you come back to the same conditions to continue your learning. The force that pulls you to the Earth is a desire to experience something that was your greatest desire in your past life.

Did you forget this? This is because you don't know that the force that is closing your mind and leading you to oblivion is fear. Only an open and receptive mind can absorb and transform new knowledge and reach the knowledge it carries within. When you don't have access to your inner knowledge, you are constantly flouncing and you don't see a way out. If you realized that it was you who chose a certain experience, you would cease to fear and be angry, once and for all. All your doubts would disappear since you would know that nothing can happen in your life that is discordant with your will. Nothing happens in your life that is not useful to the growth of you and your soul.

You chose each of your experiences, no matter how difficult they might seem. Only learning through our own experience is well-remembered by the soul. This is why they are much more important than knowing what is right from other people's experience. You, the Great You, operating at higher and deeper levels, knows this but you don't realize it because you decided to rely on you little external self.

If you still think that your life is different from what I am writing about here, this just means that you aren't listening to your soul. You don't use your free will and you do only what your external senses or other people suggest to you. You probably don't know that only when reason submits to a soul, a mind grows, develops, and ascends to higher levels. It does so for its own benefit and the benefit of all life. Otherwise, you would not have a chance to grow and everything that you do would only stop you and take you away from your own Higher Divine Self.

You don't have to seek this knowledge because all the knowledge you pursue is inside you. When you wish to discover it, it will begin to wake within you anew, at increasingly deep levels. You will become extraordinarily wise, dear reader. However, you must not let fear stop you on your way to this enormous treasure.

Accept the fact that fear has long been present in your evolutionary process that you got used to it, and now you think it is a natural and obvious element of your life. This is not true, of course, but since you were certain of it at deeper levels, your external part thinks it has to be so. Don't condemn your fear when it shows up, however. Don't think that the fear within you is wrong because then you will start to fight it, which is not wise.

Everything you fight with gets attracted to you, which makes you more attached to it. Accept that there is fear in you but don't submit to it. Every time you submit to your fears and let them take control over you, you must pass through them in order to experience everything you feel to overcome them.

You won't learn what I write here from other people. Only God's Mind contains all knowledge and all Truth. It is the only Mind. It is the Source of all existence and It knows everything from the beginning of life. It knows the whole Truth and the Mind that knows the whole Truth cannot be wrong. One can be wrong only when they know a fragment of truth. This is why you must reach deep within yourself to get to the whole Truth and discover It anew. It doesn't matter that the Source of Life is inaudible, invisible, and without smell to most people. If you desire to see it and dare to reach it, it will become tangible to you.

However, know that no matter how hard you look for this Truth, you won't find it in the outer world. I cannot give it to you, either. I will just show you the way in this book so you can realize what mistakes you made so that you can correct them. Discovering the truth is like turning the light on in a dark room. You blindly stumble on everything that is inside, while everything becomes clear and simple when the light is on. Don't be afraid to discover Light. God wants you to act in Light and not to wander blindly since living in darkness leads you astray.

When I talk about God I mean God who is our Creator, the Source of All that Is, in Whom we live, move and exist. I'm not talking about the God that religions teach about or God that is far away in some inaccessible Heaven, whom we may reach after our physical death.

It is true that you are a free, independent man, but it is also true that you are not an organism independent from God because you cannot be so. You are unbreakably united with the whole. When you imagined your isolation, this imaginary and unreal isolation became the source of your imaginary separation. In Reality, you are always united with God, your Source, because you live, move, and have your existence in Him.

The God that I am talking about is Spirit, the Creative Principle of the Universe. A human that is united with God, his Father, is also united with the Spirit that penetrates all. It is only this Unity with Spirit of God that brings the harmony in which a human experiences a continuous flow of thoughts, Life, Power, and Wisdom from Spirit to his mind and body. When you realize *Who You Are in Essence*, your Spirit is free, active, and unlimited since it dwells in unity with his Creator. When you lack this basic awareness you close the way to your spirit and imprison it in the net of delusion. Dear reader, even your religion tells you that you are made in the likeness and image of God and so, you are a spiritual being like God, not material like your limited external senses suggest to you. And though your external senses deny it, you know the Truth deep inside. This Great You knows what the reality of Life is like and it is only your small, external self that doesn't realize this Truth. The Great You knows everything because it knows your whole Life and not only the small fragment of your present incarnation.

When you remember all of life, your Great Self realizes that you are One with the eternal Life, Mind, and Power that your small external self knows nothing about. It knows that you are permanently bonded to the only Intelligence that God is, that penetrates all substance and brings vitality, coherence, and purpose to all of existence.

God is present during every moment of your life. The Great You knows that it is God speaking when you say that it is God who is active when you act, think, or move. When you become aware of the perfect and right order of new things, all the rest will be given to you. Everything is a matter of consciousness since it contains everything.

Without realizing this basic Truth, you live in delusion. You let your little you lead you astray all the time. How do you reach the Truth? First of all, discover your beliefs concerning God. You will probably see that your beliefs concerning God have nothing to do with God the way He is in Reality.

God is Love. However, your subconscious fear of God that started long time ago changes the God of Love into the God of hatred, punishment, and revenge. Your panic is guided and intensified by your wrong and expired beliefs coming from your ego. Because of your wrong beliefs, the God who is your loving Father and best friend becomes an enemy that you blame everything for. You fear Him terribly but you don't realize it. You will learn how it happened in the chapter „The Fall of Civilization."

While reading the following, don't let yourself be guided by the wrong belief of being separated from God. You are unbreakably bonded to Him and you don't need or have any reason to fear Him. Realize that you emerged from Him and that you come from Him. You are His beloved Son. He feeds you and cares for you. When you unite your consciousness with God, your Father, you are present within Him and He is present within you. You become one.

When you become one, you are surprised to see that there is no fear within you whatsoever. This is because God is the Source of all Power and the Source of all Power cannot fear anything. However, every time you fail to unite your consciousness with Him, you feel separated from Him and fear awakens in you. If you fear Him, realize that this feeling of separation created by you is the only source of your fear and that it is not God by any means.

When you are aware of the Spirit, you are self-confident and at peace since only the awareness of the Spirit is a peaceful state of consciousness. It is so clear to your consciousness that there is no place for fear anymore. You cannot liberate yourself from fear when your consciousness is separated from the Power of His Spirit. While feeling separated, you feel an all-present fear sneaking into every domain of your life.

Submit yourself to God with all the trust you can gather. He will give you everything you can open yourself to. God wants the desire that awakens inside of you to be fulfilled immediately and He fulfills it. It is up to you whether or not you use this gift or choose something else because you have free will. It is God's intention for humanity to maintain this wonderful, perfect state in which it dwelled at the very beginning of its existence and which it owned for eons, but I will write about this in the next chapters.

When you trust God completely, you will discover your inner world governed by your own Higher Self. You will experience something else and you will see everything from a different perspective. In time, when you are ready, you will reach new knowledge.

You will realize that your own Higher Self is a part of the Infinite Self being Universal Energy, Spirit, or what most people commonly call God. You will realize your relationship to the Spirit. You will get to know God, your Father, by experience, almost tangibly.

You can get to know God your Father in one way only, namely by being aware of His Spirit. Uniting your consciousness with the Spirit consciousness, you get a chance to know as much as the Spirit knows, to see what Spirit sees, and do what the Spirit does.

Being aware of the Spirit, you will see that everything belongs to you and that nothing is impossible. A false belief will fade if it is separated from your true consciousness. Power will penetrate your words again and you will speak like a man who has real authority.

When you let consciousness, this Eternal Consciousness that you are in Reality, or the Great You, control your objective and subjective mind completely, you will become an example of health, peace, wealth, and wisdom.

Your true Self (Great You) is a part of an Infinite Self, and this means that you are of spiritual nature just like the whole Universe is, and not of material nature as your limited external senses suggest. It is obvious that you cannot be imperfect in any sense, though you think so. You are also not unworthy of God as your religion persuades you. You won't say: „Lord, I am not worthy to have you come into my home..." (Matthew 8:8) since you will know with all your heart that He is with you already.

A question may arise within you. Why aren't you aware of all of this? Why is your Higher Self, that is your inner Wisdom and that is gifted with so many talents, not able to contact you so you can learn the Truth?

Well, it has been calling you continuously, but you—your little external self—are not able to accept this contact, since you are not aware of it. It is only when you recognize and understand *Who You Are in Essence* that you will reckon this contact possible and you will consciously accept it.

You must first accept this fundamental fact and acknowledge your true identity and only then you can demand the contact or help of your Higher Self (your Great You). You will understand and realize then that the essence of your staying on the Earth is contained within something much greater than what your little personality is able to understand, your little external self.

It is only when you realize the knowledge residing in your inner reality that you will be able to take it. This is the treasury I mentioned before. It is only when you reach, realize, and absorb this knowledge that you will become the one that possesses Power and Wisdom. Your previous knowledge will transform into Wisdom. You will possess not only the ability to see hidden possibilities but also the Power enabling you to manifest these possibilities in both your inner and outer world.

You will be able to do everything you wish and that is necessary to your wholesome harmonious growth. The unlimited Power is all-present but until you become aware of it, it is static and you cannot use it. It is only when you are aware of it that you can direct It at will.

When you understand this Truth and assimilate it, you will become free. You will not only bring more power to your life, you will also acquire the power of consciousness. There is a lot written about this power of consciousness but only a few people are able to understand what it means. Hence, listen now...

You desire health but you will never acquire *permanent* full health if you are not aware that you have it already. Know, dear reader, that health and consciousness of health are two different things. The point is that there are people who are healthy even though they don't have the consciousness of being healthy. They notice that they lack it only when they lose it. Everyone who has fully developed their spiritual or cosmic consciousness is healthy and lives in peace, wealth, and strength.

You may pursue happiness but cannot reach it, and when you think it is at hand, it runs away from you. You then try to pursue another thing that you think will make you happy, but it is exactly the same with everything. As long as you don't acquire the consciousness of happiness, you will never reach it and it will always be a step ahead of you. It is identical with all dependencies. You won't be able to live in abundance without the consciousness of abundance. It is similar to perfection, wisdom, etc. Without consciousness confirmed you cannot own them permanently. Do you know why?

Well, you were healthy, beautiful, and full of energy when you were young, but were you conscious of these conditions? You probably were not. It was only when you lost your health, youth, and agility that you realized that you once had them and that they passed irrevocably. Do you understand what I am writing about now? In order to keep anything for good, you must be fully conscious of this condition, otherwise you will lose it and only the memory of it will stay with you.

To keep a particular condition, you must live the spirit of the condition until it becomes your own. It is only then that it becomes true wealth that no one will ever be able to take away from you. Analogically, the things of this world will become obedient to your inner Power and you will be able to rule them freely only when you gain the consciousness of Power.

It is only the consciousness of Power that gives this unswerving certainty, similar to a peaceful mind and the feeling of an absolute obviousness at the same time. Every time you fear or doubt something, however, it means that your consciousness is separated from Power. All doubts concerning success in doing something shows only when you think that you are separated from Power. It is only when you are conscious (delusionary) of separation that you may feel fear. As you can see, it all depends on your state of mind.

Dear reader, you don't need to acquire any power or to look for it outside yourself. It is yours already. You must wish to understand it, use it, and control it; you must want your inner Power to penetrate you and saturate you so that you can freely grow in the results of your actions.

It is obvious that understanding and perseverance are necessary for working with the material contained in this elaboration but if you take the courage and acquire understanding, you will be inspired with new light and strength and you will gain confidence and power. You will see how you can come closer to the realization of your hopes and dreams every day, and your life will become deeper, fuller, clearer, and more meaningful than ever before.

Dear reader, you are on the brink of the birth of a new consciousness, power, and relationship with yourself. I hope that after studying this book you will willingly accept the ideal human within yourself—the one that was made in the image and likeness of God and that you will appreciate the Mind, in which everything begins. I mean only the Mind that shapes, keeps, nurtures, births, and creates everything that exists. I trust that you will understand that everything is a part of an astonishing whole whose body is the whole Nature and whose soul is God.

You have lived so many times that you probably were one of the people I will write about. I know that you don't remember it consciously, but don't worry because your soul perfectly remembers that period. If can access those times if you wish because they have existed in the untouched corners of your memory. On the basis of what happened then you will begin to realize where the mistake is and you will get a chance to do something positive with your life.

THE BEGINNING OF YOUR
STAY ON THE EARTH

Dear reader, this is your story.

God has created a Perfect World, commonly called Heaven, and a Perfect man in it. Only Love ruled, everything was Perfect, and it was static in a way. It didn't have a chance to grow. You probably understand that it was extremely easy to love God in Heaven, where there was nothing except Love and Perfection. It didn't bring anything new to Life as a whole, though.

This is why in the infinite God's Mind, in the Source that we come from, a plan was made concerning all people at the same time. God designed the Earth as a free will zone. Because of this you gained the opportunity to manifest your perfection in the art of using your reason and thoughts. This is why it has been a place of such wonderful possibility.

It is only here on earth, during your numerous experiences, that you can learn deep and permanent love. Your soul not only shapes this, it also fosters your spirit's sensations. You can experience everything your soul desires. Nobody can forbid you to do that since you benefit from the law given you by God Himself.

In order for you to walk through life in a physical form, you need a body. It consists of billions of single cells that form large, more complicated sets. Have you ever seen a spectacle on a stadium, where thousands of people join together to make some patterns? In the same way, millions of cells join together to make your hand, liver, eye, and every other organ. They live their life but they are totally subjected to you. All of this in the name of love. Because of this you can live your life and they can live theirs. In the second volume I described evolution and involution. Although they were created to manifest perfection, they are completely obedient to your instructions.

On the Earth and in the new conditions, you never lost anything. On the contrary, you gained a lot. Having free will, you had the opportunity to reach deeper and deeper within, penetrating deeper levels of consciousness and love so that you could grow in strength. You know Love since you come from it but you could get to know it better on Earth by your experience.

You adored, worshipped, and acknowledged God as your only Source by continuously developing love and wisdom. Your attitude was a signpost of light showing the way to those who descended to the Earth after you or who lost their way. And so, you descended to Earth a long time ago while the Earth was being shaped. You were not banished to it by any means, as some religions teach, but you were invited here as a guest. God wanted you to walk the Earthly Way as an incarnated man and to try everything that is to try there. For He said: „My will shall be done when you, together with your brothers and sisters, will benefit from the Goods that I gave to you."

You rejoiced in this opportunity and you reckoned it to be a great honor to. You gained the possibility to together care for life on the planet Earth. You acknowledged It as a living, feeling, and constantly growing Being. You could grow with It and develop along with It in the name of God's glory. You cared for each other's needs.

Living on Earth, you remained the same soul you had been while living in Heaven. You descended for a good cause. You brought your spirit to this new planet and along with others, you created a great, wonderful civilization.

Let us emphasize once again: you didn't find yourself on Earth because you were exiled. You found yourself there because of your own free will. The Plan to descend to the Earth was offered to you to accept it and not imposed on you as a necessity. You accepted it with joy as a chance for your further development and growth.

While sending people to the Earth, God didn't send a single man away from Him, nor did he leave anyone on their own. He has been cooperating with each individual for his own good and for the good of all of humanity. All action serves one purpose, which is the progress of all Life as a whole.

While descending to Earth, you were fully aware of the purpose. You put on a physical body to be able to exist in matter. Only the body enabled you to experience Life on Earth.

While putting on your physical body, you never went away from God nor ceased to be His beloved Son. You emerged from Him, since you come from Him. Nothing will change this fact. Although you manifested in physicality as an individual stream of life, you still lived in God as you do now. Though you are naturally a son, you are not united with Him automatically.

In order for the unity with God to manifest, your consciousness is necessary. It doesn't happen naturally. Some effort on your side is necessary, too. It is only when you consciously unite with God, your Father, that you reach unity. The God is present within you and you, as His son, are present within Him.

You probably wonder what the benefits are of this unity. Well, you get the chance to live in Truth. When you are connected to God by your consciousness, you become one. Jesus confirmed this: „God is your Father that feeds you and cares for you. Be his children in your minds and will, as you really are".

When you don't unite your consciousness with God's consciousness, however, you feel separated from Him and you fall into delusion. Each of these conditions brings totally different results. What are they? You will see on the following pages of this book.

God didn't abandon a man, nor ban him. He said to people descending to the Earth: „I intend to give myself to you. You go and generously give so everything you create in the Universe understands its essence as My identity." You serve God every time you express this superior order.

And so God, Beloved Presence „I Am", has always expected you to act according to the Cosmic Law, to pour love from your own Stream of Life to all life. It is part of your obligation to God or Life in general since all Life exists exclusively because of the Love we emanate. As you can see, love is not an alternative meaning you can adjust yourself to depending on your whim, it is an obligation you undertook while descending to Earth.

Your holy duty then, just like it is now, was to constantly draw the Holy Flame of God's Love and to send It further: to the Earth you walk on, the physical objects you use, the air you breathe, and each human being that helps you acquire Perfection. In this way, you do something for your own good, the good of all humanity, and the good of all God's creation.

If you didn't pour love from your Stream of Life into another life, the Light of your Flame of Life wouldn't grow and your love wouldn't have the chance to flourish in fullness.

It is the same when we look at it from a higher perspective. If Greater Life didn't pour Its Love to you, your Stream of Life and your ability to create Perfection wouldn't have a chance to spread. This is the part of the Eternal Divine Justice and Balance of the Universe. The bigger always supports, protects, and blesses the smaller.

This is why it used you to bless everything you had contact with. Because of it you grew in love and wisdom and you never experienced disharmony.

While putting on your material body, you were not deprived of anything. You still had the same Divine Spark called Christ that God gave to you at the very beginning of your existence. The Divine Spark is Love. Because of it your soul is the same spiritual reality it once was and always will be. Only your perception of your own reality can change, but not reality itself.

You were made in the image and the likeness of God Himself. You were fully aware that, although you had a physical body, you remained a spiritual being, not a material one. You then perceived your body as the light and energy that it truly is and not as the solid body that your external senses have suggested.

You came to the Earth to experience. You have the chance to get to know Love even more precisely than you knew It before since Love flows through each experience. When you experience something under new circumstances, the Divine Spark can glow with a truly strong flame. If, for some reasons, Love couldn't flow through you because of your fear, anger, or other negative emotion, you would inevitably fall into disharmony.

This is why you believed with all your might that it never happened. And even when there seemed to be disharmony at some point, you immediately replaced it with the Holy Flame of God's Love that couldn't be hurt with evil. Evil never had a chance to reside in your life nor your world for long.

And so, Love is the power of the Universe. It is like a Treasury that every Perfect Idea comes from. Within this Love the Presence „I Am" dwells. This Divine Self is the Creator of your Individuation. Within Him, each of your desires dwells that makes you happy. It is unchanging and everlasting.

All other earthly desires are temporary and short-lived. Although they make you happy the moment they get realized, they make you unhappy when they pass away.

You once perpetually sought permanent desire. You knew that only Desires of God's Love are the ones that create constant happiness and satisfaction.

You once came to the Earth to learn and your soul took this time and this place to support individual growth of the spirit of both you and the entire human family of the time. You knew that you could experience as much as you wish of everything your soul could wish for, since your will was the will of God.

And even if you did something wrong, you knew that God would never criticize you. Even if you would hit the rock bottom. He would say with love: „Stand up, son, and try again" or „It doesn't matter what you do, I love you anyway."

You chose this lesson like one chooses the direction of their studies. You were driven by a strong desire to learn about a deep and permanent love of God by experiencing various forms of your creativity. Thanks to your free will, the Earth's evolution became a part of your cognitive process and you participated in the cognitive process of the Earth itself.

In order to help you to learn God sent His messengers—

Transcendental Beings so far beyond your understanding that it is not possible to describe in words the Majesty of Love, Wisdom, and Power of The Great Ones.

As you can see, dear reader, the brave decision to descend to the Earth was beneficial not only to yourself but to the Earth itself. You came to live on It because it was the only Being that challenged you wonderfully so you could learn and grow in a wonderful way. You fearlessly used your Power and Authority given to you by God and you were free. You couldn't gain or keep the perfect Freedom by any means other than practiced knowledge.

You consciously united your mind with the mind of God, your Father. Many call this state the cosmic consciousness. Thanks to this connection, the Father was present within you and you were present within Him. You did everything according to His will. You existed in unity. Although you would speak the words and make the workings, it wasn't you who acted; it was the Father acting through you that was present within you.

You descended to the Earth because, by putting a material cover, you wanted to learn to love God with the same absolute devotion you did until that time, when you were in Heaven. You prepared yourself for it with deliberation. First of all, you promised yourself that no matter what you experienced on the Earth, you would always remember God and you would try with all your might to never ever break your bond with Him.

You loved God with all your heart, soul, understanding, and might. You worshipped Him always and everywhere with love and gratitude. Doing so, you experienced the natural World which is the World of the all-present „God in Action." You made this the superior purpose of your life and you fully succeeded in it.

OCTAVES

Although you descended to the Earth, you felt with all your heart that you never left Heaven and that you were still residing in it. It was not a delusion by any means; this feeling was absolutely true. You lived in the octave of Happiness and Love, and these were exactly the same octaves you resided in while in Heaven.

There were only those two octaves in Heaven. After descending to the Earth, another one formed: Tolerance. These Octaves are thought layers and they lay themselves in the atmosphere similar to geological layers under the earth' surface.

Dear reader, in order for you to better understand what I am writing about here, I will return to the second volume for a while. I described life in the mental world, in which you resided after your physical death. I presented single octaves then as walls. If you have anything of a particular octave within you, you have an open window through which you have a chance to experience its fullness. If you don't, you are deprived of this experience and you are not aware of their existence.

In order for you to understand it well, I will give you an example. Imagine that you are taken to a wonderful palace in an airtight closed box that is carried from one place to the other. Although you visit all those wonderful rooms full of wonderful people, you are not aware of what is there and what happens there. No matter how much you want or try, you don't have the ability to participate in anything that takes place there.

Imagine that the box with you inside it was put at the table with the most fanciful, most delicious dishes. Could this be of any use to you even if you were most hungry and thirsty? No! And if the box was put in the middle of the ballroom, where wonderful music was being played—could you take part in this wonderful ball? And if you were carried along to the most wonderful garden in the world, would you be able to admire beautiful views around? Would you smell the flowers? You would be present there but you wouldn't realize it. You wouldn't participate in anything but this wouldn't be because of disinterest. First of all, you wouldn't realize what happens around you. Secondly, your actions would be limited by the box.

It is similar in your whole Life. While you're physically living, you don't benefit from higher Octaves because you are not aware of them. After your physical death, you cannot access them since you haven't worked through it during your physical life. As a result, you lack proper „windows" through which you can experience this wonderful world. You then return to the world without realizing that you don't reside inside these octaves. This begins a vicious circle.

You can use these higher octaves during both your physical life and after the death of your physical body. You must be fully conscious, however, because it is not enough to reside in them unconsciously. When you are conscious, you cease to live in delusion because it is delusion that separates you from them; a wrong belief is a wall in an exemplary box. You are closed within it as if it was a deep well and you wrongly think that what is around you is your whole life. This is why it is so important to constantly raise our consciousness so that now, while you live on the Earth, you can open the windows to the octaves mentioned, that will bestow eternal happiness on you.

More octaves are formed while we're alive. I mean these of lower frequencies, but I will write more about them later.

Do you understand now, dear reader, why some people are happy even if they have nothing in their physical life, while others that have all the material goods they need are depressed, frustrated, and ill? The first group has access to higher octaves and fully benefits from them. At first glance, it might seem that they are people living a life of self-abnegation or poor men with nothing. They have access to something better so they don't need what the physical world offers to them. They are conscious of all of Life, and not only its tiny material particles. The first one is eternal and makes you happy; the second is temporary and leaves behind only grief, suffering, and trouble. You obviously understand, dear reader, that not every ,,poor man" you meet at a street has such wonderful opportunities.

Nothing changed for you when you descended to the Earth because earthly conditions were identical to those in Heaven. You still lived in the world of God, in a true reality, in your true home. It doesn't have anything to do with what you experience now as your reality, dear reader. You lived in Truth then and you consciously resided in the world of a Spirit, while today you live in the world of delusion. It was your great Divine Self guiding you then, and now it is your small external self. You are stuck in a deep well of delusion, thinking that what you experience that is your whole life. Your false belief that you are separated from the whole forms the walls of the well you experience as limitations.

Many people live next to you, who have entrenched themselves like you have. The light doesn't reach you so you lack consciousness. Your delusions make you think that this is the only life you have. You may even be pleased with yourself for being resourceful. You've decorated your well but it is still just a well. There is no freedom in it. There is an abundance of wonderful things around you (as in an exemplary palace) that you don't realize because of your false belief.

You once were One with God and you were guided by the Love that you lack now. You didn't acquire knowledge. It was inherent in your original identity. God gave you (and humanity) Love so your external self also could protect you from disharmony. Whether or not you use this chance given to you by God, however, depends exclusively on your self- consciousness. When you are conscious, you have access to His whole Splendor and Abundance, and when you are not, you are deprived of all this.

You must know that only Love is your protection. The only one and unique. Nothing but Love can keep the energies of the world of your feelings in balance. Only Love carries within the Power blocking destructive forces from bursting into your emotional world. It can block the road before them so they don't get the energy of your feelings. If you didn't allow Love to keep your feelings in balance, disharmony would immediately burst into your world. The same happens now. As you can see, dear reader, Love is the only Cleansing and Guiding Intelligence that keeps the human world in Purity of feelings, thoughts, and actions. So in any place that Love ceases to exist, disharmony immediately appears.

You had got physical body then, you lived on the Earth, but you resided in the same Garden of Perfection that existed in Heaven. It was possible because you kept in mind the fact even as a human being, you have remained the same God's Son – Christ, as you had been in Heaven. However, you didn't attribute the source of your power to uniqueness coming from your birth status (as God's Son), but to being one with Spirit consciousness. The Power you had made you act according to God's Will, the Cosmic Spirit. It was possible because you constantly kept the consciousness of *Who You Are in Essence.*

It presently seems to you that you reside in a different place than before, which doesn't change the fact that you are still the beloved God's Son. Everything changed for you externally, but nothing changed inside of you. You were born of His Love and you still live in God, move and have your existence in Him. This condition is given to you forever, no matter what you experience or where you are.

You can walk with God again, your Father „I AM", as you did once, but you cannot let anything pull you back from recognizing, acknowledging, and using this Powerful God's Presence that you are.

You don't feel God everyday although He is always standing next to you, ready to act. It happens because the Inner Presence of God never imposes itself. It has to be invited by you. You must open up to it, you must want and allow God to act through you.

Since you forgot *Who You Are in Essence,* you continuously let yourself be governed by disharmonious feelings. It is them that cover your consciousness and destroy all the benefits you could receive every day.

This condition has never changed for people that have kept their consciousness of Being the Son. For others, it lasted as long as they could keep this fundamental fact in mind. It lasted very long for both. When somebody started to forget God, his Father, he immediately broke contact with Him and his conditions began to radically change to the worse, but I will write about this in further part of the book.

THE BEGINNINGS OF THE LOST CIVILIZATION

When you came to the physical world you knew you wouldn't be alone there. You wouldn't have an opportunity to experience what you desire if you were alone. A great number of volunteers came to the world along with you—pioneers who agreed to the same that you did. You needed each other because it was the only way you could learn and express increasing love and wisdom.

You had your free will and you could do whatever came to your mind, but you consciously chose joining your will with the will of God. You acted exclusively in accordance to His Plan. Under His Guidance you created one big family of light, in peace and love. You made the Earth a wonderful place to learn, where love and wisdom found an ideal chance to grow and be expressed.

I may surprise you, dear reader, at this point. You didn't

come to the raw, undeveloped Earth. God, our Creator, wouldn't put any of His creatures on the Earth before the conditions necessary for their ideal growth are fulfilled. (As you can guess, life on Earth didn't start from Stone Age, as they teach us at school, but rather much later. You will learn about how it reached the point of powerful human egress in the following pages.)

Don't you believe? Look around and see the great love and solicitude. God cares for his creatures. „Look at the birds of the air; they do not sow or reap or store away in barns, and yet your heavenly Father feeds them." (Matthew 6:26) People that trust in God don't worry every day like most contemporary people do. They are always trustful and believe that food is awaiting them. They know they live in the Heavenly Kingdom so they all have equal access to the Goods that there are There.

Isn't it strange? They are not even partly intelligent as people and they never lack food or a place for themselves and their families. If they fought each other, anxiety would sneak into their lives and then they would lack everything. You can observe this behavior among animals living with people.

God is our Father, and other people are brothers to us. He also feeds us and takes cares of us. Realize it. You don't have to fight for a place at God's table just to get scraps. When you treat it with love, there will be enough food (and everything else you could wish for) for yourself and everyone else around, no matter how many of them are there. It is enough to trust. It is distrust and not lack of things that creates in your life shortages.

If you cannot trust that there is enough good for you, you are filled with fear and anxiety. The Great Principle of Life says: you attract what you fear. Shouldn't you have an easier life having such a wonderful intelligence, or better, shouldn't you feel safer than other forms of life? You are a beloved Son of God.

Realize this fact: You have been persuaded that you were

exiled to the Earth. It is indisputable at the same time that God gave you free will so you had the right to decide whether you want to descend to It or stay in Heaven. Following this way of thinking, you would not undertake this mission if you were not absolutely sure that both in Heaven and on Earth you have always been under God's perfect and permanent care. You just forgot about it for a while.

While descending to the Earth, you knew that you wouldn't have to seek the fulfilment of your needs, that God is the only force in the Universe, the force Omnipresent, Omniscient, and that as the Only Source of All That Is, He will always takes care of you. You were completely aware of the fact that your being is in God, your Great Father or Maternal Principle of all things, for everything is one and the same thing.

Once, when you dwelled on the Earth, you knew beyond all doubt that you lived in God and you moved in Him. You could feel God with all your heart the same as you had felt Him before in Heaven. You experienced and recognized God as Divine Power, Love, and Substance that is all in all, penetrates all, and spreads around you. Then the Earth and Heaven were the whole to you.

You were guided by Love in everything, which wasn't difficult since you come from Love. It is Eternal, Immortal, and Perfect. And since you lived in Love in Heaven, you could still do it after putting on your physical body. Although you were guided by It like you were before, you had to consciously open yourself to It while putting on your physical body. Only consciousness of Love gives you access to It and it is only by being conscious that you can use It at every moment of your life.

Your task is to open up yourself. Although God is present all around you and there isn't a place where He is not present, He never imposes Himself on you and doesn't force you to do anything. He gave you Free Will and He expects you to contact Him freely, wishing to benefit from His Divine Energy. God is Love and you can contact God only through loving God or through unlimited Gratitude. And you can be grateful for everything. The Energy gives you everything you wish for in return. Once you could control It and use It the way you wanted. You obviously did it only with the correct higher purpose.

You did nothing out of low, selfish motives, as you probably do now. First of all, there was no egoism within you whatsoever. Secondly, you didn't have a reason to act this way. You trusted and you had everything you desired.

You turned to God like your own Father. You did it like a child turns to his Dad. Each child believes that its beloved Dad has everything that it needs to live. A child knows with all its heart that its beloved Dad loves it so much that he wouldn't ever say no to it.

And if you asked God with such confidence and trust, He would immediately answer your call and bring you everything you needed. How could it be different since you and Father were one? You were His beloved son and you had everything the Father had. You believed life was absolutely natural and common and you couldn't conceive of it in any other way.

You knew the Laws of the Universe (which I will write about in the fourth volume) established by God and you followed them. Listen closely, dear reader. It is not only the fact that you knew them. One can know something intellectually but they don't have to follow what they know. You followed these laws daily, they were the content of your life, and you lived them during every moment of your day. You were saturated by them so deeply that there was nothing in you that wouldn't be the higher law itself. Using these laws was automatic and almost mechanical for you. You didn't ask if there was any other option, because you knew and wanted only this one.

One of the Laws says that you have a complete, unlimited right to freely use all things necessary to your spiritual, mental, and physical growth. This is why every wish to use your potential in the best possible way for you is an inseparable element of human nature.

You looked at Nature as a great, living, continuously growing Presence and you saw the community around you exactly the same way. You knew that all is One and that it comes from the same Source, that both you and everything else are made of the same matter that God is made of. So everything that God is, is also a part of you. Each Power that God has is also within you. You can grow like God grows because you carry the Source of all power within you.

You did everything in a grand way before. Everything, even the most ordinary things, you did the way that God would do, each word you spoke as if God spoke it. You met women and men both of high and low positions in the same way that God meets other Divine beings. You lived like God lives among Gods.

You always acted as if everything you did was your highest, purest, most perfect goal, as if your highest good and greatest chance depended on a successful outcome of everything you took part in. As if every event was planned for you, so you could progress in growth and consciousness. Acting this way, you achieved your maximum potential.

You never avoided willing to be everything you could be. This made you constantly strive to become the person you wanted to become. You did only what you wanted to do and you had all you wanted to have. You used all things in an unlimited way and everything you succeeded effortlessly in everything you put your mind to.

While doing something, you never feared that your desire wouldn't be satisfied or that somebody else would take away anything from you out of envy or greed. For you realized that each man can stand in Light and attract what already belongs to him.

You approached your desires in a way that made them all be satisfied at once. This was due to the proper way of thinking. You controlled yourself and you clearly demanded what you desired. This is how you received everything you needed and accelerated your growth. And since every man had the same potential to realize his own desires, you never wanted to take away someone else's desires or to make them yours because you had no reason to do that.

This is how it was then. Each man has potential to realize his true desires but he can do it only if he believes and knows with all his heart that God is vast abundance. The Bible says: „According to your faith, it will be given to you."

You had never doubted nor feared because you felt protected by your bond the Source of all Power. You also knew that nothing happens in your life that you don't consent to.

While joining the Source of all Power, you had no doubts. You knew that you were able to do everything you could imagine and that you would deal with all circumstances. And you were right thinking that there was no such thing that all Power couldn't accomplish.

You drew all wisdom and power from the unlimited God's Reservoir. You submerged yourself in It and drew Its riches according to your will and needs. This vast Ocean of Divine Substance was active and accessible to you at any moment. While submerging in It, you became ONE with your Father. It was only this closeness with the Father that enabled you to draw and use all the resources of His Powerful Energy with ease and without limits.

While you were in close contact with God, you were fully aware that the life Energy flowing through your mind and body is the same Powerful Living God's Presence that rules the vast Universe. Its Powerful Stream of Life not only supports your physical body but all other activity is passed through it to the body. Do you understand what it means, dear reader? It means that all Life (meaning all Activity anywhere) is God in Action. It means that all the Energy you use every day, even the energy necessary to move your little finger or take a step forward, is God in Action. It has the Presence I Am within, and the I Am is the activity of the Whole Life.

It is thanks to God's Presence that your heart beats and blood circulates through your veins. It makes your liver, kidneys, and other organs work. It controls your mind and keeps you in Truth. Its Essence as God in Action drives and activates your external body. God's Presence manifests in the form of Light Presence. You can see It as the Golden Thread of Light that anchors the Powerful, Masterful, Higher, Divine Self in your heart and brain.

As God's son, you are the individualized creator. You have not only the right but the responsibility to create along with Him. This is how you help your Father rule the Universe. This is why whenever you say „I Am" and feel Him with all your heart, you liberate the Source of Eternal Life that flows through you freely. It doesn't matter how you express this I Am—whether you speak it, think it, or feel it—since it is only thanks to I Am that you have the opportunity to recognize Your Own Victorious Divinity.

The boundless faith in the Powerful Presence I Am once gave you that confidence, the guarantee that you will accomplish the desired results. How could it be different since you knew that you had the Powerful Intelligence, Power, and Activity of God within you that nothing could resist? It all depended on the state of your mind. What you felt and how you perceived reality determined your reaction to it and the way you eventually saw it.

And so every time you said or now say „I Am" or „I Am that" you set Gods Unlimited Powerful Energy into motion. Once you say „I Am" you set the Source of Powerful Presence of God I Am into motion, from which you could take without limits.

When you say „I Am not" or „I'm not," „I don't have," „I can't," or „I'm not able," you immediately choke the Great Presence of God I Am and you cannot use His Benefits since the Source becomes inactive and idle.

The secret of your power to create once got in the way of your thinking. First of all, you always lived here and now and you were absolutely self-conscious. When you said „I Am" in the state of consciousness, readiness, and openness, you knew exactly and empirically what these two words meant and you united your mind with God's Mind.

Knowing this Truth, you not only gained knowledge, you also got to know the right goals for your life. Thanks to the Truth, you found the measures to accomplish them and the Power or the abilities to use these measures.

You used It with all your achievements—both the big ones and the small, quotidian ones. It is only when you became absolutely conscious and permanently united with the Powerful Intelligence the Power of Mind that you became the creative force giving you the opportunity to create consciously. You let God act through you and by opening your heart to Him, you enabled the Flame of your Life to unite with the thing you desired.

Whenever you created anything, you didn't take anything from anyone. God doesn't work that way. He makes everything more abundant than necessary so it is enough for everyone. If you don't believe it, take a closer look at how Nature operates. It creates two, three, or even more plants where only one used to grow.

The Higher Power of Mind operates in the same way. When you are United with It, it enables you to operate in a creative, harmonious way. What's more is that when your consciousness is united with the All-present Spirit, all the powers of Heaven and Earth hurry to serve you.

While striving for success, you remembered a full, harmonious, spiritual, mental, and physical growth. You knew that all those zones are equally important and necessary and that none of them should be neglected or forgotten. The excess in one domain would immediately cause lack in another.

This is why you didn't satisfy the needs of your soul at the cost of your body and mind and you didn't focus on only your body or mind. You maintained perfect balance, which made you grow harmoniously in each of Life's domains.

Your purpose was LIFE complete, and not just the life you lived then. You were only interested in the existence that realized the potential of your body, mind, and soul in the most complete way. You knew that there was only one Force, one Life, and one Intelligence. Since your consciousness was almost constantly connected to this Intelligence, you had the access to all Knowledge and Wisdom. You could transform your body into a new desired form. You could also heal others when there was a need to do it.

Dear reader, let us translate it into more modern language so you can understand it. Let us assume that your greatest desire is health and that desire is the most correct. Behind a desire to be healthy a desire to live in abundance should be placed, and behind that a desire for God as the Highest Intelligence not only to live within you but also to work through you. Then it will be the understanding, experiencing, and expressing the love, joy, and inner peace that becomes more important than anything else in your everyday life.

And when it happens, you will start to realize the true purpose of your Life and not just the whims of your present, external, little you. In your inner worlds a perfect harmony will rule. You will grow in love and wisdom, and this will protect you from all evil you created in the past. You will need the ability to control your thoughts and to decide on the meaning you want to give to each of your experiences.

When your consciousness was united with the All-present Spirit, you knew with all your heart that God is the almighty, boundless, inexhaustible Source of All that Is. You reached for Him whenever you wanted or needed it, believing that you would receive everything you desired or wanted to have and knew that there was enough of everything for those who trusted.

You benefited from Him without fear and limits, knowing that you weren't hurting anyone with your deeds. You realized that each man was equally equipped and could reach not only for everything he desires but for others' desires, too. If a man didn't reach the Source, it just meant that he didn't want to do it for some reason (he closed himself to God, felt unworthy of Him, etc.) and not because he couldn't or didn't have the right to.

Everybody called on God constructively to get an immediate answer. If the thing you ask for doesn't come to you, the only reason is that there's a conflict in your world since you don't let what you ask for to become the part of your experience. What cut you off from His answer can be all negative emotions like fear, anger, hatred, pity, jealousy, etc. The answer to your request must hang on in the atmosphere, awaiting the moment that you open it.

You are like a magnet and you constantly attract various things. If you experience negative emotions, you close yourself off and push away what is higher and positive, including your own requests for improvement. You open yourself or attract what you fear; the atmosphere around you is saturated with this vibration.

You always attract either what you believe or fear with all your heart. It doesn't matter, of course, if you desire a particular thing or run away from it. You attract it because this is how Universal Laws operate. However, God's answer to your requests awaits the opportunity for you to consciously let it reach you. This is why people sometimes receive things after a few years after they had originally asked for it. As you can see, there is no cause without effect and it is not possible to understand the effect without understanding the cause.

You must understand that you are individually responsible for everything that flows through the energy of your external self in the form of thought, feeling, and spoken word. You cannot escape your own creative activity. With every thought, feeling, or word, you create something, every moment of your life, even when you are asleep. It doesn't matter whether you are aware of your creative process or you create it unwittingly. And so, while you are awake or sleeping, conscious or unconscious, the waves of vibrating activity constantly flow from the Flame of your Life to create.

This is why everything that is a part of your being will hurry towards you and become a part of your experience until you decide to emanate only some levels of vibration. This is why it is so important to live here and now. Only when you are

constantly aware of yourself that you can continuously and skillfully control your thoughts and decide what you wish to experience in your Life.

You once knew that the World was your mirror, so you
looked at it and ordered only God's Perfection to be shown in it.
You gave your external world God's Acceptance, or Beloved
Cherished I Am Presence, and the outer world acknowledged
God within you.

As you can see, it all depends on the state of consciousness. When you were conscious of your unity with God, your
Father, you were also conscious of everything else, since everything else is already included in His consciousness.

Nothing but your mind (through your thought) is the creator, architect, and constructor of absolutely everything that ever
existed and will exist in your world, in your present home. Realize that everything you have and are was created by your single
thought that is the only power able to produce all things. All
riches were created from the universal substance.

You affect this substance with your thoughts and make it
take the form of a visible shape. If you see wealth, beauty, and
perfection in various forms in your thoughts, your life will be
the same way. If you see anything less than abundance, it will
manifest in your world, too. This is why poverty and misery are
caused by your thinking of what you don't want to experience
and not by actual lack. Abundance is everywhere; you just cannot open up yourself to it. This is why you experience poverty
instead of wealth, misery instead of happiness, etc.

All the things you see around you were made the same
way. You live in the world of thoughts and the world you perceive is part of a greater universe, also consisting of thoughts.
We owe it to the thinking substance that everything was created
from. Everything was created in the Perfect Divine Order.

You first attract what you focus on and then you transform it through your judgment and send it in order to create. It happens because the Flame of Life liberated the Life Energy directed to the external self, in order for the thing you focus on to be created. It happens in the conscious or unconscious way, whether you attract something through desire or realize the things you cannot bear. Then the Power and God's Substance fills the form that you created this way.

Although everything comes from God, it passes through you and is tainted with the depth of your inside (positive or negative). This is you and your consciousness, however, and not God, who determines what traits you wish to develop and keep in your world. In this way God, emanates through you and others. It is not personal God, as some religions falsely teach, but an all-encompassing, all-penetrating God.

THE LIFE CONDITIONS

Every comfortable, charming house and every comfort such as light, heat, and the dishes you eat on were created with the help of the powerful cosmic energy coming from the divine Source of All Things and All Power. How comfortable it is to know that God is accessible to you at every moment of your life and that He wishes to satisfy all of your desires! Everything you had then you got directly from God, from cosmic space.

You fearlessly used the Authority and Power given to you by God and you were free. You couldn't acquire and keep this perfect Freedom otherwise by consciously using knowledge. Its foundation was an unswerving confidence and an absolute consciousness of your power. This is why you continuously controlled your own being and precisely declared your demands concerning what you desired. By doing so, you got everything you needed and you accelerated your growth.

God as Life itself is Perfect action that radiates through

Love, which is the power of the Universe. It is a Treasury that every perfect Idea comes from. In Love to your own I Am Presence each desire dwells that makes you happy, and only the Desire of God's Love is the Desire that creates permanent happiness and satisfaction.

Although you used to get everything directly from God and from cosmic space, you would never describe this phenomenon as unusual, unnatural, or a miracle. On the contrary, you believed it was absolutely natural and if things didn't materialize in your life, you would think something wrong was happening. You thought it was obvious since you realized that the external world was an exact reflection of the inner world. You clearly recognized that what manifested outside had existed inside of you.

You lived exclusively in your inner world and you didn't identify yourself with external things or even your physical body because it was deep inside that you found infinite Wisdom, Power, and Resources for everything you needed and what awaited discovery, growth, and expression. It was only when you recognized the possibilities in the inner world that they took forms in the outer world and you made your physical body a channel for the Pure Essence coming from God, your Father, to outflow continuously.

Before you could receive anything from the cosmic space, however, you had to unite with the thing so it could manifest outside yourself. And so you can „do" as much as you „are" and what you „are" depends on what you „think" which is the result of your level of consciousness. You never diminished yourself. You reckoned yourself to be the Song of the Highest God. You realized that you were Universal Intelligence, individualized. One can call himself Son of God only when he is fully conscious of God's Spirit and you were fully conscious of It then.

You also appreciated and admired the value of each man you met, even if it was a beggar or wanderer. You treated everyone with the highest respect since you saw God in everyone. You believed that everything you went through was an experience that helped your soul to learn *Who It Was in Essence*. Each experience is important to the soul, no matter if it makes its ascent or falls.

And so you knew that each woman and each man, no matter their present condition, are as perfect as God. Since everything is God and there is nothing except God, you turned to people like god turns to other gods.

The secret of all power, success, and possession is in the way of thinking. You cannot manifest any power you didn't have already. The only way to secure a power is by acknowledging it. And you will never realize a power if you don't understand that all power comes from within. Both of these worlds, inner and outer, are inextricably linked.

And so you once had everything you desired. You never hid yourself behind others and you didn't fear possessing things that others didn't have yet. You knew that you lived in Abundance and you were absolutely sure that there was enough for everyone; you even thought that everything was in excess. You let Divine principles work within your body and you became a living example of Light to others. When you let the hidden purpose of Light emanate from your body, you became an example of what others could accomplish or achieve.

When you got spiritual and material gifts on your path, you never thought that you were luckier than others. You just cared for the Divine principles to work in your physical body. You said to others „You can follow my example." You thought that a man who doesn't prosper at a certain time is as good as the one who prospers. It couldn't be otherwise. You lived in a perfectly good world, and there was not a person or thing that wouldn't be absolutely right and proper.

And while you saw only the good in everything that happened around you, your mind emanated Light and widened increasingly. You were absolutely conscious of your Divine condition. This is why you lived like god and you saw God in others.

I am writing about it because I want you to understand from example of the life described that there are no limits on Earth. Even now, each human can act in the spirit of cooperation and uniqueness of his existence.

You once knew that God's aim is constant progress and growth and that it can proceed only through yourself and your needs. You felt with all your heart that God within you wants to live fuller and more perfectly. It explains why, although you already had everything what was necessary to live to the fullest, new needs would come to you. This is why you continuously exchanged what was „good" for what was even „better" and more perfect.

So you satisfied the ever-growing need for a richer, fuller, more abundant life. You thought that you should have everything that served life, strength, elegance, beauty, and wealth. Doing so, you grew and the whole Life grew through you.

You were absolutely right to think that accepting less and remaining with what was smaller was a sin against God. It presently seems that you totally forgot about it. You limit yourself and therefore limit God and the Universe's growth. You previously satisfied your desires with joy and now you are ashamed of them.

Living in this splendid way, you didn't describe your existence as unusual or unnatural. It was just a good life to you, a natural consequence of following the way marked by the original and righteous order. Each manifestation of the righteous order has its natural cause and evokes a natural effect. Nothing but inner harmony reflects harmonious conditions, beautiful things, and everything that is the best in the outer world.

All those „wonders," as we call them today, are nothing but the results of Powerful, Omnipresent, Cosmic Law in action. When you accepted and acknowledged God within, you knew those Great Laws and you knew how to activate them in order to receive manifestations of all kinds.

It was God's intention from the beginning for humanity to keep this perfect condition forever. He wanted to fulfill every desire the moment it arises.

God as the only substance is living, acting, and enjoying through yourself and other people. He still wants you to abide in wonderful buildings, play divine music, sing wonderful songs, and travel and see the beauty created by Him. This is why all divine potential seeks expression through people.

Each human can have a different set of skills. One can create instruments and another can play them. One can sing (or paint, sculpting, etc.) while the other appreciates his beauty and admires his voice (or the painting, sculpture, etc.). One designs, the other sews, and the other still can see the beauty of the garment. One can cook tasty dishes and the other savors them.

God wants people to surround themselves with beauty to savor it because all things are the workings of His creation. God wants to play, sing, travel, take delight in beauty, wear beautiful clothes, and eat good meals through you. You can certainly say that God influences your desires and will to express himself through you. Your only task is to focus on God and to communicate your desires to Him. Doing so, you unite your will with God's Will and this will bring the most wonderful results.

You are God's beloved child and your Divine Self always has free choice. What you get from Him depends exclusively on how far and how high your imagination can reach and the will to possess. Since you once realized that the World was reflecting your deepest self, you can put everything that you desired inside it in order for it to return to you. The world is yours and you shape it according to your wishes.

You knew with all your heart, without a slightest doubt, that you live in an unfathomable ocean of the plastic Mind Substance. This Electronic Substance is always alive and active. It is most sensitive to your thoughts and whatever you form in your inner world submits to the condensation law, becoming your individual world expressed by action. Universal Substance of the Universe can take any form you can dream of.

Everything you see made by human hands had been made before in the human mind. You once knew perfectly well that a thought is this creative force and that it makes things transcend into the physical world.

As you can see, dear reader, your life was limited only by your desires and not God's potential. All that exists is the manifestation of various thoughts but it is made of the same basic substance.

It wasn't only you that prospered, of course. Other people also lived in wealth if only they desired. A simple conclusion can be made: God, your Father, doesn't expect you to be generous, give other people alms, or deny yourself and perform your duties at Masses or Sabbath, as your religion orders you to do. He wants each human to independently reach for the Divine Goods that will satisfy all his needs.

Dear reader, I hope you don't believe that you came to the Earth because you were banned or punished, so that you are forced to suffer, sacrifice yourself, and live in a constant worry.

Shouldn't you enjoy each challenge that you meet in life? Didn't you come here to sincerely care for creating and cultivating all forms of life? Their purpose, as well as yours, is constant growth because all that lives has the right to achieve its intended level of growth.

CREATIVE COOPERATION

Knowing what was written above, you devotedly and passionately created goodness and beauty in every domain and in every form. You helped others develop and grow, bringing everything to the highest level of prime that your imagination could reach. You supported accomplishing and owning everything that enabled people to grow. Your work was a joy not only to yourself but to God. You realized that He experiences beauty through you only and this is why He wants you to never stop seeking it.

Comfortable houses surrounded by most beautiful gardens used to stand along wide and perfectly maintained streets. Although you could have everything, your right to possess could be limited if you hurt another man with what you did. This is why you always supported accomplishing and possessing what enabled growth and you didn't support anything that could hurt or diminish anyone.

You constantly followed the cardinal principle that said: „Each member of a society must have an access to everything he needs, what he wants to use, and what he can use." When people generally followed this rule, everything was abundant, even excessive.

If we were to transcend these conditions to present times, all poor families would immediately get everything they needed for a noble life, a beautiful property or a house and land they could cultivate themselves. Everybody would have their own cars, there would be an easy accessible railway everywhere and airplane connections. People would own yachts or other things for recreation and enjoyment only if they wanted to.

There would be tools for growing and reaching one's potential in every house—libraries, musical instruments, paintings, sculptures, etc. You would enjoy everything, even sunlight. You would care for the Earth and It would become a great paradise garden again. Its beauty would make people happy and in return for your actions it would let you live in the same Kingdom of God that you lived in before. I hope that you're beginning to understand more deeply what I am writing about, dear reader.

There was a perfect Heavenly love ruling the Earth because every human focused on his spiritual nature and loving God, consequently and constantly. It wasn't a mental understanding but rather a cordial feeling of deep love, attachment, peace, and joy. God saw your great attachment to Him. Although He is Omnipresent and Omniscient, He gladly looked into your world to be close to beings differing from Him by their size but so similar to Him by what they felt. You could feel this great God's love yourself and you saw it all around you.

You were satisfied by God's special Energy. It nurtured you, gave you life, and you gave life to It. You were absolutely grateful for everything you experienced daily; you thanked God that He gave you life.

You didn't have to eat much to maintain these vibrations and there were people who didn't eat at all. They fed on energy only. It wasn't any special phenomenon. They simply grew to such a level of perfection that they were able to absorb the energy and to keep it thanks to the substance drawn directly from space.

Many legends and myths known today were drawn from the life of those great people who lived as real gods among other gods. This is why following generations called them gods. Those myths and legends are truer than contemporary people are ready to accept.

Dear reader, I don't know if you realize that people that feed only on energy still exist today. And I don't mean the Great Ascended Masters but people living in the physical bodies. Others feed normally but they can absorb everything from the cosmic substance in exactly the same way that it was done in the past. They know the Principle of Life and they strictly follow It. They receive the results they need the most in return.

Dear reader, Divine Love is omnipresent Energy but you can benefit from it only when you open yourself to it. Everybody was once aware of it but now there are only a few. In those times you joyously used the continuously beaming energy streams to perfectly strengthen God's being within you, relying on love and wisdom. It is the Principle of Life, the Perfect Divine Order. It is a strictly scientific domain. Its foundations are as strict as the basis of mathematics, physics, or chemistry.

You knew that God's Substance is thinking intelligence that it works through all, is present within all, communicates with all, and affects all. This Substance always wants a more complete and inclusive life so it is always willing to cooperate. It activates its influence, however, only when a human activates it by his desire, faith, and righteous conduct.

WHAT ABOUT TECHNOLOGY?

Dear reader, if you looked into this distant past, you would be very surprised to find yourself in a primitive retarded stage now. You wouldn't see anything there that would indicate technological progress. There were no communication devices, industry, pollution, electric wires, open construction sites, or other traces of technological progress. You wouldn't find any of the technologically dominant devices that you find in „modern" industrial times.

It's hard to fathom how there was no technology in the distant past. But if you studied this civilization and deeply contemplated it, you would understand that they didn't need technology.

Transportation wasn't needed then but this isn't because people didn't move around. People did travel long distances but they didn't need transportation to do it. It was enough to just think about a place and arrive there instantly. It is similar today:

you think of some place in the world and you are there. You think you do it only in dreams but you are wrong—a part of you is there already.

Dreaming of a distant place is nothing else but moving in space. Once people could take their physical bodies with them but now they can't anymore. Masters claim that you could move like that today if you became permanently united with God, believed that such movement is possible, and didn't allow fear to tie you to your current location.

If you dared to use this kind of transportation, you would avoid many stressful factors. You wouldn't have to bear tiring long journeys, crowded train cars, or traffic jams. You wouldn't hear street noise because there wouldn't be any. You once moved more quickly and comfortably than you do now, even though we have so many wonderful accomplishments and scientific developments around us.

You didn't need telephone either since you communicated through telepathy. The same concerns radio and television. As an all-knowing person (beyond being just clairvoyant or clairaudient), you could see and hear whatever you wanted from a distance.

You didn't need a kitchen and all its tools because food would appear at your call, as well as clothes and household devices. It was up to your creative invention to determine the kind of house you lived in. You could live in a palace or a simple ordinary house, depending on your needs and fantasies.

There were no wires to send electric energy since nobody needed it. You used another energy that was all-present and always accessible. You satisfied all your needs by using spiritual powers alone.

You were so used to light and heat appearing that you never thought twice about it. You could have even gone into a cave, deep inside the earth, and have it well-lit and warm as a flat with many windows in the summertime. The light would spread in all directions, was all-present, and didn't give shadows. When you wanted to sleep and needed darkness, it faded away.

The energy you used so eagerly was sensitive, intelligent, and it reacted to your every thought. Nothing changed concerning the infinite resources and flow of this wonderful Energy. You ultimately get everything that you think of. To being able to access it is not problem, but using it in a careless way.

If you don't like what you get, change your thoughts. You must guard them cautiously, though. They often wander like stray dogs and bring back what they find on their way. To live at the same level as you did before, you must be perpetually self-conscious. If you succeeded in acquiring full consciousness, you would immediately break through delusion and reach the Truth itself. You would then know God personally as well as *Who You Are In Essence.*

There was no noise in the days of ancient civilization since higher forces operated noiselessly. There was no dirt or odors since there was nothing to produce them. Such was life when you were permanently united with God. You lived God's life. You didn't waste time; you devoted it to gaining a better understanding of love and wisdom.

You believed that every plant, animal, mineral, and living thing was your brother. You realized that every speck of dust and every particle is as much a part of God as higher things.

You may not really understand what I am writing about, because you see the world in fragments. You see the Sun, the Moon, a man, a tree, an animal, a stone, a speck of dust. It was different then. You saw Light everywhere and you experience this intelligence with your heart. You felt that everything was

the same Substance, Love, and God. You realized that everything, both big and small, are from the same God substance.

Everything that exists is related because it comes from
the same Source. Everything, including people, are one big
whole with an All-Encompassing Mind, with the Substance being God and eternal Unity.

We all make one big family. Each child, no matter their
color, is a member of this great earthly family. Each newborn or
grown-up, no matter their status, religion, class, caste, or whatever, is a member of this great family.

We all exist in the same God. Each one of us lives,
moves, and exists in Him. The only difference between people is
their level of consciousness. You cannot say that an oak is better
than an apple tree, a rose better than a lily, or that a dog is better
than a cat since everything is equally beautiful and equally necessary to God and us.

Dear reader, you may think now that this old way of
thinking was close to fanaticism but this is how you felt then
and you accomplished wonderful results.

You didn't consider whether God really exists, like you
may do now. You knew beyond all doubt that He was real because He was constantly present in your life. You could feel
Him with all your heart and each cell of your being. He was
closer to you than your physical hands and legs, closer than your
own breath. You not only felt Him, you could see His manifestations with your own eyes everywhere you looked. You would
never doubt the existence of the power that God is. This made
you feel that you lived in Heavenly Kingdom although you lived
on the Earth.

PREVAILING CONDITIONS

When you appeared on the Earth, the climate was mild. It was sunny and warm, and a light pleasant breeze was always blowing. Mild rain would fall from time to time just to supply plants with water. The earth was a safe, powerful, wonderful location of infinite beauty and love. It resided safely in the soft, unpolluted arms of the atmosphere.

You lived among friendly, joyous, peaceful, balanced, and God-focused people. Everyone's bodies were beautiful, magnificent, and ever young. You were wonderful, not only because of your perfect looks but because of the inner light emanating from you that was outwardly expressed in the beauty of your character.

Thanks to the fact that you were permanently united with your inner being, you found yourself in the condition of absolute peace and satisfaction. You can certainly describe it as an eternal happiness.

Your mood was expressed in the most beautiful rhythm of your movements. Your walk was so light, one could think at first glance that you were floating in the air since you almost didn't touch the Earth.

You lived in kindness and decisiveness at the same time, controlling yourself and being cheerful. You persistently pursued your goal but you would take only the direction that you and other people would benefit from. It was more important for you to understand, experience, and express love, joy and inner peace in everyday life than anything else.

If you returned to this good spiritual mood today and held on to it permanently, it would bring you fortune, talents, health, and happiness. Don't be surprised that your soul sang with joy and danced in admiration of you. God sang and danced along with you.

Although you spent a long time on the Earth, you didn't need words to communicate with other people or God. You used images, sound waves, and beams of light the way you used to do it in Heaven. It was possible because, although you descended to the Earth, you kept your former abilities that we commonly call medium.

Nowadays there also happen to be people who have got partial, minimal abilities of this kind, manifesting in the form of clairaudience and clairvoyance.

SEX

During the times I'm writing about, you had got your external body as you do now, feminine or masculine. No matter the body you inhabited then, you were neither a weak woman nor a strong man. Your inner character manifested itself as the strong masculine and your love was expressed as feminine characteristics. These two were joined together, making you a whole being. You existed as a fulfilled, independent wholesome being that joined masculine and feminine characteristics in one wonderful body.

We can observe everyday how important it was on the streets of our cities. We can easily understand what power is deprived of love. It is brutal, ruthless, and deprived of feelings. And love, regardless of its size, is not constructive if it is deprived of power. When those two traits combine, they give the agential power. These people are not common. When it happens, ordinary people perceive them as super-humans.

You need a sexual partner in order to procreate. Once, people used something like breath in order to procreate. You may start to understand what the immaculate conception mentioned in the Bible is about. You didn't waste your life energy for sex because you thought it was too precious.

God designed a man to be in His Image and Likeness. It is extremely important for you to understand this. God gives you energy so it flows through you freely. It is life energy.

When you let Divine energy flow freely through all your chakras, from the base of a spine to the crown of your head, you combined the Earth's energy with cosmic energy and you lived in absolute harmony. This caused your mind to be filled with the most wonderful ideas and you had the Power to fulfill them all. This gave you unusual faculties that you offered to all of humanity.

Today, you often block this Divine energy. These blockages formed as the result of lessons you haven't worked through, which I wrote about in the first volume. And when you block It, you feel that you must discharge It in some way so It doesn't blow up at any moment.

The more you block the energy flowing through you, the more severe your feelings. You cannot sit in one place, you are restless, and you don't know what to do with yourself. You usually feel this energy as a stimulus to take action to achieve sex or another earthly pleasure.

You discharge it, though it's more accurate to say that you waste it. Instead of using it to fulfil the needs of your Higher Self so It can make something constructive for you, you waste it on sex, work, various pleasures, or the whims of your little, external self.

The younger you are, the more difficult it is for you to control this ever-flowing energy. Some people have a clear, almost tangible problem with that, while others almost don't feel it at all since they ignore the energy flowing through them and are totally cold. It is their way of dealing with an incomprehensible problem.

No matter your case, you shouldn't feel guilty by any means. I, too, wasted this energy until I understood what it all meant. The problem is not that you waste it but that you block its flow. The energy blocked causes diseases, pains of all kind, stressful coincidences, and accidents. What kind of accidents? Look at the first volume. I wrote about the chakras' functions and the causes of blockages formed within each one of them.

Dear reader, within the body you presently inhabit, no matter what it looks like, there is everything. You don't have to do or obtain anything else since everything you need for your life to be fulfilled is already within you.

No matter if you live in a feminine or masculine body, you have both masculine and feminine characteristics. You should just balance them so they work in perfect harmony. If you don't, you are just half of a wholesome person.

You can change it by deciding to return to God. You will become enlightened then. You will not only transform your material physical structure and transcend your form to a more luminescent one, you will also balance your feminine and masculine character. You would still be able to live in this world, but you will not be of this world. You will become the whole being again, the way God created you.

People who don't really understand this phenomenon call this moment ascension. I will write about it later. You lived in such a luminescent body in those distant times. You ascended nowhere. You lived every day in the indestructible body of light, in the world you called the Heavenly Kingdom.

MASTERY

In modern times, it happens that a man accomplishes absolute Mastery. Some Masters are well known, e.g. Saint Germain, while the others transform to this state unnoticed by the external world. In every case it is a result of working with themselves, overcoming their own little selves, and crossing delusions on the way to the Truth.

Don't become impatient, though, because it seldom happens that someone accomplishes this within one incarnation. When the Perfect Divine Energy lightens up the physical body of the adept, he doesn't die, he remains still in his body of light, in the same world and in the same way that you used to live. What the Masters accomplished is a natural order, the next stage in every man's evolution.

And so the Masters are wholesome immortal Beings with balanced masculine and feminine characteristics. Dividing the body to separate sexes followed much later and encompassed only those who turned themselves from God, but I will write about this later.

The ideas expressed by those great masterful souls are the ideas that truly guide people. In the span of the ages, there were many of them. They didn't do anything unusual beside the fact that they accepted and used the teachings of Masters on an everyday basis. This knowledge was previously accessible only to a few but now it changes. Dear reader, know that no one but the Masters can give the direction of progress to our world. It is them who stood behind every milestone in the history of mankind.

The Masters are obviously not the same as ghosts. While accomplishing mastery, they didn't go through death and they didn't ascend their bodies. They have lived in the same bodies they had while physically living. You may not see them because their bodies are illuminated with a very high vibration. These spiritual, luminescent bodies are indestructible. They are so perfect that they live eternally and they are eternally young and beautiful. As angels, they reside in a stream of vibrations that are so high that the ordinary human eye—even a microscope—cannot see them. Everything is a state of consciousness. When it is low, it is difficult to see them. When you raise it, and, more importantly, get rid of fear, the chance to meet them opens up.

Dear reader, the fact that you don't see them obviously doesn't mean that those higher beings don't exist. When you raise your consciousness to the reality of the fourth dimension, you will accomplish the faculty of seeing the forms of life inhabiting it.

CHILDREN OF THIS AGE

Each newborn child is good and perfect. They are all good because they all come from God. Each one is born of light and universal love. There are no evil children. The way they are conceived doesn't matter. The only thing that matters is the way they were brought up. If a child is properly guided, it will grow fast, seeing only perfection around.

Everybody can guide a child, but the mother that has got the greatest power in modeling her child to become the most wonderful and perfect being. She can start doing this from the moment it is conceived. This is the way it was once done.

When focus was on a Perfect Being, a child was shaped into a perfect being. It was guided and protected by the Perfect God's Intelligence, the Powerful Presence I Am. This is the Great Natural Law. Every mother understood this wonderful Truth and followed It. Presently, this Wisdom is recognized by few mothers and even less use it practically.

Since all mothers used to do it in the past, a wonderful, majestic race had the chance to be born. If mothers did the same presently, they would get the same results. It is never too late for change. You can even see grown-up children as perfect beings. Many contemporary mothers discovered that when they raised their grown-up children from the depths of drug addiction, alcoholism, and many other disorders.

When children were born in the past, the elders of the community cared for them in addition to the parents. With great care, as if it was their greatest treasure, they made sure that the child didn't break contact with God, its Source, and remembered always *Who It Was in Essence.*

In those times, people knew that each child had the gift of spiritual clairvoyance and ensured that they recognized reality the same way that they perceived the material world. They made sure that the child remembered perfectly *Who It Is*, why it came to the world, and what is task was.

All souls remembered their divine background. They knew *Who They Were in Essence* and guarded any newborn child against forgetting it, too. Bringing up a child meant then keeping and maintaining the wonderful light of its soul as much as possible. They guarded the children's minds so that they emanated a true Divine love.

Children brought up this way never felt the temptation to turn from God, their Father, nor forget Him. Presently, it is the other way round. Bringing up a child means killing what it came to the world with and forcing it to model the behavior of adults. Why? Because grown-ups, in their ignorance, think that by living longer in this world they know better than the child. Is this true, though?

You should not blame your parents, grandparents, or great-grandparents, though. They were brought up the same way you were. You finally have the power to break this enchanted circle of life in delusion and this needs great courage and determination. You can do it only when you know *Who You Are in Essence*. You can attract a perfect child that will also be ready to live in Perfection by living in this way.

It was much simpler in the past when the people around you experienced what they were talking about. They were perfect, exceptional, knew *Who They Were in Essence,* and they followed it every moment of their lives. The all-present good example worked just like a bad example works today.

You came to the world and you instantly knew that you were a part of the family of light and that the key to success was Love. From the first moment of your life you were reminded of *Who You Were in Essence*. They talked about how exceptional and perfect you are so often that you were unable to forget it.

A child brought up this way didn't need to be constantly reminded that it was loved, expected, and absolutely safe since it could see and feel it with all its senses. Each child, without exception, knew that it could realize the Divine Plan it came to the world to realize.

This is why you did only what was most pleasant for you and what made you feel good and satisfied. You led your life so that you absolutely accepted yourself and that it was in accordance with your Inner Being, because you were *Who You Were in Essence*.

You did everything with childish joy and simplicity. You lived and worked according to indications of your Higher Self that manifested outside by being guided by Intuition. Intuition, however, didn't appear to you in the form of a pale, subtle flash like it does now. It was a clear and easy-to-read signpost.

Only what you wanted to experience mattered and not what other people thought you should. Nobody pressured you, either.

There was no currency in those times. Civilization was so spiritually advanced that money was useless. You gave everything that was best in you with love, not thinking of payment or a prize; what was best came back to you from other people. This is how you served others. You didn't need money since everything would come to you or you produced it directly using Universal Substance.

That life and its workings can be compared to the current lives of wealthy men. Many of them are rich because they developed a strong field of intention around them. It is formed of joyous expectation of Abundance.

These people learned to expect wealth, success, glory, and fame, and believe that they are natural and obvious. They don't even consider any other possibility. They don't think they can fail in accomplishing or succeeding.

It comes from the strong patterns they have within that they automatically follow. This is why their life is filled with enthusiasm for new ideas and they succeed in everything since they are not afraid to try.

It was like that with you. You never feared to undertake even the most risky action. You didn't even think that you could fail in anything, that something might not succeed, or that you could lose anything. On the contrary: you were absolutely convinced that whatever you did, you would succeed. You never took failure into account, thinking it was impossible or even absurd.

You created everything that you imagined and desired because you knew that you could be anything You Wanted to Be, do anything you want to do, and have everything you desire. In this way you made everything around you bright and beautiful.

Eternal Youth

Dear reader, the spiritual life filled with love and joy was eternal. While truly loving, you remained eternally young. Your body showed great vitality and never became senile. You lived eternally since you were absolutely conscious of God and through Him you were conscious of Eternal Life. Only one God and one Perfect Pure Life existed to you. You were conscious that It was present in everything, that it penetrated all existence, and that God was a living substance you were made of, too.

While fully aware of Life you were also aware of Health because Perfect Pure Life is Health itself. It is unthinkable that the flow of pure Life could create anything, but health. So you have always been healthy.

No senility or decay approached your body. Although you were aware of your physical body, you never focused on it exclusively because you knew that you had a spiritual body and that it was indestructible. That's why you were eternally healthy, shapely, beautiful, and young.

You still have this spiritual body and it is eternal, inde-structible, beautiful, and young. You probably don't see it in its real form or as it really is since you covered it with a hardened physical shell made from your false thoughts.

As you will discover on the following pages of the book, this dense physical shell that your physical body is today ap-peared much later. You began to form it only when you forgot *Who You Were in Essence*.

Living in such perfect conditions, you didn't see the need to die. Age was not a problem to you or anybody else living in this society. Everybody was respected and loved, especially old people. They gathered more Wisdom every year that couldn't be learned through anything but experience.

It is the other way around nowadays. People are valued for their knowledge, but only few respect Wisdom since they don't realize what It really is. A man that lacks Wisdom cannot evaluate it since he doesn't have a benchmark. That's why masses of people have knowledge but there are few people in the world that are truly wise. This is why we are marching quickly towards doom.

Every year lived by a single man enlarged the treasury of Wisdom of the society as a whole during those times. Presently there are not enough people with enough experience to acquire the Wisdom I am writing about. Contemporary people who live „long" are old men that have knowledge but who haven't gath-ered wisdom because they still haven't lived for long enough to attain it. People acquired Power and Wisdom as the years passed, which made their Love grow. Presently, old people are mostly empty shells lacking Love, Wisdom, and Power.

Those who managed to gather wisdom, however, left. They can't see a place for themselves in this world since there is nobody here who could use their wisdom. No wonder most young people march to their doom each year. They don't have anybody to learn from and they lack true patterns to follow.

In the old days, the so-called aged people were „old" (as we would say today) only when it comes to the number of years. They were not old in spirit by any means or appearance. Their reality expressed itself in eternal youth, joy, and satisfaction. Each of those aged people knew and understood higher spiritual law that triumphed even over death.

You lived in the dimension that was free from physical death and that we call the fourth dimension today. The third dimension we presently live in was formed much later but I will write more of it in the following part of the book.

Dear reader, where there is proper understanding and use of God's power, there is no senility, disease, nor unfortunate accidents. There is no death, either.

There is no natural law of death or decay in Nature. Death did exist then but it was an experiential phenomenon only for some individuals. Death, just like life, must be fulfilled. It was once much easier to fulfil life since it was much more wonderful and unusual.

Death comes only when the vibrations of the physical body step down to the level at which Life gets simply suppressed and pushed out of an empty shell unable to operate.

When someone „died" during those times he could become resurrected in the same way Jesus Christ did much later. If someone wanted to die and leave, he could do it, of course. However, he didn't stay „in the other world" for long, like he does now. He eagerly came back to the Earth because it was only here that he could realize his true activity. It is no wonder since the Earth was truly a Heavenly World then. It was filled and surrounded with such beauty that even Heaven itself wasn't attractive.

Dear reader, you lived extremely long then but you never turned into a disabled old man. This was only because of a deep understanding of the protective power of Love that you used constantly. You created an internal archive of wisdom. It was like a deep, refreshing well and you drew your true reality from it.

There are people in the Bible that lived for three hundred, five hundred, or even two thousand years. Many of our legends and myths were drawn from their lives and the following generations called them gods.

FURTHER LAWS

I don't want you to get the wrong impression that every-thing happened without any human effort. A firm decision was necessary to continuously keep in mind the knowledge that reas-sured you of God's existence and remind you of its Source.

Whatever you did then, during even most insignificant or prosaic things, you always remembered that you were not the author. You remembered that it was God's Power and Intelli-gence working through you and your body and mind were only channels for Its activity. This is how you realized God's true nature within you and you manifested it outside.

Everything you created came from who you *were* and that depended on what you were *thinking*. And so, whatever came to you from the external world existed within your inner worlds previously. As you can see, dear reader, how you react to reality depends on your feelings, perception of reality, and thoughts.

A proper inner reality not only enabled you to act, it also built your courage, hope, enthusiasm, confidence, trust, and faith. This is how you gained the opportunity to create and read the visions you then translated to external world.

Dear reader, you have probably already noticed and understood the following matter. The foundation of health, wellbeing, all greatness, power, accomplishments, gains, and successes is harmony in your inner world. You don't have a chance of accomplishing anything positive in your life without it. Lack of harmony in your inner world causes total chaos, poverty, pain, and suffering.

You cannot be truly happy or satisfied if your body, mind, and soul don't live in total harmony. It concerns each function performed by your body, mind, and soul. If these three don't operate in total harmony, you don't have a chance of satisfying your desires.

And so a real life, as you once had, meant full expression of everything you ever desired and what you could give yourself using your body, mind, and soul.

A desire is a drive for both your life and any other man's. It is a potential seeking expression and a function seeking fulfilment. Without desires there is no life. And so, a man suppressing his desires doesn't live according to what God wants for him; he satisfies himself with poor relation.

It can happen that external, physical things are of no use to us. Were the people in the lost civilization poor? Did they lack anything? No. They lived in God and with God as close as their own breath, hands, and legs. In return for this God realized their every desire.

In order to use causal power, besides living in Unity with God, you needed a true animating thought or ideal because nothing comes into being without starting as an idea. And it had to be born first or to come to being inside you. You had to identify yourself with it and live with it. It was only then that Power was transferred to the outside world.

You couldn't express anything externally that you didn't already have inside of you. You couldn't possess Power without power consciousness. You didn't seek any power outside yourself since you were aware of the Power flowing inside you.

Understanding your inner world, you had the ability to see your hidden possibilities.

Even if you realized that you had inner Power, you knew that nothing would work by itself and that you were the center that activates it all. Since you understood it completely, you lived with the consciousness of your heritage and authority as God's Son, as Christ. You not only had authority of God, your Father, you also inherited everything He had.

You must understand a basic Truth. Although you created just like God creates, you were fully aware that you were not God. You were His extension and not God Himself; you were God's Son and not a Source. In the whole Universe of universes there is but one Source and this is the Highest God. You were fully aware of the fact that there was only One Presence, One Intelligence, and One Power working in your mind and body and it was God.

You expressed God in an active way, during everyday activities like eating, breathing, and walking. You made your outward expression and activity a channel for the unbroken outflow of Pure Essence coming from God. Whatever you did, the attention of your mental and feeling world was exclusively on the I Am Presence.

This enabled you to live in the perfect world, with perfect people, in perfect conditions in which you realized and experienced your desires. You united with the thought that was itself absolute beauty, power, and peace when you desired something. You desired only what was most noble. You never took into account the whims of your lower senses. You didn't let them speak.

You made sure you didn't hurt others while pursuing your desires. You didn't want to harm another one of God's children in some wicked way since you realized that you would pull down the lightning piercing to your own heart first.

Dear reader, you can see that the one who loses is the one who wants to hurt someone else. Harm can only be done to someone that wants to be a victim and that attracts what someone else sends to him. The one who doesn't feel such a need will never get harmed. You once had the opportunity to precisely and immediately observe this phenomenon since your desires manifested almost instantly.

Although you presently need to wait some time to see the effects of your actions—both positive and negative—they are delayed, sometimes by a lot, but each man always gets back what he sent out.

VOCABULARY

You didn't need words to communicate with other people in those times since you could communicate with others through images and sound waves. You could also communicate through spoken words.

I would like to emphasize an important fact here, though. There was not a single negative word in the language you used then. These began to form much later. They were formed by adding the prefixes no–, un–, and im–" to existing words, which is how pairs of words such as perfect/imperfect, healthy/unhealthy, etc. were formed. This system has functioned until now.

There was not a word describing past or future, either. You always lived in the eternal now and something like „before" or „after" never existed. You will ask how this was possible. Well, you didn't live in your past because it passed away like a river so there was no need to come back to something that had already passed. You didn't go into the future, either, since you knew that nothing could happen that wasn't in accordance with your free will. The present was interesting and engaging enough for you to focus on it exclusively.

There were no negative words but this doesn't mean that there was no negativity. You could express negativity and you had the right to do it. It was just known then that by using negative words people profaned God within them. Even if there were words describing negativity, nobody would use them and it seemed as if they didn't exist.

You didn't create negative words because you thought that it would cause great irreparable harm to you. Why? Well, at this time you knew for sure that God's Substance was reasonable, thinking, and intelligent. In its original form (invisible to the present eye) it penetrated, saturated, and filled all the space in the Universe. It was intelligent and it reacted to whatever you thought in every moment. And so, each thought became a form that imprinted itself on God's Substance, which made your thoughts become reality.

And so, if you thought that you were incapable of or lacking something, you would close the door to realization and receive the opposite of what you wanted. Divine Energy works continuously and when it is wrongly directed, it creates things you really don't want to experience. You once used only positive words, because your way of perceiving things was totally different than it is now.

You presently see only what is apparent, visible, and tangible. That's why you see the lack of what you presently need before anything else.

You never saw with your physical eyes since you had higher consciousness and believed it to be a delusion. This was correct thinking. Being able to change or improve what you saw outside at any moment by your internal action, you looked exclusively at what you desired to acquire and what God could give you. The abundance of Divine Energy gifted you with whatever you turned your attention to.

It is always present in your life. You receive everything you focus your attention on. The only difference is consciously looking. If you turn your attention towards what you lack, rage against, or fear, you receive the opposite of your truest desires.

Let's assume that you desire health more than anything else but instead of becoming healthy, you become increasingly more ill. It happens because you don't focus your attention on health but on ailments you presently experience. It is the same with all other things, such as money. If you often wonder where you will find money to pay the bills, you obviously fall into bigger debts. You focus on lack instead of on abundance and so that's what you receive.

When you desire something (such as health or money), it immediately manifests in your spiritual world, though it is still invisible to your eyes. If you persisted in desiring something for long enough, you would certainly transfer it to the physical world. But you lack faith and patience. You nip your desire in the bud because it takes too long to become apparent to you. You end up settling for less. You end up focusing your attention on what you lack instead of infallibly persisting in desiring.

If you thought about lack in those times, you created a form out of your thoughts, something like a seal. God's Substance also created such an imprint; it created lack. Such thought would produce unwanted results until you destroyed the seal, or in other words, changed your thoughts.

If you presently get the same negative results all the time, this means that you either don't think right or you haven't destroyed the previous form, a „seal" you may have created long ago. This is how the Life Principle works and nothing can change It. I hope that you understand now why your manifestations were once so different and why you presently get the opposite of what you desire.

LIFE PRINCIPLE

A Life Principle is God's Principle of Acting in the Universe. It operates exactly the same as the principles in mathematics, physics, or chemistry. If you follow its rules strictly, you always get the same result, regardless of the world's opposition. This manifests, however, only if you approach it with the same confidence you've employed while declaring that two plus two equals four. You cannot have the slightest fear or doubt concerning its realizations.

A Life Principle manifests in I Am which is the action of an absolute God. It operates through all forms of conscious living and expresses itself through I Am. That's why It is much more important than claiming „I exist." While saying with complete understanding „I Am," you open yourself to your own Divinity plus much more. You also open yourself to the Source of Eternal Life at the same time so that it can flow through you freely. When you say „I Am not," you immediately close off access to Divine Energy and the wonderful Source cannot flow through you.

As you can see, while turning to God, your Father, you must know the Life Principle and follow it strictly. A Perfect Divine Energy that you once used every day with excellent results continues to surround you. Contemporary science calls it mechanical energy. Although It is everywhere, you don't benefit from its presence in any way.

You don't have access to It because It becomes Power only when you reach for It consciously and consciously use It. It will never work any other way. It works just like an electric current. It is also everywhere but it doesn't work itself. In order to be able to use it, one must first reach for it and organize it.

I will say it in other words. In order to realize your desires in the name of God, you first had to ask for it, desire it, and reach for it. If you didn't do it, the All-present Intelligent Energy would await, neutral and inactive. That's why you find constant exhortation in the Bible: „Call Me and I will answer you. Ask and it will be given to you. Knock and it will be opened for you. Seek and you will find."

It is not enough, however, just to ask, thinking shallowly or intellectually. One must desire with all his heart, mind, and soul.

As you have probably guessed, your decision cannot come exclusively from reason. Your desire must come from the whole of your mind and heart, which means that you should use the entire Flame of your Life and not just a tiny part of it. You must desire with all your soul, which is the whole energy of your feeling world, and also the force that surrounds all Light resting in your Causal Body.

You see, the value of your Light consists of many more elements than what you have achieved in your present life. It is a sum, or a collection of your whole Life. It consists of every single act of creation, the whole of your Existence. Therefore, you are the result of your all incarnations gathered in one whole and not just the one you presently live.

The Effects of Positive Thinking

You once used only positive terms and they made positive effects. You saw only good in everything and you experienced only good. You emanated deeds filled with love, which made life precious and joyous not only on Earth but everywhere. Your attitude towards life emanated harmony and kindness. Nobody was sad, poor, or conflicted with illness in this environment.

You were surrounded by people that provided themselves with goods directly from space. They joyously cultivated the land and nurtured their crops. You cultivated edible plants with true passion and love; there were fruits and nuts that were amazing to the eye and joyous to the mouth. You grew every plant that you could think of. Nature supported you with all plants abundantly. The soil was fertile and rich. While cultivating anything, you didn't need to work as hard as farmers and gardeners do now. Your engagement in growing plants was fruitful since the wonderful crops returned the energy you invested in them.

There were only such plants and forms of animals on Earth then. That served the common good because Its inhabitants loved with all their hearts. They were One with everything. Love ruled among everything, not just people. All nature loved you and was friendly to you. Weeds and poisonous, prickly, and harmful plants did not exist yet. There were no animals attacking humans.

Each year, many people die because of snakebites or animal attacks. We used to have such a powerful love that all animals, including dinosaurs, didn't attack us. They were friendly towards us and each one of them served humans the best they could.

There was great love between humans and animals. Love conquers in every condition. You thought this life was the most natural so you would be surprised if it was different. Animal behavior began to change when human behavior began to change. It was then that prickly, poisonous, and harmful plants appeared, but this wasn't until much later. Imagine a beautiful rose without thorns or a lion playing with your children like a dog and you will understand what I am writing about.

While you lived in harmony with all of nature, everything served you since you served your environment, too. All was abundant and you never lacked anything. You never considered worrying about what you were going to eat, what you would wear, where you would live, or how you would get the things you desired. You knew perfectly well that God, your Father, would take care of everything you needed to live. What's more is that He was going to give you a thousand more chances than you would be able to use.

Remember the times when the age of glory and unimaginable beauty ruled on Earth. These were long years of adventure, learning, and glory serving as the results of a perfect cooperation. This perfection was reflected in the energy fields of individual people. Together they were raised into the sky with a surprising and wonderful glow. The Earth seen from the above looked like the brightest star.

THE INTENTION FIELD

No wonder the Earth glowed since all people living in those times lived in a perfect harmony with their spiritual ideas and followed only the rule of love in relation to their neighbors and everything that existed, perceiving all their thoughts as holy in everyday life. This is something disproportionately greater than what most people reckon to be a prayer nowadays.

Over innumerable eons of such conduct, a great reservoir of goodness was created. It presented a peculiar energy field made of desires, intentions, and the prayers of everyone that existed. You can easily say that it was a treasury filled with divine attributes, characteristics, and principles.

This powerful reservoir of goodness, divine energy, and original purity is indestructible. It exists even in our times. It is a pillar and cannot be attacked by any negative condition or evil spirits. It is always ready for you to draw from it without limitations. You just need to attune yourself to God and be United with Him in order to do that.

The first step in achieving anything was passing your desires to God, your Father. I will explain further since not everyone may understand.

When you turn to God, it doesn't matter how you call Him. It doesn't matter if you direct your desire to God, your Father, your Higher Self, to I Am Presence, to Eternal Spirit, to the Highest Mind, the Highest Intelligence, Jesus Christ, Allah, Buddha, or any other Great Master because All is One.

It is important, though, for you to turn to What is Higher. You can ask for everything literally and it doesn't matter if what you ask for concerns what you want to be or what you want to have, know, see, feel, or learn. You can ask while doing any of your daily activities.

When you once consciously used the energy of your Life's Presence you knew that you used It in order to achieve things you wanted to achieve, since „whatever you ask for in prayer, believe that you have received it, and it will be yours." (Mark 11:24)

I now realize that many people never receive the things they asked God for. This is because they do it differently than they had before. The main difference is that once God was as close to you as your own breath and body but now you treat Him as if he were far away, inaccessible, and strange, living in some distant Heaven you can't reach.

You then trusted Him with all your heart just like one trusts their beloved Father. Now you fear Him and believe Him to be severe and retributive. You once devoted yourself to Him and there wasn't a moment that you weren't thinking of Him, while today you only think of Him occasionally, if at all.

When you turned to Him, you did it like a child that turns

to its Dad. There is no child that doesn't believe that its beloved Dad has everything that is necessary to live. The child is absolutely sure that its Dad loves it in return and will always meet its needs.

Now you probably don't ask for what you need often. You think that you are resourceful enough to deal with every trouble yourself. You only ask when everything fails or everything buffets.

When you asked God with the confidence of a trusting child, He immediately answered your call and provided you with everything you needed. How could it be different if you and Father were one? You were His beloved Son and you had everything your beloved Father had.

Such an attitude towards life was natural, ordinary, and common to you. You couldn't imagine that you could live differently. You allowed God to act through you when you trusted Him. You achieved this state of conscious Unity through the constant pursuit of living with Him in Unity. You didn't achieve Unity spontaneously, though. You first attuned yourself to your soul's vibrations. It was only when you were totally united with it that you could consciously unite with God. It is not a difficult task. The moment you think of this Great vibrating and pulsating Principle that God is, you realize It within you and get immediate access to it. Although continuous living in the state of expanded consciousness demands a constant, mental effort from your side.

That is the only condition under which effort put into uniting with the Spirit becomes a prayer. A true prayer is the working of human mind wanting to get to know God. It is not the effort put into forming a relation that didn't exist before, but into a complete understanding and recognition of the relationship that already exists. The state of unity has always existed and its recognition depends on human consciousness, however.

When you were aware of your unity with God, your Father, you were automatically aware of everything else, since everything else was contained in His consciousness. The true and sole purpose of prayer is to intentionally and consciously unite one with the Spirit. All other aims are contained within It.

So you didn't pray to live in health, peace, strength nor wealth, but to keep contact with God. When you were united with Him, you were automatically healthy, peaceful, and harmonious. You had strength and wealth since all of this and even more is contained within Him. These qualities show naturally and perpetually when you are conscious of them. You don't need to ask for them.

However, you had to believe in this Unity with all your heart. You didn't have to repeat your prayers twice concerning one intention. When you believe that you will get what you ask for, your request becomes a decree, not a prayer, the moment you ask it. You ask for something when pray for it and you create it when you decree it. And when you believe with all your heart, you don't ask twice, you are just grateful that you got what you asked for.

The Bible confirms it. All prayers contained in It are not requests but decrees. Let's take the Lord's Prayer as an example. You speak the following words: „Your will be done, on earth, as it is in heaven. Give us this day our daily bread, and forgive us our debts." Do you plead for something in this prayer? No! If it was pleading prayer, you would say different words. You would ask for something to eat or for forgiveness of your sins. And so this prayer, just like every other decree, only determines what will happen. It wouldn't happen automatically, though. It is you, nobody else, who make what you say in a prayer, become realized by believing in the fulfilment of the decree. You once got

everything because your faith was true and deep, and not shallow like it is nowadays. You think you believe but doubts and
fears hide the deep layers of your subconscious.

Uncertainty shows only when you think that you are separated from God's Power. It is only in the state of separate consciousness that you can feel fear. You once believed truly. You
and God, your Father, were One, and your prayer became a fulfilled decree the moment you spoke it. This is why you pursued
the achievement of your desires with joyous determination. You
never doubted nor gave up since you knew that every desire and
its joyous expectation is the energy field that attracts a desired
thing to you like a magnet.

You didn't let your mind imagine disadvantageous things
that could happen. You knew that this works just like a prayer in
that it could bring you what you didn't want to experience. You
understood this Truth hidden in this enormous, unified energy
field. You strengthened this field with your conduct, knowing
that this energy can grow to an unbelievable size only though
creative multiplication and common use. You received power
from it that helped you realize your desires.

You knew that you could not lose or fail. That's why you
tried with all your might to raise your energy level and send it to
others. This is how you aligned your energy with other people's
and helped it grow. This way of conduct was „contagious" in the
positive sense of the word.

You first attracted God's energy, transformed it within,
and sent it away. Other people could draw energy both from the
intention field of both you and God and send it away, also. Both
actions were generally the same. They brought a multiplied effect, making the energy field (or an intention field, a prayer)
continually expand.

Everybody was bonded in one, powerful, unified field of

God's energy. This is why the energy of a single person, because of creative multiplication and common use, was much
larger and reached much further than a personal, single, individual energy, since it was powered by the amount of people participating in the field and it encompassed the entire society.

We made something like a perfect community together
in which everybody had equal access to God and His Wonderful
Goods. This field was like a Great Divine Money Box, bottom-
less and filled to the brim. It fulfilled the expectations and desires of the entire civilization. Everyone wanted to benefit from
this prayer or intention field. This field protected, supported, and
provided us with everything we needed.

You desired for the others what you desired for yourself
because you knew that what you sent would return to you. You
guarded this very cautiously. Others did the same.

In order to understand it better, imagine an ideal family,
where there is just one Father-Mother and the rest are brothers
that spread throughout the entire Earth. Imagine people that live
with God and in God and your mind may form an image of the
world made to the likeness of the Heavenly Kingdom you lived
in then.

Or imagine a church that encompasses the entire Earth.
Imagine people it that are united with and devoted to God, not
contemporary religious practices. The image of a civilization
that used to live in the Heavenly Kingdom will be formed in
your mind.

There is no hunger or suffering caused by evil there.
Everybody is conscious of eternal life, health, power, and wisdom so they live eternally and are healthy, powerful, and wise.
Everyone is conscious of Wealth in His Kingdom so they live in
the prosperity and abundance of His Goods. You presently don't
have the access to Abundance, not because someone doesn't let

you get there but because you don't realize the enormity of God's Abundance.

The more you thought and acted according to the Divine Plan, the larger your own and other people's strength grew. This made things show almost immediately. As you can see, it all depends on the state of mind.

The general level you reached then depended on both yourself and everyone else. You knew that nobody could stop their manifestations, so you focused your visions, being the inner activity of God, on the goals you set for yourself.

All of society created this. It was a time of great satisfaction for everyone. Dear reader, as you have probably recognized, Heaven is not for lazy people. There are various activities there. Cooperation is expected from everyone inhabiting It. Only perfect organization can a masterpiece in good shape in the form of the Great Family of Light that God created through man.

EXPERIENCE

You knew that you would never have your desires fulfilled by God if you were not in accordance with the Universe's intentions. You wouldn't be able to satisfy your desires if you didn't follow the direction intended for humanity. Other people were in the same situation.

Knowing *Who You Were in Essence,* it was easy for you to discover your part in the Great Plan of God. This is why you eagerly did your job. You always undertook the tasks that you wanted to do and that nobody could do for you.

You never counted on others to do your job because you knew that you were the manager of your life. You remembered that you could freely use your personal strength that you owed God. You continually decided anew every time what to desire. The Power of God in those times manifested in your life even in a small, single, or trivial activity.

By realizing that you can ask for everything allowed you

to live a creative, fulfilled life, the one you wanted to experience. As you went forward, you gained momentum, your inspiration deepened, your plans crystallized, and you acquired greater understanding and consciousness.

If you ever forgot that you created your life yourself, you would become just a performer and not a creator. You would go along with the motions, accepting everything life brought you. The point is not only that you might not like your experiences but that you would lose authority in your own life and you would start to drift instead of maintaining control.

Since you knew that nobody can live the life of nor grow for another person, you never worried about anyone's individual fate. Even if someone made a mistake or did something the wrong way, you reckoned that it was God working through him and that only good could come out of the apparent evil. You never saw things in a binary of good and evil, regardless of the activity. You saw the Higher Good in everything.

You never feared making mistakes since you knew that you benefited from them and you learned a lot. Even if you felt discomfort while experiencing something, you never felt disappointed or disillusioned since you knew that love would immediately heal all your wounds. Besides, you could always share your feelings about your failures with others.

You always acted in faith and you never let fear get to you. You approached everything with great trust since you knew that God guided you through every decision you made. You never paid attention to appearances regardless of how big or serious they seemed since they seemed to be to your external senses. You accepted only God, which was Perfection in your Life.

You never rebelled. You knew perfectly well that struggling against some ,,unwanted" thing would lead to loss of control over it. If you fought, rebelled against, or resisted anything, the object of your struggle would immediately be revealed to you and the rest of the world.

You probably don't believe me but you immediately felt that you were forced to experience everything you paid attention to and struggled with. How does this mechanism work? I will try to explain.

You create an image of things that disturb you by showing interest in and observing it. Your feelings react to it and you begin to fight with the unwanted image. You don't get rid of what you don't want by doing this, however, you actually get the opposite. You not only bond with the disturbed feelings of a person confronting challenges, you attract them to your own experience, too.

You don't like this experience, however, and you don't want to go through it. You are interested in it because you don't like it so you get excited. This is your last opportunity to pull yourself away from it because when you start to fight a destructive condition, you open yourself to every other destructive condition of other people, which multiplies your experience. Only focusing your attention on the unwanted thing is enough to bond your Life Stream to what is disharmonious which causes you to attune yourself to receiving disturbances generated by all of humanity.

It happened before, of course, that your attention unwillingly focused on the conditions you didn't want to experience. Whenever you became aware of it, however, you immediately called on the Law of Forgiveness and demanded Its wisdom and strength to keep you from making the same mistakes twice.

You turned to God with everything, even the smallest things, because you didn't fear Him like you do now. You knew that He is all Love and had Infinite Patience. You knew that no matter how many mistakes you made, you could always turn to

Him. You believed in His Unlimited Love and Freedom and you benefited from your privilege as the beloved son of God.

Dear reader, you have probably now come to understand that there are only two activities in life—Inner and Outer. If you don't let your Inner activity rule according to your Own Perfection Plan, it is the outer activity that takes control over your fate and rules according to your imperfect senses. This brings about serious consequences.

You notice „something" and at the same moment you agree to that „something" and you accept that „something" since you let your mind become united with that „something" through your attention.

Whatever your mind accepts and agrees with, such as things or conditions, is immediately attracted into its world. You agree to accept something you don't want when you let your attention rest on unwanted conditions. It happens independently and automatically.

This is why it is so important to live in Love every moment of every day because only Love prevents everything that is evil and cleanses and protects everything that is good.

Good and evil, however, are not separate beings. These are just words you use to describe the results of your actions. Whenever something „bad" happens you simply forget that these actions were arranged or determined by the character of your thoughts or they we inspired by someone else's thoughts.

Your thoughts create your world constantly, twenty four hours a day, no matter whether you realize them or not.

I'm writing this so that you realize this fact, not to make you fear your own thoughts. A thought itself is neither good nor bad, it just is. If it is positive and harmonious, it manifests good. If it is destructive and disharmonious, it manifests evil.

There is a difference, however, between those states. A

positive thought always has vitality and life. It always grows, expands, and develops. Since it is creative, it attracts everything it needs in order to manifest into the ultimate shape.

Destructive thoughts, however, include the germs of their destruction. They eventually die because there is no Life in them. They bring all discordance, disease, and misery upon you. When it comes to that, much energy is necessary to break free from such negative conditions. A simple conclusion comes out of it. Preventing „evil" at the very beginning certainly needs less energy than repairing what this „evil" managed to make.

You once prospered wonderfully because you knew that there was only one thing in the Universe that could limit you. It is an acceptance of outer appearances instead of the Powerful and Active God's Presence within you. Being absolutely aware of it, you didn't waste your time for temporal things of this world. Although they haven't existed for a long time, they have left misery in their wake.

You approached other people's experiences with great understanding and forbearance. You never butted into other people's business and you didn't impose your will or get angry when someone wanted to experience things you may not have liked.

On the contrary, you not only respected other people's free will, you perceived everything through the lens of higher good. You saw other people's existence as an opportunity to experience *Who You Were in Essence*.

Analogically, nobody imposed anything on you. You were the only factor that determined which characteristics you wanted to manifest and keep in your life. You constantly brought new information into other people's lives and affected the growth of the entire Earth by growing and developing.

You sent love to everyone. You never considered wheth-

er a particular man „deserved" it. You even lifted the lives of the
people that did wrong. You raised them up so the apparent evil
would turn to Higher Good.

Darkness disperses when even a small amount of light is
let into a room. This is how you lifted people to Perfection so
that earthly things didn't last long on Earth.

You realized a Love of Immortal Perfection was im-
planted in mankind from the very beginning. You knew that the
lack of this Perfection would create absolutely unnecessary tragedies and sufferings like it does now. This is why your Life was
filled with Love, Forgiveness, and Mercy.

When you forgive everything that is apparently evil and
your life is filled with Love, Forgiveness, and Mercy, you don't
feel disharmony, even for a while. Jesus said this much later:
„Love your enemy as you love yourself."

You considered people's experiences from a higher perspective and saw nothing wrong with it, no matter how „evil" it
seemed. If you saw only evil in it, you would have to experience
it yourself, so you preferred to see only the Higher Good.

It was difficult to see evil or be evil because you immediately experienced positive emotions whenever you focused
your thoughts according to your Inner Self. These emotions
were unconditional Love, which meant that you automatically
united with God, and there is no evil in God.

A force that is neither good nor bad is liberated every
time you have a desire. It is contained in feelings. It is simply
energy that you can direct at will. It is only when this neutral
force acquires human traits that an emotion is formed.

You diligently guarded yourself from judging this holy
neutral energy of feelings so that human emotions didn't disrupt
your insides, no matter the appearances in the outer world. It
didn't happen independently. You constantly trained your mind

so it didn't judge in a shallow, human way and saw only the Higher Good in all.

You controlled your life only when you took responsibility for everything you did. You knew people never did anything unwillingly. For example, if you hurt someone with your words, you didn't try to excuse yourself by saying you didn't mean it. You knew that you wanted to say what you did at the deepest level of your being since it was necessary for the growth of yourself and other people.

It was the same when you forgot something. You didn't blame yourself; it was the opposite, in fact. You accepted your responsibility and diligently examined your unconscious motivations. You became a fully conscious, enlightened person again. You submitted your body to your mind, you submitted your mind to your soul, and you submitted your soul to God.

If your mind didn't positively react to something, you assumed that this event could bring only good and that there was a conscious intention of God in it. If something disrupted your emotions, you didn't worry at all. You realized that God worked in and through everything and that He would transform all undesired conditions for the benefit of yourself and others. You reacted to every situation with love and forgiveness, no matter how 'evil' it seemed.

You knew that nothing but Love keeps the energy of the world of feelings in harmony. Destructive forces can't control nor bring disharmony into the world. Love has always been your only protection since It is the only Pure Thing in the domain of feelings.

You once knew that Love was the only Cleansing and Directing Intelligence. Love is a Master Force; it is a Cosmic Law. God gave It to humanity so that the little, outer self could act in accordance with the Great Law. When it is properly directed, it becomes the Directing Intelligence itself that can protect you against all disharmonies due to positive action.

You knew that there was only one way to invite Love to action and it was your feeling of deep devotion and love. This was the only way to reach and liberate It.

You always respected your feelings. You approached them with understanding and care. This attitude towards life stimulated your growth, made you grow, and helped you understand yourself and others.

If you didn't have feelings, you wouldn't see reality around you. The intensity and color of your feelings come from the way you perceive the external world. They are absolutely necessary to you because they give color to your life. Without feelings, your world would become bland and gray at best.

You once avoided moiling in your feelings with the judgment of your external self. Your feelings were always pure and neutral. That is why you never submitted your feelings to moral evaluation, no matter what they were. You judged only what you did, not what you felt.

You were always imperturbable to whatever happened around you. You knew that all experiences, no matter how hard or „evil" they seemed, are necessary for both yourself and others because they enable you to grow. Besides, we should experience each situation from all sides—we must give in order to receive.

Experiences are for learning. It is hard to believe in many things without personal experiences. Experience is necessary since intellectual understanding that is not supported with the charge of our own emotional experience fades in time, unfortunately. We remember our experiences throughout our Lives and incarnations because true knowledge is imprinted on us from practice. True knowledge is not a shallow, superficial image that comes only from observation.

You joyously passed through all challenges because you knew that you cannot learn anything from other peoples' experiences. This is how you learned in totality, not just fragments. To learn and not moil, to learn and to overcome oneself—this is the art of growing. And you desired to grow as much as possible.

Do you now understand the reasons for your imperturbability? Do you know why you didn't condemn, judge, or become angry with other people? You knew the Laws of the Universe perfectly well and you understood the principles of the School of Life. How could you be angry with anyone if you knew you did the same thing once or would do the same thing in the future?

Each one of us goes through the School of Life, although few people realize this. We are all learning how to live in growing excellence. This is why immediate forgiveness is so important. The point is not to be forced to go through the same experience second, hundredth, or thousandth times.

We all do, did, or will do things we would eagerly condemn others for. If we want people to forgive us, we must forgive them ourselves, even if we don't completely agree with them. And we don't agree only because we don't realize that we will be, are, or were in exactly the same situation.

THE OPPOSED FORCES

In the whole Great Universe, one neutral force skews things into opposing directions like a clock's pendulum. You perceive it as two opposing forces. If it wasn't for those two apparently different kinds of forces, human growth would be impossible. Everybody would be the same and identical without them.

There wouldn't be such a variety of sensations either, and the lack of stimuli would result a lack of desire. However, we have an entire spectrum of these. You perceive something (wanted or unwanted) and a new desire immediately rises within you.

Each of your actions comes from a variety of inspiration, and growth follows because of the knowledge you gained. This was the reason we gained the ability to evaluate contrasts created by single experiences. If you didn't have the opportunity to compare what you desire with what you don't, you wouldn't be able to draw any new conclusions.

This would mean lack of growth for both you and the entire Earth. New desires are born inside of you on the basis of the experiences of other people. As you see, you got the best possible conditions when you came to Earth. You can realize yourself any way you want and your own desires stimulate you in order to do it.

Each contact with someone else's experience evokes some feelings within you. You often declared: „I like what this man experiences and I would like to experiences something like that, too." This was how the desire to possess the goods you saw was evoked inside you. It happened also that someone else's experience didn't evoke your admiration and you said: „I don't like it at all. I wouldn't want to experience anything like that." You however never criticized what you saw since you knew that you would attract the unwanted experience this way and you would have to go through it. You did something completely different when you saw the unwanted incident—you let the desire to create something completely different arise within you. Instead of criticizing what you didn't want to see, you thought about what would be good for you in that situation and what you would like to experience. This is how you realized your desires.

Dear reader, I would like to show you an important difference in how you experienced things then and now. Because you remembered your Inner Being and cared for your permanent contact with it in the old days, you had the fullness of God's power and every desire would be fulfilled almost immediately. You immediately recognized the cause (your desire) and the effect (your experience), which gave you an easy choice. You could continue what you desired if it was a pleasure to you or desire something else if your experience turned out to be unpleasant.

Everyone's lives operated around a tangible moral economy. You could have done wrong as much as you wanted. However, you avoided evil because it didn't pay off. The so-called evil was an unpleasant experience and brought nothing constructive to your existence.

Your good was everybody else's good since we were one big family of light and love. You always focused on what brought you closer, not what separated you, from others. The key to success was love because only true Love creates and keeps everything in harmony and perfection.

TECHNOLOGY

As I wrote already, dear reader, everything you needed was created with the power of your mind. You got everything you desired directly from a cosmic Substance by thinking the right way. Food, clothing, and the comforts of home and work were always nearby, ready for you to use them at any moment.

It all appeared in your perfect, Divine form and in such abundance that you could give your good to other people. The Bible describes situations like this. It regards them as miracles but you, living in this reality and meeting it every day, didn't see it that way. You used such forces every day that the contemporary, ordinary man usually taunts, fears, and distrusts.

Seriously, how could you regard these occurrences as miracles if you saw them all the time and knew how to use them? You approached them the same way you perceive contemporary devices today. If a man living in the nineteenth century was shown a mobile phone, television, or the internet, the same thing would happen. These would be miracles to him but they're completely normal for you.

After a period that lasted eons on Earth, people that weren't advanced and couldn't understand the working of Divine Laws began to incarnate. I will explain the reasons why later.

Technology developed for them. However, it proceeded to the stage that enabled them to expand their human faculties, not substitute them. For example, a cane was supposed to support people while walking, not substitute legs or the ability to move on one's own.

It was thought, then, that the true purpose of technology was to develop mental and spiritual capabilities. It was not to substitute them by any means. The most important thing was to develop innate human faculties. They were not substituted by artificial means because it was well known that faculties are like muscles to a man. The ones that are not used slowly deteriorate. They were taken care of and respected as if they were the greatest treasure.

You spent your free time with other people, devoting it all to spiritual growth. While discovering more and more truths concerning your existence, you reached through deeper layers of love and wisdom. This created an approach to Life that was spiritual in all its aspects.

It was guaranteed that no man would bring technology that could potentially harm people or the environment. They only designed devices that served all of civilization.

Technology developed in a wonderful manner but everybody was still aware that everything that was gained through technology could be created by their own mind. If you used technology, you did it to support your creative power, not substitute it.

This civilization achieved a lot in the domain of science

and innovation, reaching far beyond our current achievements because of their noble conduct.

Such a high stage of growth was possible because nobody stopped in individual person's pursuit. Each person of that time was aware that everything in the universe was developing and that no person or thing could stop in the midst of their endeavor. If you stopped for even a short while, it meant that you regressed in relation to constant forward progress. All of your actions were based on your awareness of personal growth and progress, which accelerated and speed up the progress of all mankind.

You were absolutely aware that everyone came from the Source and made one whole with the All-Encompassing Mind with God. And since you formed one big human family, you were free from the rules of kings and other authorities. You rejected the idea of the human kingdom for God's Kingdom.

These were golden times for the Earth and people. Everybody lived in prosperity. This idyll lasted for eons. The culture of this lost civilization seemed absolutely natural to people of that time, although it seems fantastic and unreal to us now.

Dear reader, I hope you begin to recognize what the existence of those people looked like. It was an example of how to use the Great Divine Law in the most natural and simple way. Each living person fully used It.

All of this happened during an earthly, physical life. Less advanced civilizations thought this happened later, after the death of the physical body in Heaven. Heaven was an everyday experience. It wasn't an unreal pipe dream, but a tangible reality.

THE SUMMARY OF THE BEGINNINGS
OF THE ANCIENT CIVILIZATION

I hope I managed to describe this civilization truthfully as the purest race that has once existed in our world. These people were the original, native race that all other races come from. It was later associated with crystal or white light.

This society created beautifully perfect conditions with its faculties in expressing beauty and excellence. It made a paradise of beauty and excellence on its planet. And it achieved it through an absolute control over all elements. It was (and still is) God's intention for all of mankind to live forever in this perfect condition of existence.

All contemporary people could use those Divine Laws if they wanted to and knew how. The only condition is that they do if consciously and with understanding. Many people have maintained true Mastery of those Laws and Truths throughout Earth's history.

More than one reader may ask himself if the history I describe could actually have been his own experience. Is it possible for a man to live here on Earth in such perfect conditions? If the Earth can be so perfect, why live differently now? What made us fall? What can I change to raise myself again? Or maybe people living then were some special nation, chosen by God?

I will answer all these questions on the following pages. For now I am just going to say that you are exactly the same soul that lived then. You still have the same possibilities and faculties you had before. God wants you to live in perfection because you are His beloved Son. Everyone, regardless of their race or background, is a child of God. Every man on the Earth is your brother.

You may ask why your body must submit to the terrible process of degradation, illness, and death.

There are many reasons for that, as you will learn on the following pages of this book. Before you get there, I will tell you that the situation of the souls incarnating is much harder. You don't descend to the perfect world; you descend to one that is far from excellence.

Although your soul remembers *Who It Is In Essence* after it comes to the world, the people surrounding you try to make you forget it.

Children that remember where they came from are often admonished. They're told not to indulge in fantasies or imagination. They're told that adults are the only ones that know anything.

There are many families that remember *Who They Are In Essence* that are under psychological or psychiatric care. People think that there is something wrong with them. Nobody wants to believe what their children tell them. It has become better lately because there have been books published on crystal and indigo children. But how many families have these books and how many deny this phenomenon?

In the old days, just after coming to the physical world, you were told *Who You Were in Essence* and that you were perfect. You could enjoy life and live forever if you wanted to. You looked around and saw that it was true.

The truth was what you knew deep inside and what other people told you because everybody lived in the same perfect way. You didn't get old nor die. You even didn't know that you can or should die because nobody persuaded you of the need for it.

Now things are different. When you were a child you were told that your body was conceived and born in sin and that you're going to suffer because of original sin. When you come to this world, however, you come to know with all your heart that God is your beloved Father and that you live, move, and have your existence in Him.

On Earth, you learn that God is somewhere far away in Heaven. They threaten that He will punish you. They say that He is a frightening and jealous God because he banned Adam and Eve from Paradise for eating an apple from a tree. In the beginning, you don't believe what people tell you because you've held onto the truth that God is pure Love to you. Even if your first earthly parents made some mistake and sinned, it is definitely not a good reason to compromise the lives of everyone in the world.

You were persuaded of so many terrible things. You finally came to believe that you were unworthy of God after coming to the Earth. This is why your body is sinful, imperfect, weak, prone to disease, and condemned to grow old slowly. You believed that you cannot live like you had lived before forever. They persuaded you that you would have to die in the future because this was the way things go. How could you live forever if everybody dies? You cannot stay on the Earth alone...

You obviously opposed them in the beginning because your instincts told you the contrary. You began to „understand" more as you grew up. I put quotes that word because I am writing about it ironically. Instead of living your own life and thinking the way your insides told you to, you began to live like other people.

You wanted to stand by your truth but you didn't want to be different from them so you started to follow along and you became like everyone else. You excused yourself by saying: „If everybody think so, their Truth is 'true', not mine..." And so, you gradually began to believe what they told you.

Nowadays, not many people realize that the Truth was deliberately hidden long ago and that great care has been taken to make you think a certain way. In modern times it was Emperor Constantine and his entourage who did this; they believed that they were god. Over the passing millennia in the history of the Earth, one could find many like him. Some 'taught' and continue to teach us their „truths" consciously, cheating us with premeditation and calculation in order to draw profits for themselves, while others did it out of sheer ignorance.

In the old times, such „teachings" were imposed on us by tortures, swords, or stakes while today it is done in a more civilized way. What way? Look around and take note of the opinions of some politicians, advertisements, and articles in newspapers or television or radio programs with your sober mind and you will realize how much of this truth is. Nothing or almost nothing.

Realize that these are mean, calculated lies and try to break free from their authority with all your might. You will succeed only when you absolutely forgive the great manipulators of mankind and erase them and their treachery from your memory. If you don't do it precisely this way, you will remain under their negative influence forever. Being angry with the ruling system will enchain you to it even more.

If you don't avoid the bad influence of television, radio, and literature, they will constantly weaken your nature, which is mainly characterized by love. Know that demoralizing and fast-spreading thoughts plaster our planet like a mold. This is the reason why the Light of God cannot break through, which is why you live in deepening darkness. Light is information and its absence is a lack of true information. You will learn where it leads in the following pages.

Dear reader, do you still think, like most people do, that our modern world is conditioned by the struggle against reality surrounding us? Do you still think that you must fight to live? Or maybe you are beginning to understand deeply that you attract the things you struggle against into your life? The essence of your existence is not a chaotic search for principles that could put your life into order, but to skillfully learn about your inner world. It is your business to use your heritage to the best of your abilities.

When you reach deeper levels of your own being, you will begin to act according to the natural order. You will integrate yourself with the Universal Ruling Principle, as you once did. It will be as if you turned a key in the door and entered a next room. You will look then and everything that was bad and unwanted will disperse like a morning fog. And when you lift yourself up you will be able to support other people's growth. I have presented a lot of practical knowledge for you here.

YOU AND GOD

Dear reader, I would like you to consider your relationship with God. I realize how sensitive the subject is, but until you take the courage to do it, you won't progress any further. You cannot avoid this question forever. It doesn't matter if you are a so-called believer or nonbeliever according to Church. For one may not visit a church at all and be as close to God as he is to his own breath, hands, and legs.

In the face of more frequent and powerful cataclysms, diseases, poverty, hunger, and wars in various parts of the world, a growing number of people ask themselves: „Who is God?" They call out for a person to blame, the one who „lets this all happen."

And so, without looking at God from a broader perspective, you cannot comprehend your own life or the things that I want to tell you. Everything you experience in your life doesn't really depend on the name of God you believe in, but on your faith in Him, whether it is true belief or belief in the image that has nothing to do with God.

God's power still dwells inside of everyone, just like it did at the beginning of existence. You read about what this Power is capable of earlier in this book. Shouldn't you ask yourself why the average man is not aware of It and why he doesn't feel and use it?

The answer is quite simple. Since he is not aware of it, he cannot inflame it within. This is why the Power concerning most people lives in the form of a merely smoldering spark. If it had adequate conditions and was whetted by your consciousness, it would immediately gain the chance to burst with a full flame. The Light would appear within you.

Regardless of whether this spark is smoldering or burning with a great flame, however, each one is equally precious since it comes from the Flame of the Heart of God Himself. It is in every heart. It doesn't matter if you realize this or not.

It doesn't matter if you are a believer or an atheist, either. It doesn't matter whether you are a good man or seen as a disgrace to society. You have God's spark just like everyone else. Your life is a part of a Great God's Life coming from the Great Central Spiritual Sun, which manages all of the Enormous Universe, consisting of innumerable Universes the same as ours. You have the opportunity to sense this God's Spark. It manifests in the form of your innate instinct, in the form of a kind of alarm clock. This is why you sometimes experience moments of deep reflection about yourself and your general sense of life. This silent, wakening signal appears inside you always but you don't always want to hear it.

When you hear it, you would rather start talking, working, watching television, or listening to the radio. You may reach for an addiction or anything else around to help you stifle this injunction. Then the next signal sounds and the next until you finally hear it.

If you don't want to stop, there will be other, more drastic ways of getting you to listen. A serious disease or accident can stop you and get you to listen. When you get stopped this way, you get a chance to think about what you had done wrong in your life.

Don't think, however, that this is a punishment for your evil deeds. No way. God loves you very much and He tries to reach you one way or another. Since you don't want to listen willingly, your Higher Self must find another proper way. It doesn't have anything to do with His whim or a caprice. It knows that the quality of your life in this and every other world depends on this knowledge.

When you agree to listen to Him, a hidden, tormenting desire arises inside you, which is the insatiable strive for something bigger, better, and more perfect. It is a desire sent directly from the Source. It appears within everybody but whether a man wants to acknowledge this depends on him only.

When I think of God, of course, I am talking about One and All exclusively, in All, through All, and for All. This is the God as Absolute, and not of Jesus or some other prophet that most people reckon to be God. I mean the concept of God as Absolute, The One who is above all religions and who manifests himself in every man in the form of the innate instinct or insatiable desire for something better, more beautiful, and bigger than what we currently see.

This innate instinct makes people disagree with their own and other religions. They sometimes argue or even fight with each other. They may unconsciously refuse to call this Enormous Power the Christian God, Muslim Allah, Buddhist Buddha, or anything else. They know deep inside that this concept is absolutely incompatible with Perfection and The Greatness of Existence of the Higher God's Power.

People unrelated to any religion describe God as the Highest Intelligence, the Universe, All That Is, Inner Being, Higher Self, Spiritual Guide, Guardian Angel, or I Am Presence. It doesn't matter what name people call Him since no name can describe the Greatness of His Power or the characteristics of Power and Energy, the One. All names refer to the One and the Same God since He is One, is Oneness: „For I said 'I Am' that Is and there is no other but me."

People fighting in the name of their religion don't actually know what they are fighting for. They divide God into many fractions. That is why so many religions were formed and new ones are being formed. But how can you divide God as Oneness into so many religions?

The God that is above all religions manifests inside you in the form of an innate instinct. Otherwise, you would never reflect on your life. You do it when God alerts you that something is wrong with your life that you wandered too far from the Source.

God is your support and Providence, He represents purity of all ideas that find expression in your consciousness and conscience. You usually organize your life according to those, though you often do it absolutely unwittingly.

God doesn't speak to you on a whim. He gave man a free will and He respects it. He sees where a man wanders and tries to guide him towards the Truth by His suggestions. Only a man who learns the Truth can understand the seriousness of his situation and efficiently break free for good.

God speaks to all people by silently whispering deep into their hearts and nevertheless there are millions of people all over the world who are lost, doubtful, and completely unaware of the fact. How can they be awakened? They suffer, not knowing the cause of it.

They are so deaf (spiritually) that they wouldn't want to follow Him, even if He was quite loud and clear. And since He cannot reach them directly, he finds various indirect ways. He uses his representatives, among other things, who can hear Him and relay what He wants people to hear.

However, God never spoke through any preacher of the Truth to make him the only God, like his followers would want. He spoke through a preacher because He thought he was an adequate channel through which the Truth can flow, so that he could be heard and understood. God never spoke through Moses, Jesus, Buddha, or Muhammad only. He spoke to all people in the world.

People who hear God's voice are wrongly believed to be His special chosen ones. It's true that they are special because they are able to hear His voice because of their efforts and pure lifestyle. This is not the reason, however, to form a new religion. It is a misunderstanding of the subject that caused several dozens of thousand religions to be formed in the world, the majority of which were forgotten. What's more is that there are more people hearing God than there are religions. And there would be still more if people having contact with Him had the clout.

God is Love, and the greatest religions, including Christianity and Islam, were propagated by war, torture, and suffering.

Writing this, I don't claim that religions are bad or that they shouldn't exist. Each one of them presents its own piece of truth that should join the rest. I believe it can be done without losing the fundamental truths and traditions of all religions. Joining all religious truths is important if the power of prayer energy is to increase enough to show and overcome dangers created by those who fear. In the chapter „The Energy Field" I described how this mechanism worked.

There are only a few people here on the Earth that keep contact with God. There are few who want to listen to them. Imagine, dear reader, that at the street of your city appears such a great Light Being like Jesus, Buddha, or Muhammad. You may find it hard to believe but people wouldn't recognize them as prophets, they would believe them to be crazy and would put them in a psychiatric clinic. How many spiritual people are oppressed or „silenced"?

Contact with God is not reserved for the Prophets of the ancient biblical times then, as existing religions suggest. New channels open all the time, through which the Truth outpours.

God speaks to each man deep in his heart, too. In order to be understood, He sends his Angels to people, or Ascended Masters. Such a contact is possible anywhere they can be heard and understood. It is a rare phenomenon, however. Not everybody can talk directly to Them. Our physical bodies block us, as well as our limited consciousness.

This is why many people experience the phenomenon of true contact and they go mad since they don't believe it can be true. Even Muhammad himself believed he was possessed for three years before he opened himself and let the Truth reach him.

There may be somebody next to you who sees Angels or talks to Jesus or to some other Great Master. The problem is that most people don't believe it and they try to fight these „hallucinations". When it doesn't help, they are forced to go under „therapy," taking psychotropic pills or going to psychiatric clinic.

Many people don't believe it since they have always heard in church that these wonderful faculties were reserved for the old biblical Prophets. They have been persuaded that we deal with madmen who are only imagining this contact. This is nonsense, of course. There are people all over the world who contact Them every day.

The church often condemns such contact since it cannot verify them. Who would do it? Most clergymen rest on a much lower level of spiritual growth than the one who has the privilege to have this contact. While they cannot verify this phenomenon, they fear it. Also, if it turned out that these contacts were real, they could become a threat to existing religions. New, more powerful religions could eventually be formed on this foundation, based on the Truth to a greater extent. One way or another, all religions were formed because we didn't understand the essence God for such a long time.

The question of getting to know God, however, is quite simple. It is regaining a lost memory. You knew God because you were created by Him. Then you lived with Him for a very long time, like a child lives with its beloved Father. Next, when you have already started to descend towards more dense activity, nothing changed in the matter. When your energy was turned down for good, a Curtain was drawn before you and the Wondrous Beauty of the unspeakable God's Temple was forgotten.

Dear reader, know that it is possible to see or hear Masters or Angels. It needs to be said loud and clear, especially now, when many children are being born with such abilities. And there will be even more of them. They need help in their strangeness. We should nurture them instead of keeping them down and persuading them that adults know better.

In order for you to understand it, dear reader, I will use an example:

Several years ago, after one of my numerous lectures, a large group of people gathered around me. It is natural and happens every time I appear in public. Some people want to thank me for my help, others ask questions. There was a woman among them that I couldn't take my eyes off of. I can still remember her lucent body and love emanating from her whole being.

She pushed her way to me and said: „I got a short pass from the clinic. Could I have a word with you cause I have to get back soon?" I consented to that. She said: „Jesus comes to me. I not only see Him as clearly as I see you here, I can also walk and talk with Him freely. It was Him that told me that you were going to be here and suggested that I should come, so here I am."

I was glad. „It is so good to talk to a person so wonderfully gifted," I said. „Very few people can do it because one needs a body as lucent as yours. Jesus's vibrations are too high and can come close to only a few people. He does this only with people whose bodies can bear His great Light."

She was surprised. „So you believe me? And they have been keeping me in the psychiatric ward for so many years now. They treat me with electric shock therapy but my visions don't go away." I said: „I believe you because many people all over the world have the same type of contact. I talked to some of them and I personally know of such cases. And since the contact is real, the „visions" cannot go away, either, because they are real, too. You are at a hospital because you want to prove to everyone, such as your loved ones and doctors, that you are telling the truth at all costs. Does it change anything? They don't see it or hear it so you cannot blame them for not believing you. Ordinary people rely only on their five senses, and your meetings occur at such a high vibration level that it is hard for them to understand it." We talked for a short while since she had to go back. I suggested that she remain open to the contacts and refrain from fearing. „You are most wonderfully gifted, you should be happy not sad, nor suffer in the psychiatric clinic," I said. „Since only a few people become mature enough to receive this message, please don't tell everybody what you see and know. Follow this rule: 'I always know what I am saying and never say what I know.' You can say such things only to people who are able to understand it and are at the same or a similar level of growth as you. Only such a man will realize this is not nonsense. If there are no such people around, you should be silent. I asked her if she had ever met a doctor that would understand. She said she never had. „So you should be silent with them, too," I said as a goodbye.

We parted because some of the people waiting wanted her to finish soon and treated her as if she wasn't quite normal, too. I needed to engage in their more mundane matters.

She called me after a few days with the news that they had released her from the hospital. „She must have followed my advice," I thought. She told me that she still had the visions but had become calmer. It turned out that she didn't have a place to go because she had lost everything in the meantime. However, God took care of her. Now she is a famous healer in the United States. She helps many people now but this wouldn't be the case if she hadn't asked for help.

Dear reader, if you are a psychiatrist, doesn't this suggest anything to you? I hope that you think twice the next time you diagnose someone. The patient may fear what they are going through themselves.

Do psychiatrists have the right to judge and claim that what their patients see and hear is not possible only because they don't see nor hear it themselves? Well, psychiatrists are no exception here because most people are not aware of higher vibration spaces.

Being a part of the majority doesn't mean being right. I think it is time to accept that extremely different people can be as normal as we are. „Different" doesn't mean „ill," „stupid," or „worse." If a psychiatrist is going to cure something that is incurable, it may be worth it to get to know the new subject in order to see an „ill one" in a new light. Such people are hunted down, they fear their otherness, and suspect themselves to be mad. It is a doctor's duty to help these people understand their situation since psychotropic pills won't solve the problem.

Not all residents of psychiatric clinics are as spiritual as the woman I wrote about, of course, but one thing is certain: each one of them truly sees and hears. The question is who they see or hear. Is it the Being of Light, as in the case of the woman, or, more commonly, the inhabitants of the astral world – ghosts?

If these are ghosts, the man needs the help of an exorcist. Psychotropic pills won't help. They work like earplugs or eye bands. They suppress sensations but they don't have the power to remove the source of unpleasant experiences, as it usually happens with ghosts.

If a patient truly sees a Being of Light, nothing needs to be done except make him realize that it is possible and natural and that it happens to many people. People seeing Beings of Light usually have a task to perform. When and what? They will know when the time comes. They need to stop fear first, however. The doctor is able to remove fear not visions like I did in the case of the woman I mentioned.

I must clearly express a very important **warning** here! Not all voices come from the Angels or Masters although they may claim to be them.

Most voices or visions come from the **ghosts of the deceased**. In order to distinguish them, one must immediately ask such a being: „**Do you come from the Light?**" and attentively wait for the answer. Nobody will dare to say yes to this question if he doesn't come from the Light or directly from God.

A ghost will try to answer evasively and this is how you know that it is not Jesus, a Master, or an Angel. Immediately tell it to leave. Don't even take time to think about what it tells you. Otherwise, such a discarnate being will haunt you, disturb you, and possibly even possess you for good.

Every day, I deal with cases in which a man once caught in such a trap cannot liberate themselves from a ghost for years. The consequences can be serious, distressing, and tragic, which I wrote about in the book *Possessed by Ghosts.*

Such a person is indecisive. He or she intuitively feels that there is something wrong with the contact because neither an Angel nor the Master can be the cause of suffering. On the other hand, a being-usurper persuades him that the matter is of great importance and although he now suffers, he should bear it. In order to prevent possession, ask the question above at the very beginning of such a vision in order to save yourself unnecessary torment.

Never let your own curiosity to guide you; rely on your intuition or common sense at least. Only the Being of Light will answer to the question with the firm „yes."

RELIGIONS

God speaks to all people, though most of them don't hear, feel, or recognize Him. It is a task of every religion to awaken this awareness. Since the time of the fall of humans during the period that I described above, all religions in their original, true version intended to become the foundation of life liberating humanity from its limits and the capacity it created.

Therefore, religions wouldn't have been created and be necessary today if people had remained constantly aware of their existence with God. People would listen to God and follow His advice. Take the example of the lost civilization that didn't have religion at all and lived with God and within God. Why didn't these people need religion? Well, in those times each man kept God in his heart and communed with Him every moment, not only occasionally, such as during prayer or church service.

Dear reader, I am not writing this to separate you from your religion. I am not trying to persuade you to new theories that are the opposite of the ones presented here, either. I am trying to awaken your obliterated memory. You will recognize that a false understanding of God's Essence offered by some religions means you don't believe in Him at all.

Realize that infidelity is not lack of faith in some church teachings but lack of faith in Truth. Upholding the dogma of the Bible is not enough. Praying by mouth only without active consciousness and proper action is worthless.

How easy it is to read or talk of love, mercy and faith! Loving truly, showing mercy, and believing in God with all one's heart demands consciousness to be transformed. I don't mean transformation though drugs, alcohol, or a momentary flow of emotions. The permanent change of consciousness can be achieved through real knowledge and understanding and only specific deeds and practices can keep it. It is assimilation of something mystic into the present consciousness that makes something become a habit.

What churches teach us nowadays leads us astray. You think you believe in God while His image has become so distorted that you don't believe in True God at all. Most people learn this when it is too late, after their physical death. What am I talking about?

Well, many religions want you to seek God outside yourself. Even if you feel Him deep in your heart, you don't trust yourself and you don't believe it is possible because priests told you that you are not worthy of Him. Long ago, before the Catholic Church was formed, they placed God far away from you in an imaginary Heaven so that you couldn't reach Him. They placed themselves as intermediaries between Him and you. If you contacted God directly, you would regain your old power and what would you need religion for? No church can let it happen since it would cease to exist without you and others like you.

In most cases, even the most devoted follower wastes his or her earthly life seeking God outside themselves and cannot find Him. Most people wrongly think that by sacrificing their earthly life, they will get a rich prize after the death of their physical body.

Some religions require people to fast and mortify themselves. Others require people to willingly sacrifice their lives by making a suicide bomb while others waste their time on Earth wrongly believing that the Savior was crucified for their sins so it is enough to regularly visit a church and wait for God to do the rest.

It is easy to live in such „blissful" unconsciousness but it gets difficult when you die and experience a huge disappointment. It's then that you see that nothing your religion told you was true. Many people seek God in the astral world, but they try in vain because they will never find Him there. They don't see God, Heaven, or the promised prize. They search endlessly and they cannot find Him since they search in places where He is not. I am talking about all of the followers, not just one that misunderstood the teachings of their church. The church led them astray and deceived them by its false teachings. Obviously priests and nuns also happen to be among the deceived.

They heard all their lives that God will come to meet them at the moment of their death and take them with Him. They seek God and Heaven but they cannot reach Him, no matter how „devoutly" they lived. They were too eager and they didn't think for themselves. The awareness that they should seek God inside their hearts was never developed because they turned to a God placed outside themselves for all their lives.

Such a devotee feels much disappointed and bitter and wishes to take revenge. These are the ghosts that make so much trouble to the church, curse, and blaspheme. The more devoted a man was while alive, the more trouble he makes for his loved ones after death. Thousands of families possessed by „devoted" ghosts serve as proof.

Dear reader, you may be very devoted and firmly stand by your religion. It is possible that my words evoke your unbelief, fear, or feeling of being lost. I think that it's much better to work through this lesson now while you still have got your physical body and can do something with it than when you find yourself in the astral world with no way out.

I would like to emphasize, however, that I am not writing this book to co-opt you. My point is that you don't accept anything blindly, including this elaboration. You have been deceived for too long. I want you to find the knowledge deep inside you and believe it with all your heart when you acknowledge it as the truth.

Ultimately, you know everything I am writing about deep inside because you lived many times before and you experienced everything I am writing about yourself. Remember, this was the intention of the Great Beings of Light, after whom all religions were formed.

After Jesus had ascended, His teachings were deliberately changed in order to achieve control over people, including you. Remind yourself about the True Teachings and your life (whether in the physical form or after death) will never disappoint you again. All wisdom is within you, collected during every incarnation you have passed through. You just have to find access to this precious treasury hidden deep within you.

You will find confidence that God is with you always and forever; that He cannot be separated from you, or from any of His other creatures. He is Almighty and Omnipresent, He is All in All, Omniscience, All-goodness, and All Truth. He knows all and is the cause of all things. How can Someone who is Everywhere not be present inside you?

You have carried this Truth within forever. Take the courage to break the external shell of your false beliefs that makes it impossible for you to reach your inside. You will find numberless layers of wisdom, love, and power there. You will achieve a deeper understanding of your physical life and beyond.

It is not easy, especially in the beginning, because there is so much doubt inherent in human beings. However, if a person dares to make a step forward, it is going to be easier for him with each step until the day he discovers with astonishment that what is wrong is left far behind and doesn't affect him in any way. Most churches—the specific names are not relevant—are stuck in the same place. They want you to seek knowledge through them because only then can they be certain that you won't find it. And even if you discovered it in some miraculous way, they will make you doubt it by persuading you that what you discovered was impossible. This is why, among other things, they persuade you that you live only once so you don't seek the Truth yourself.

Dear reader, you came to the Earth many times before. Did you find God through religion, even though you sought Him so devotedly? Did you, being at the mercy and disfavor of the church and its priests, come closer to God by a single step? Do you feel better, more satisfied, and happier? Well, you won't find your destiny but following the signposts outside of yourself.

As I wrote before, you are here to love, learn, and grow. Do you really think that a soul comes to the world just once and then praises God forever? Would a soul be happy with such a life? Would a single existence limited by physicality of the body make any sense?

A True Life is full of constant progress and growth. The

apparent death and loss of the physical body is just the next attempt at making you realize that even what most people reckon to be the end is only further transformation and growth. In reality you are immortal. And wise. And you become even wiser every day.

Religions want us to believe that the Prophet, a Great Being of Light such as Jesus, is God. Jesus knew and preached the Truth of God and taught us how to use the Divine Law daily. He didn't reckon himself to be God and us to be people. He said that every man is God, since God is Spirit dwelling in every man. We read in the Gospel of John that Jesus said: „You are Gods."

God didn't speak through any of the great prophets to make them Gods but for you to hear the Truth from their mouth. It is pseudo-followers that made a God of the Prophets in order to take control over the movement. The true followers were mostly killed. Besides, it is much easier to control people using the tripartite relation: God (Jesus) – intermediary (priest) – sinner („ordinary" man).

None of the Great Masters and Prophets (like Jesus, Muhammad, and others) claimed to be God or felt that they were His special chosen one. I don't negate nor discredit that these were (and still are) Great, Wonderful, Lucent with Truth Souls. I bow to each one of Them. They were striving for excellence through numerous incarnations and achieved a point where they could clearly hear God's voice and translate it into human language so everybody could understand Him.

It demanded a huge effort on Their part. They desired it deeply and we fulfilled this desire. At the beginning of their journey, each one of Them had times of doubt, just like we do. This is why every one of Them deeply studies all religions that they had access to. They did all this so they could be prepared to hear God's voice.

The Prophets taught about God but none of Them, except for Muhammad, formed their own religion. None of Them claimed to be God, either. They preached the same. They indicated that God that was One. I don't want you to believe things you don't have the chance to verify for yourself. You lived during various times and you can find the access to this knowledge, you just have to open yourself to it. Don't believe words, even mine. The Truth is deep inside you. It is also contained in various historical notes for you to confirm It.

Dear reader, I am sure that you lived in times when one of the Great Beings I mentioned preached. If you understood deeply and absorbed the Truth they preached, you would also become an enlightened being and you would ascend like They did.

Since you returned to the Earth, it means that you should either learn more since you closed yourself to God or that you desire to help other people to understand Him. We live in peculiar times and we need all the help we can get. Setting a good example helps other people more than anything else.

If you are here to help people turn to God, remember that you cannot impose anything on them. You can try, show, encourage, but nothing else. Accept the fact that no matter how hard you try, some people won't join you. They have not matured enough to wake up. It can make you sad but it is your high duty to respect their free will.

Remember! You cannot press them in any way, even if their wrong choice seems to indicate spiritual loss in the future. You must accept the fact that since they don't follow the good example, they will probably have to learn from their own mistakes. You won't help them otherwise and you can hurt yourself. I will write more about it in a later part of the book.

You may wonder whether religions today fulfill their tasks or are unnecessary. The answer is yes and no. Although they do it wrong, they nevertheless turn people's attention towards God. If it wasn't for religions, a contemporary man wouldn't realize what God is. I repeat, though: a false belief in God can be as wrong as no belief at all because it leads people astray. Many people think everything is all right with their lives since they are religious people. Many people boast that they believe and practice their religions to the fullest.

The more he tries, though, the further he goes astray. Religions had to find to find a way to keep their followers from rebelling and leaving the church for good.

Here it comes: the founders of the greatest churches knew that religion wouldn't make anybody meet God in the earthly life, so they moved this moment until the time that was to come after the death of the physical body. Souls that passed through the transformation called death were disappointed that they didn't possess what their religion had promised them. The devotee has been convinced that he is too sinful and unworthy of God. When he dies in devotion, however, God will take him. Then he will get the prize for being faithful to his Church.

As far as we know, he can live through his earthly life but after his physical death he gets caught in a trap made of lies concerning God. He trusted his religion and now experiences horror until something about his understanding of the Nature of God changes. I deal with such disappointed ghosts every day, and I have met innumerable hosts of them in my life. These are not only lay people but also priests, nuns, and monks.

Every religion indicates another God and another Heaven. It seems absolutely normal in our physical reality but has serious consequences after the loss of the physical body. I will try to explain it to you, dear reader.

Thousands of people die every day all over the world. They live in different parts of the globe and follow different religions, which are plentiful. Can you imagine this chaos after their death when everybody tries to find the way to their own Heaven? They behave like someone looking for his glasses while having them on his nose. This is the reason, among others, that so many souls wander through another world.

Heaven is a state of consciousness and not a particular place. It is a consciousness of God and Truth one can achieve for good only while being physically alive, though not with the help of the religion.

And what if lack of faith is better than false belief? Certainly not, since lack of faith makes the soul fall. There is no life without God. A man who does not believe wastes not only his present incarnation but all the other ones that he doesn't change. It continues until he wakes up.

Believers are awake and though they seek truth in the wrong places, they nevertheless believe that God exists and they are open to Him. Nonbelievers don't want to wake up. They think that death is the end of everything that only nothingness follows it. Even if such a soul wakes up after the death of its physical body and discovers that it still exists, it won't know what to do with itself. It won't have a goal. So it is going to wander forever until it doesn't need to raise its consciousness anymore.

Some readers may ask how it is possible for so many religions to exist, each indicating different Gods. Even common sense suggests there is something wrong here. For God is One: „I Am That I Am, and there is no Other than Me." God Is One, being eternal progress, worship, and ruling. The house of God united keeps this condition permanent. Were religions formed in the lost civilization? Did people fight with each other? No, because its representatives lived in Unity with God.

All religions teach that God is One, so they all confirm this basic Truth. Where does the idea that followers of differing religions should fight to prove that their religion is the only true one come from? Do their bodies suffer differently from diseases? Do they get well in different ways? Or maybe they experience emotions and mental problems in different ways?

I think that most people will agree when I say that we all fear rejection, loss, or treason in the same way. That anger is equally poisonous for the body of a Muslim, Buddhist, or Christian. We all share the desire to love. We don't differ concerning our body and spirit. Why do religions make us different?

Each home that is divided, no matter how powerful its religion is, must collapse sooner or later. And this threatens its followers with failure and death no matter which side of the barricade they stand on. You will learn by reading this book how it happened many times in the past. The only way for all religions to unite is to acknowledge that the true God is One.

Nowadays, the church doesn't fulfill its duty since people begin to desire to experience God personally, not through a priest, on their way to enlightenment.

No person or priest can transfer any of their rights to another. Besides, there is no reason to do it since everybody is equally equipped. You may not understand it completely at the moment, dear reader, but it will become clear to you when you raise your consciousness. A priest trying to transfer his rights to contact God to a follower is inconsequential. First, he tries to pass something he cannot give, since this value is inalienable. Second, nobody needs it because they all have it inside. The only thing a priest can do is to show how to expand one's desire for absorbing the Good that God is within one's heart, which is what religions should exist for.

In conclusion, at some stage of our life or growth each one of us grows beyond all religions, since none of them can satisfy our inner desire manifests as the need to constantly strive upward to God, to Light.

Besides, how can an ordinary priest know God? He studied various subjects at theological schools, trying to get to know Him through his mind only. After graduating, he focuses on theological problems and he sometimes studies other religions so he can compare them. And so, most priests spend time on reflection and learning.

I have received incredible information on the matter since I get many letters from priests that say that that they went to seminary to find God but couldn't find Him there. Other people write me saying that they can't find God at church. Unfortunately, many truly devoted people have become disappointed with their religions and have left them. For there is no way to analyze the Creator in detail, trying to intellectually discover that God is the Heart emanating Love. This is why rationally defining God and experiencing the Love that He essentially is are two different matters. Many followers practicing until now „grew" beyond most religions mainly because they stopped in their growth. Life, however, is a continuous progress and nobody can just stop since they would regress in relation to the development of everything else. This is why a man knows deep inside that a soul must walk alone on his journey towards God.

This need is so strong with some people that they sacrifice their whole life to it. It is necessary to have a lot of courage, which not everybody can afford. Some people prefer to turn back or to stop than dare to go further.

This is why the timid part of humanity (which is the majority), is lost and feels as though they've been caught in a trap. It feels a strong inner desire, almost a pressure, but it cannot realize it since it is not aware of it. Something in them strives for what is higher but they cannot precisely name it. They don't understand themselves and they begin to fear themselves.

They fear leaving their religion yet they don't have the strength to remain stuck in it. They begin to fear everything but they fear God most of all. This is why one needs to find the courage within to raise themselves above religion while studying the Principle of Life that God is One. It is only then that he will reach a True, Great Wisdom.

I will try to explain to you, dear reader, why a different image of God appears in every religion. Well, each of the great prophets—Moses, Buddha, Jesus, or Muhammad—indicated the existence of the One God. Their followers understood what they preached while physically alive and agreed with them because otherwise they wouldn't follow them.

Each time one of Those Great People ascended, however, the Truth was passed from mouth to mouth by followers and lost its meaning along the way. It wasn't as obvious as it had been while the Prophet was alive. The Truth was lost over time and instead of believing in One God, as the Prophets advocated, they made a God of Him.

And so, for example, Jesus preached the truth about God, His Father. His revelations were very uncomfortable while He was alive. They didn't want to accept them. Jesus and his followers were tortured and killed for these teachings. And since the Truth has the great power of attracting people, a great movement of people following His rules was formed after Jesus left. When this group grew in number, the Roman emperor Constantine desired to control this movement.

You can directly conclude that Christianity wasn't born in the times of Jesus but three hundred and fifty years later, when He wasn't on the Earth for a long time. It was Constantine who smartly used the movement of Jesus's followers. Instead of worshipping the Only God, as Jesus taught, God was made of Jesus who preached of God.

Not just Christianity but almost all religions were formed long after the death of the Prophet. And so, every religion was the result of Him preaching the Truth of God, not the cause of it. This is why we should approach it cautiously. Religion is not God, but history made of experiences and messages of its followers. It was formed when its followers couldn't reach the Preacher anymore and He couldn't verify the values included in things such as the Gospels.

GOD

It is impossible to limit God to a human being such as Jesus Christ or some other Great Being of Light. God is Omnipresent, Omniscient, and Almighty. However, none of the great Prophets had these characteristics to that extent. They were Great compared to humans but not compared to God.

The truth is that the Prophets were Great Masters. They mastered their bodies to achieve such excellence that they were able to stock up and live only off the substance drawn directly from the atmosphere. They did it not only for themselves but for other people in need. These abilities were perceived as miracles by the people living at that time so the following generations considered them to be Gods.

I repeat, however, that none of Them were the Limitless God. None of the Prophets felt that they were doing the privileged workings of God. Jesus often said: „You are going to make bigger things from the things that I make." This means that he perceived himself as a man equal to us. He realized that everybody could achieve the same level of mastery He had achieved or return to the condition people had enjoyed at the very beginning of their existence. I wrote about it in the chapter „The Beginning of Civilization."

What each of those Great People like Moses, Buddha, Jesus Christ, and Mohammed achieved didn't come of its own accord. They reached this level of mastery because of the enormous energy they put into making themselves better. They mastered their external selves and made themselves free from the delusion that everyone else was stuck in. They might have had better predispositions to do that than other people of their time had. They might have come to the Earth with a plan to do it but one thing is certain: they achieved Mastery by doing an enormous amount of work in their prior incarnations.

Dear reader, I am not writing this to diminish the merits of those Great Beings in any way. The Beloved I Am Presence constantly expects you to act according to the Cosmic Law. This means that everyone is obliged to always remember not only His Presence but the Presence of all of His messengers—the Great Master Beings caring for the Earth and Everything That Is, since we All are One.

Since Jesus and other Great Masters of Light were not One God, does it mean that God is a shapeless gas cloud like some scientists say He is? No, although they are a bit closer to the real image of God than those who worship the Great Lucent Being in the form of Jesus, Moses, or any other Great Master. They look at God from a wider perspective than other people do. God is a real Being but He doesn't have a human shape. He goes beyond human understanding so much that a man cannot define Him.

It is difficult to define God because He fills all Heaven

and Earth with Himself. He is the highest knowing power penetrating every shape in the whole Universe. He is the Life, Wisdom, and Energy of each creature. God, or I Am Presence, is the
Source of all that is. This means that we live, move, and have
our being in God.

Do you disagree with me because your religion tells you
otherwise? I encourage you to study holy books and inspired
writings of your religion. You will soon discover that I am not
wrong. Every religion speaks of an Omnipresent, Omniscient,
and Almighty Force, a Source or Energy that has many different
names in different languages. It is most often named God.

Most of these teachings say that God is continuously
growing, expanding, and gathering more power. This happens
because each creature grows as a part of the whole. Even physi-
cists seem to understand that.

Jesus had perfectly interpreted the concept of God when
he said to a Samaritan: „God is Spirit but He doesn't need to be
worshipped in some special place, on some consecrated mountain. He is Spirit that can be praised everywhere and one can
reach Him within his soul, thanks to the Truth."

Dear reader, I will try to explain it to you in other words.
You will agree with me that everything that lives in the ocean
has a right to say: „I live, move, and have my being in the
ocean." And just like an ocean embraces all Life contained in its
domain, the air also embraces all forms of Life belonging to its
domain. And God Almighty embraces all Life in water, air, and
all other domains that are there. You seem to be a separate being
but you are living in an Omnipresent, All-penetrating ocean of
the Spirit.

You really do live in an unexplored ocean of a plastic
God's Mind substance that is eternally alive and active and sensitive to your thoughts. This Cosmic Mind is the Creative Prin-

ciple of the Universe—the Divine Essence of all things.

I hope you understand the true nature of God better now. You cannot live without Him just like you cannot live without air and as fish cannot live without water. What's more is that the life-giving Spirit is much more necessary to life than air, food, and water. You can survive without food for a few months, a few days without water, and a few minutes without air, but you cannot survive for even a split second without Ether or Prana, which are the basic elements of Life. Those who manage to live without food feed themselves with Ether or Prana.

We, people, think that we have reached the highest level of growth compared to other creatures around. It is true that we have reached the highest level but it is nothing to be proud of. We are the only element among all of Creation that deliberately brings disharmony and wastes the energy of God that keeps us alive. It's like we cut off the branch we're sitting on or poison the water we're drinking deliberately and purposefully.

Humans are the only creatures in the Universe that have taken control over their domain and claim themselves to be independent of God. I mean only the external (physical) human domain and not the internal one. I am talking only of those people who actively refuse to acknowledge God's Presence in their life.

I do not doubt whether or not you know God. I'm talking about gaining access to knowledge. It is within you even though it has been effaced in your memory. Getting to know God is not discovering something unfamiliar. On the contrary, it is continuous searching, uncovering, and bringing Him back to your memory.

Dear reader, you know God because you were created by Him. You used to be close to Him every day and you were absolutely aware of His Presence. You might have remembered a bit of your Father while reading the text about the lost civilization. Read it from time to time and you will discover more.

You will reach this knowledge much more quickly if you dare to get rid of the fear that was imposed on you long ago, not just the fear of the knowledge of God but Himself alone.

You must know you believed long ago that you had sinned mostly in relation to God himself. You presently think that you were separated from Him. Religions commonly call this original sin. They ignite fear in every man while proliferating a false belief. According to this false belief of separation, you subconsciously think that God is going to punish you for that. This is why you constantly panic about having done something wrong.

Long ago, our religious forefathers included parts about God's anger and revenge and blocks to the Truth in the Bible. If you got to know it, you wouldn't need your church anymore. The belief in a punishing God doesn't have anything to do with God as He Really is. God is Love. It is only your subconscious fear of God (directed and ignited by your ego) that changes a God of Love into God of hatred, punishment, and revenge. This false belief changes God from your friend to your enemy.

You should understand, dear reader, that God didn't invent all of this. People invented it while seeking advancement. It is difficult for you to uncover this perfidious manipulation because it was done with extraordinary premeditation. The main intention was creating this false belief in people in order to evoke the greatest panic within them to steer them and control them.

Realize that no matter if you are a so called believer or an atheist, deep inside you have this (sometimes absolutely unconscious) feeling that you do unbelievably evil things. It is time to recognize and confront this fear. This terrible, unbearable feeling has been accompanying you for thousands of years.

Although they constantly threaten you with sin, know that it is not a deed itself that is sinful. No matter what „evil" things you do, it is never a sin but an experience of some kind that you learn from. It would be nonsense to punish anyone for learning. You must experience things because there is no other way for your soul to grow and develop.

What you commonly call a sin is not a deed but a reaction to the judgment of what you did. You can think it was unclean or unethical. It becomes a sin if the way you decide to express it brings feelings of anxiety and guilt to your heart.

You do wrong when, instead of striving for internal excellence, you follow egoistic whims of ego or your external little self. When you compose yourself after the first incentive your ego suggested, your own intellect will blame the mind for wrong conduct and judge it to be false, immoral, and unintelligent.

As you can see, a sin is nothing but your own negative thought that insults your dignity, disturbs the peace of your heart, and fills it with fears and guilty conscience. It just happens to you, so turn back inside towards excellence.

God is the Omniscient Spirit. He is Omnipresent and Infinite; there is no place where he doesn't exist. This means that you cannot oppose Him nor ignore Him because He penetrates all. His Intelligence is Unlimited.

God, who is One, governs both the enormous Universe and your body. You feel Him as a domain of the deepest, most noble motivations in your activity. You usually don't have a clear and permanent consciousness of this domain present inside you. You can feel it only intuitively like a foggy and indefinite desire, as a mysterious, unconceivable force pushing you through life in a direction you often don't understand.

You don't understand it consciously because you forgot

about the purpose of your desire you descended to the Earth for long ago. It is this part of life that some people fulfil as a mission, sometimes apparently against common sense and their own business.

God's Powerful Presence governs and controls all growth in the Perfect Divine Order. I Am Presence is such a vast Source of Power that it gives earthly and eternal life to everything that lives. A spark of this enormous power of God, as I mentioned already, is also present inside you. Everyone, even the world's biggest pervert, has a Divine Self within them.

You don't realize that because your Divine Self is sometimes covered with an exuberant ego and sometimes with layers of anger, hatred, fear, and other low emotions. There is no one on Earth that is unworthy of God or His grace. There are only those who turned back from Him, denied His existence, and fell into delusion.

God is not male, as many religions present Him. Our Father-Mother has both masculine and feminine traits. His masculine characteristics are Will, Strength, and Activity while the feminine are God's Love and considerate Care. This means that the love of the Mother and the strength of the Father coexist and act simultaneously. I mean spiritual content, not material.

God, Father-Mother, is surrounded by a glorious Brightness that is impossible to express in words. There is nothing on Earth that can be compared to it. This is why no living person can come close to Him with their physical body because they would be immediately annihilated.

Only very lucent and loving people like Moses, Jesus, Buddha, Muhammad and others whose names we don't even know were able to come closer to Him. This happened in their spiritual bodies, however, not their physical bodies. His image was imprinted forever in their hearts. They kept Him forever this way and haven't forgotten Him, even for a moment after coming to the Earth. This is why they could praise His Glory.

They taught that every man should carry such a portrait in his heart. If you have bad associations with the word „God," you can call this Omniscient, Intelligent Spirit some other name such as Goodness, Highest Intelligence, your Father, or whatever you like. People must name things in order to have an image of it.

Dear reader, carrying the image of God in your heart is the most important thing in the world. When you understand Him properly, you can turn to Him directly, like you would turn to your Father-Mother. It is only when you contact Him that He will give you all the good things you ask for. Try to remember how easily you did it in the lost civilization.

God penetrates all conditions. If you let Him manifest inside you, you would feel with all your heart that you are connected to Him. You would truly worship Him. You would worship God of the whole human family and not just the God of one religion.

To worship an external god, as some religions teach, is idolatry. To worship God inside yourself and see Him manifesting from the inside to the outside, even to the whole world, is to create and rest in the conscious contact with the emanations of God, Life, and Light existing everywhere.

So many religions lack a true image of God. They tell their followers to seek Him outside themselves, where it is impossible to find Him, which is nothing but worshipping idols. You don't venerate a true image of God then, but a human image. And the commandment says: „You shall have no other gods before me." (Exodus 20:3)

A man searching for God outside himself doesn't see the sense in his own life. I am talking about Life in general, not just the physical part but the existence beyond the physical body. Such a man feels lost, fearful, frustrated and doesn't know the cause of it. God is not some external being that needs a man to bow to him, but an integral inner aspect of your own being. The life of every conscious man should focus on those truths. The man that can understand this will stop fearing God, which will make it easy for him to imagine His magnificence, power, and potential. This will enable him to regain control over his own life as a result.

I am talking a lot about the inner experience of God. I don't want to give the impression, though, that the Great Principle dwells only inside an external body form. I am saying that His Wondrous radiance can be, and often is, felt there.

As I have said before, God cannot dwell inside or outside only since He is Omnipresent. He is the Highest Intelligence and Thinking Substance that everything was made of and that is everything, constantly seeking expanded expression and life. It is the Source of all Energy and Power that enables Life to flow and animates all things, including yourself every second of your life.

While trying to feel Him, you will first sense something faint, almost intangible. As time passes, you will be able to feel Him with all your heart as the powerful Current or Stream of Life flowing through your brain and heart.

If you don't do it and you search for Him outside instead, your five senses will tell you that He doesn't exist, which will trap you in delusion. This delusion pushes people towards external theories claiming God to be out of reach dwelling in some distant Heaven so they don't feel a complete emptiness and hopelessness. I hope, though, that while reading this book you reminded yourself of the splendid life you had in the lost civilization, when you joyously satisfied all your needs and enjoyed great abundance. You felt God and shaped His Substance at will, consciously and with all your heart. You did it trustingly because you knew that God desired to live and to express Himself through you and the rest of the people. You also wanted to live in His completeness. When your little will united with God's will, your mind existed in harmony with God's mind, which attracted His Substance to you.

Forces responsible for all of Life gathered around you, and the Only Life filled you and everything around you. You transformed it inside and expressed it outwardly. This is how you obtained abundance, which began with healthy, wisdom, physical and mental energy, vitality, and life's force. To the external senses, you were a miracle worker in the complete sense of the word.

Nothing has changed since then. It is God's intention for you to live in the biggest possible abundance. If this is also your goal, you can cooperate with the Highest, bringing clear optimism and welfare to your inner world, which will soon transfer to the outer world.

One must attune to all that is when harmonizing with Him, which will result in a bigger desire for abundance for yourself and everyone else. If you think only about yourself, you won't acquire anything. If you do, it will be for only a short time. This is the Truth. This is how the Principle of Life works and this is what a Perfect Divine Order is.

You will gain wisdom if you harmonize with the Highest Intelligence, and I don't mean knowledge of facts. In my opinion, Wisdom is the power to perceive Truth and the ability to use it in the best way. This is the power of the immediate choice of the right purpose and measures best serving its realization. Your Wisdom is directly proportional to your level of harmony with the Highest Intelligence.

And so, one must acquire Wisdom himself; he cannot inherit or gain it in any other way. You can pay others to do a job for you if you are rich but you cannot make anyone think for you. You cannot buy Wisdom nor take it away from anyone.

Having true Wisdom enables you to choose the right way, know how to satisfy your desires, and lead yourself towards the best way with the best results. You also know how to realize your dreams and plans.

Wisdom is then the most desired gift you can receive from God. It leads to the achievement of balance, righteous thinking, controlled thoughts, and the ability to avoid difficulties from false thinking. Wisdom, however, is not the only value you can obtain from the Highest Intelligence. Other characteristics that It can give you are: physical energy, vitality, strength, and everything else you could ever wish for.

Since Intelligence is all and it manifests in all, you can access Its Wisdom by harmonizing with all. All your goals, however, must be of the noblest nature. You don't have a chance of acquiring Wisdom if you want to hurt another man and your intentions are discordant with the Will of The Highest One.

God's energy, or a shapeless Substance, is inexhaustible and penetrates all. The level of your resources and chances, however, is not dependent on what God wants to give you, but on how much you want to have and absorb. God gives you everything. That's why everything is dependent on your will to draw from His vast Source.

People usually draw Energy automatically and instinctively but they could get much more of It if they did it wisely. Remind yourself again how you did it in the lost civilization, when you were using the Energy with no limits whatsoever. You are still creating like you used to, and you are doing it during every second of your life. The point is that you were then conscious of yourself and God, while presently you let your creations be negative or accidental.

It all depends on the quality of both your conscious and subconscious thoughts and emotions, negative or positive. You don't know everything that you subconsciously feel. When your thoughts and emotions are positive, all is well since you are satisfied with the results they bring.

When you get negative results, you complain about God and evil fate and you almost never consider the fact that it was you that created the unwanted thing.

If you don't have the image of God or if it is distorted, you can now imagine that God is the most beautiful Being of Light and feel Him in your heart as your Father-Mother. You are a child of this Wonderful Being, who loves you very much and cares for you. It is just love and it shows Its unconditional Care to everyone It created and not only those who somehow deserved that Love.

The Great Beings (Jesus, Buddha, Muhammad, and others) who you may call Gods are then His messengers only. They descend to the Earth every few hundred years to remind people of God. They want to share the Truth about God and make you realize *Who You Are in Essence*. They are not content with teachings; they exemplify what Divinity in man is. You lived on the Earth so many times that you must have met them already, since they came to you, too. They didn't want to just reveal this Truth to you. They wanted you to remember it. If you understood it completely, you would become as enlightened as they were. Since you come back to the Earth all the time, it is a sign that you don't want to know what God wants to tell you. You submitted to the delusion of your own ego, which is why you can't find the way to Him.

Most people have forgotten *Who They Were in Essence*, their purpose on Earth, and what their direction is. They cannot open their minds and hearts to God and His Divine Plan. The Great People of Light descended to the Earth since they wanted you to follow them because this was much easier than marking your own way. Each one of Them emphasized that loving God, our Creator, is fundamental and most important. The point is not to love God but to love Him above all since only then can we love everything else. They taught love, sympathy, and devotion. They didn't mean seeking God outside but within one's heart, of course.

Since God is Omnipresent and dwells within each person, you cannot divide something that is inseparable. You cannot separate God from a man. Although we turn our back on Him when we cease to love, this doesn't mean that we are separated from Him. He is still in your heart but He doesn't impose Himself on you. You must believe it yourself and find Him there.

Always, at every moment, you can return to Him. Do you remember the story of the prodigal son? It is a story that relates to everyone. In order for you to be able to return, you must love God with all your heart and soul. It is impossible, however, if you don't love yourself. The point is not to love your little personal self, but yourself as the whole, meaning both your physical body and the Great Divine Self, God's presence inside you. Fasting and mortifying your body is nonsense since it usually expresses the fact that you don't love God and yourself.

God wants you to live to the fullest, enjoy Him, and stay close to Him. When you are joyous, satisfied, and fulfilled, God knows that you are happy and that you live the right way. By denying self-love, you deny God since you don't really let Him dwell inside you. Love is God and God is Love.

It is up to us whether we open or close ourselves to It.

This is the condition. To love and accept God, you must first love and accept yourself as a whole. Then your love will turn to God and other people. When you love God within you, you also love God in another man. It's never the other way around.

If you love others in order for them to love you, you will totally fail. What if others loved you with all their hearts? You wouldn't feel their love since you don't have it in your own heart. Analogically, you also cannot feel God's Love that surrounds you, even though it is Omnipresent.

It is up to you only whether you open yourself to It or reject It again like most contemporary people do. You have free will and you have the right to use it as you wish. Is it worth using it to hurt yourself?

This is why the Great People cared so much for sympathy, for both other people and themselves. When you understand your lessons with sympathy, you will also understand the lessons of other people.

If there is no sympathy in you, you begin to take pity on yourself and others. This is how you burden yourself or them with this negative emotion that pulls you and the one you take pity on. It is a big mistake. When you take pity or feel sorry for anyone, you send them a signal: „You don't have the way out." This is like clogging the only way out with a huge stone. It increases the sense of hopelessness instead of looking for a way to break free from a negative situation.

The matter changes radically when you feel sympathy. You are sending a completely different signal by saying: „This situation seems to be very difficult. I know, however, that I chose this lesson. When I understand how I attracted it I can get the chance to work it over and break free once and for all."

This gives you the strength to lift yourself to a higher level instead of getting down like it happens in the beginning.

When you act like this every time, you will suddenly discover that God created a perfect world and a perfect man. It couldn't be otherwise since He created him in His likeness and image. In order to see perfection in all, however, we must first recognize it inside and accept it. „Be perfect like the Father Is perfect," Jesus preached.

It was the mission of each of those Great messengers to bring the Reality created by God closer to humanity so it could encompass It with its consciousness and live everyday according to this Truth instead of delusions like it did before.

At the time when one of those Great Ones appeared, people understood Him and this was why they followed His teachings and followed Him in great numbers. So they followed Jesus, Buddha, or other prophets at the time of Their incarnations on the Earth. The Great Ones established signposts for all humanity using their own experiences of using Light and the Power of God.

MESSAGES

After any of the Great Beings of Light left, and the process was the same every time they did, people would cease to understand His messages. Instead of following the life He lived and suggested, they returned to their old habits. It was easier for them to assume that He was God than to dare to live Truly. In honor of the Great Being, religions were formed that exists until now.

I don't see anything wrong with paying tribute to those Wonderful Beings. It is our duty to revere Them and love Them for what They tried to do for us. It is time, however, to liberate Them from being Gods. I repeat that none of the Great Ones and nor their apostles ever formed any of the religions existing.

I don't condemn religion, of course, I am just suggesting that the intentions of Jesus, Buddha, and Muhammad were misunderstood. All religions were formed by people who didn't have anything to do with the any Great Being since they were born many years after It left. They knew Their teachings only from messages passed through word of mouth. They were not written down since writing was not common then.

And a message can be understood in many ways, depending on the understanding of the person that receives it. It is very well illustrated in the game called „Chinese whispers." When we pass some longer text, its content changes so much while being passed by a few people that in the end you don't know what it originally was.

It is similar with gossip. There are different intentions at the beginning and end. Even if we pass a message personally, we cannot be certain that it was understood correctly.

People interviewed by the press can understand what I am talking about well. You say what you want to be written down, and while reading the article you are surprised that the journalist understood almost nothing of what you said. It also happens that your words are given a completely reversed intention than your own and you can do nothing about it since the text is already published.

There are editors, of course, with an opportunistic approach to your ideas, though sometimes there are serious distortions in the interviews being published. The people reading them are misguided no matter your honest intentions and good will on the part of the editor.

It is similar with the Bible and New Testament. There are many errors coming from translating the „original" texts (or notes). Every translator writes the text the way he understands it. In order to understand a spiritual text, though, one must achieve a very high stage of growth himself or at least to live at the time the text was written. Many errors in translations were caused by misinterpreting some letters and symbols since translators lived at a different time than the Prophet. Such errors are understandable even though they cause much trouble to us, readers.

This is not the only cause of the problem, however. Unfortunately, most of the Bible is just a mean and deliberate forgery. At the time the Catholic Church was being formed, Constantine deliberately ordered many distortions of the Bible that hid the real message of the Gospel. This was done on purpose so people would seek God outside themselves (where they would never find Him) instead of inside their own hearts.

Five popes were killed because of that and subversive people were put on their place to hush everything up. When the next pope would be chosen after a suppositious one, he would endorse everything he found while taking the position. It doesn't matter whether he did it out of fear for his life or out of ignorance. The fact is that you presently use and rely on the distorted Bible text.

These days, particular religions and their theologians teach about God as Creator that created a Perfect World but made a mistake in His work. He created imperfect people who could sin. Can you see any logic in it? I can't.

How could God who created all things with such an unusual precision and perfection, both the greatest and the smallest ones, be wrong and create an imperfect man? To punish him through eternity?

I am writing this because the Bible may be a valuable signpost for many people because it describes how to go all the way from our beginning to enlightenment. People interested in it should skillfully avoid its distortions. How do you do it? One must open himself to his own intuition and it will unmistakably guide him and suggest what Truth is and is not.

I discovered how important this knowledge was in numerous conversations and interviews concerning the New Testament. For many people, the interpretation of single words or of some bigger fragments of the Gospel is important. They reckon them to be a perfect and infallible guide. This leads to many unnecessary conflicts. Wars have been fought about that in the past.

Conflicts could be avoided if people realized that words today had a different meaning during Jesus's time. We should know that Jesus spoke and taught in Aramaic language only. It was a dialect that was not really understandable during those times. Although Aramaic was only a dialect, it totally dominated the official Hebraic that Jews spoke in Palestine these days.

We should also know that the words of Jesus were passed only by word of mouth. They spread like stories or gossip. They were written down in Greek manuscripts only seventy years after Jesus left. The words were probably translated to have different meanings than Jesus had meant because these two languages and cultures are very different.

The Bible was translated into English in the fourteenth century and into Polish in the seventeenth. Differences in understanding were present in the original version and increased when it was translated. Does it make any sense to focus on single phrases or fragments if the words have been taken out of the context of their original meaning? I think we have a better chance of understanding Jesus's message when we read them as a whole.

Besides, at the time that the New Testament was being written down, thousands of false interpretations of true events were written, which replaced the original texts. Historical facts were distorted and blurred. Not for good, though.

A Bible similar to ours existed in every civilization. This means that many civilizations left their Bibles. It doesn't matter whether they were written down on porcelain, clay tablets, or papyrus. If different versions of forgery were compared, the words changed could easily be seen.

Archaeologists searching lost civilizations had found them. This is why so many researchers have the true and complete versions of the Holy Scripture that debunk forgeries. Many of them are terrified by the forgeries they discover.

The forgeries are generally quite easy to find because all civilizations have used the same chronological system throughout the ages. Although the texts of other civilizations were written long before our Bible, they nevertheless describe the same events. As you can see, dear reader, the Holy Scripture is timeless and follows the scriptures of all religions. It has been this way since the beginning of time.

Not many people may know that all this knowledge is kept also inside the Great Pyramid, which is the true, indestructible record that reflects the many achievements of the people living with God. It is a Bible engraved in stone and meant not only for one race but for everyone living on Earth throughout time. Although a forgery once made was revealed long ago, the contemporary Church still persuades people of things that are not true and orders them to believe them. Although it acts in the name of Jesus, it relies on His false image. It was prepared and imposed mainly by medieval priests in the times when religion accepted slavery, evil, and oppression.

While writing about history, the Church doesn't rely on the four Gospels to present Jesus Christ as He really was. It quotes Isaac's poetry, where this false, untrue pseudo-ideal was taken from almost intact. This is why only few people know that Jesus as an educated, well-dressed, rich, noble man of an impressive appearance, full of power, influence, and authority.

Instead, even the contemporary Church wants us to follow the example of an isolated, poor, contemptible, man of low background and miserable social status, neglected by people of a higher social ranking. Our ideal became a man who didn't have friends and saved fishermen, workers, sinners, and outsiders. We see Him as someone who often was naked and hungry and who meekly tolerated insults and harassment. He raised his hands as a gesture of mercy whenever the world despised him.

Times have changed and the Catholic Church stood firm and still stands by its image. Instead of presenting Jesus as he really was, filled with Power, Love, and Might, it presents His alleged meekness, humbleness, and docility, the characteristics that enabled Him to withstand evil and injustice.

Religion made Him a God in order to separate Him from people. He overcame death, the greatest human enemy, and was resurrected. Religion, however, obstinately celebrates His death and suffering. He dwelled among living people for fifty years after His resurrection, but religion is silent about it. Why?

Is to encourage its followers to 'be as meek as a lamb, bow to your oppressor, submit to the one that wants to hurt you, turn the other cheek' If believers accept this ideal, isn't it easier to control them?

You don't believe it was different than your religion tells you, do you? Read history. You will learn from the Talmud that every Jewish rabbi and teacher at the time of Jesus had to culti-vate some craft. This was what the law ordered them to do. Saint Paul was a tent weaver, and Rabbi Isaac a shoemaker. The fact that Joseph was a carpenter was not a detriment to Jesus but an honor. Beside their profession, every one of them was a well-educated and respected celebrity.

Jesus was the highest. He was a man of an impressive, majestic, and strong look. We will find these words in the Gos-pels: „He taught them like one who has authority and His words were filled with power." And so, constantly talking about Jesus as someone who was poor and despised is sheer ignorance.

I don't blame priests for that. Not many of them were reading historical scriptures to learn how it really was. Most of them rely on what they were taught in seminaries. They pass on this „knowledge" to their followers. They preach even though they get caught in a trap themselves, becoming the victims of their own preaching. They preach of God while they don't really believe in Him. If they did, would they still be stuck in delusion?

This explains why educated priests, enlightened with Truth after discovering and understanding It, immediately leave their priesthood. They know that they cannot serve the Church as it is now anymore because it opposes the Truth. Dear reader, unfaithfulness is not a lack of faith in the teachings of some Church, but a lack of faith in Truth. Sin, disease, and poverty are neither virtues nor Truth. They never were and never will be, although the Church orders us to believe those mean lies.

After Jesus had ascended, His apostles dreamed of creating God's Kingdom on Earth, the same as I described in the chapter of civilization lost. In God's Kingdom there is neither hunger nor suffering caused by evil. So they dreamed of a world where a common effort would make a single man grow.

God's Kingdom is a kind of a perfect community where everybody has an equal access to God and His Wonderful Goods. Has the Church ever fulfilled this task? No! Because it worships temples, religious practices, celebrations, and holidays more than people.

God gave a man greater task than to celebrate certain days and places as holy. The whole Earth is a holy place and all days are holy time. They were sanctified by God's love that fulfils a Divine purpose and reveals a higher destiny to man. It is thanks to this vision that the apostles' teachings were as filled with power as the teachings of Jesus Christ.

While building the original Church, Constantine, the founder of Christianity, wanted to adopt the spiritual power the apostles had but he didn't want the vision, which was its basis. If Constantine followed this vision, the Church would also gain the spiritual power of the apostles.

Constantine didn't know that this spiritual power was contained in the vision itself and not in the institution of the Church, so when he rejected the vision, the Church immediately lost its spiritual power. Putting it differently, the Church has never had the spiritual power, since it hasn't assumed to have a vision of building God's Kingdom. This is why it placed God far away in Heaven and ordered its followers to pray to Him while he became their intermediary.

The Church would have the power to be reborn if it started to build God's Kingdom correctly. It would transform and rise up its followers instead of confirming their delusion.

It's no wonder that people doubt God nowadays. It is quite obvious with the Church like that. Many great people, even those reckoned to be saints, have said that it took a long time before something enlightened them enough to feel closeness with God.

Even Mother Theresa from Calcutta, whose life we consider to be holy, didn't feel Him for almost fifty years. This is why experiencing the absence of God, and even doubting His existence, is a natural thing on the way to faith. It is a part of becoming mature—sometimes painful but necessary.

THE DOWNTURN OF EXCELLENCE AND THE DIVISION OF CIVILIZATION

The next chapters will show you how you started to grow apart from God. When you understand how you did it once, you may find a way to correct this unreal separation. I am not writing this to make the reader feel guilty, of course. I just want him to draw conclusions from his mistakes. He may be able to avoid them in the future, either partially or completely.

The golden times of the civilization described above lasted for entire eons. However, none of the civilizations existing until now were endless. Why? The reason is simple: single men became increasingly inactive after a period of magnificent prosperity.

It doesn't matter whether it came out of crapulence or ordinary laziness. The fact is that instead of being interested in the creative plan of their own Great Divine Self and following Its advice and guidance, those people became interested in the pleasures of their external senses.

While turning toward the external world, they lost consciousness of God's Power. Their inner light slowly shrunk, which made them fall into a greater oblivion. They looked like people struck with lethargy or hypnosis. This apathy or brain fade snuck in slowly, unnoticed. If it was different, things could have been another way.

Some people began to care only for their bodily needs, others for the needs of their minds, while the other still totally forgot about themselves and worked for others. It was a mistake, since when you submit only to the needs of your body, you act unwise and cease to live in harmony with God. If your aim is just a cool intellectual pleasure, although you act according to ethic rules, you are also unwise and not living in harmony with God. It is the same if you practice only altruism and devote yourself to the service of others.

You are a whole, consisting of a body, mind, and soul. You need to develop all these aspects simultaneously, since it is only then that you grow as a whole. When you devote yourself to one domain only, you behave like a bodybuilder who builds just one muscle. Sooner or later, the rest of your body will show that you are not growing evenly.

There are only two activities in life: an Inner activity that is guided by your Higher Self and an outer activity guided by your external senses. No matter the reason, you turned back from your Inner activity completely facing outside, submitting yourself to the ruling of your external senses. It wasn't important before if you did something for yourself or worked for the others later because you enjoyed the feeling of your job being well done. Later, you couldn't or didn't want to take the necessary effort to create simply for the joy of creating.

Before, when you had your complete consciousness, you

knew perfectly well that you were born from the Light and God's Love and you eagerly expressed Them. Everything you did, you did out of love and you generously gave the fruits of your work to yourself and others. You gave without thinking about the reward or payment because this was the way you worshipped and expressed God. This made you conscious of being one with Him and united with society. Everybody approached life the same way, so together everyone made One Big Family of Light. Your civilization was founded and guided by the Great Being of Light. This Great Life's Presence constantly reminded your external self that the Cosmic Law of Excellence and Authority is the Law of Love.

It began to change later, since you started to ignore this Great Law completely. Persistent exhortation was wasted since your happiness and welfare didn't come from God anymore. It seemed that you didn't remember Him anymore.

You were constantly reminded, though, that if you don't love God Inside with all your heart and cease to worship Him, you will lose everything. You were told many times that if you want to be happy you must return to Light; there was no other way. But the other conduct was becoming contagious, expanding in bigger circles.

Seeing that a growing number of people had become entangled in the net of satisfying the whims of their own senses, the Great Being of Light decided to withdraw Its activity and let people learn from their own mistakes, even if it had to bring hard experiences to them.

It appeared for the last time in its Lucent Body so everybody could see It, even those who had lost their inner light. It said something like this:

,,I was teaching, enlightening, blessing, and bringing abundance to your people over innumerable years. At the beginning, you were all benefiting from the Light and Energy of Goodness that God is. However, as time passed, more and more people began to expropriate and misappropriate this Wonderful Energy. This has lasted too long and expanded too much. That is why everybody must choose their own way that they are going to follow.

If you choose the way of God's Light and you act as you have been acting, everything will prosper in your life and bless you and everybody else through you.

If, however, you don't keep your Love of God, of Him who is One, the Highest Divine Self, that is eternally dwelling in your heart and you won't acknowledge Him to be your ruler, everything will fall apart and you will be led to darkness.

Remember once and for all: You are God's son. You were created from the deepest Love and Wisdom, of the same Love that brings forth all Life. You exist in order to live in this Love and Wisdom.

By rejecting the Original Cause that God is, you deny your identity. You hurt yourself badly since you make your spirit vestigial. You must choose to either live in unlimited Love or run away from It. Remember, though, that the consequences of your decision go far beyond the time you commonly call an earthly life. God is giving you a free choice. You must decide yourself whether you still want to live in the Heavenly Kingdom as you have been until now or if you want to leave it. If you forget God you will have to forget this wonderful Excellence you enjoyed for those innumerable years. The choice is yours.

You know the Truth since you have been using it successfully. If you don't want to be aware of the Original Cause and act against Its rules, you will experience only suffering and pain. You are standing at a crossroad with others and either more glory or a fall to doom is awaiting you. God is Light and if you don't wake up in time, His Light will blind you.

Being God's son, you are the individualized creator. The Flame of Excellence of your own Life was placed in your heart. You came here as the one who is to guard the Earth and care for It, and to be a fruit of Divine Love, Joy, and Beauty for It. Your planet will generously provide you with good things in return.

You were appointed to be the Earth's guard—this is your task. Don't waste it. You are co-responsible not only for what you create on It but also for the way you help manage the Universe. The world is your mirror, so you can place everything in it you want to come back to you. The world is yours and you mold it according to your wish. Everything you mold in our inner world will be transformed into condensation made of the Electronic Substances and it will become your world of manifestation.

You have free will and you don't have to listen to me. You can push it aside, refuse it, be dissatisfied, or do whatever you want to do. It stands always in its Eternal Order, saying that Love is a Benefactor and a Gift and the Ruler of All.

If you still love, you can be sure that you are safe. You live in Light and you are Light. If there is no Love within you, you won't be able to keep yourself going at this level. Your body won't be able to bear Light if there is no Light inside it.

This is why it is so important for you to love God. It is only then that you are going to experience completeness like you once did. If the feeling of Love becomes strange to you, you will vanish because people acting discordant to Love cannot remain in the condition called Heaven or the Heavenly Kingdom.

It is not too late. Forgive yourself, forgive others, and release the energy resources inside you that are being wasted on anger, fear, and guilt.

Be strong. Stay infallibly in faith and realize that people will be confronted with the wave of destruction. Soon a spiritual purge will sweep away everybody who don't worship God and don't hear His voice inside.

I can assure everybody who wants to listen to me and seek love that they will know what to do next, regardless of what happens. We will give them all the help possible.

Love opens a soul to God's voice, and contact with Him assures safety. Without free access to the inner voice of God, people will meet spiritual death. What are they going to do without Him in the face of the dangers threatening Earth? Without this contact, they will meet too much pain and suffering.

It disheartens me that many of you won't answer my call. You won't believe that you went astray and will delay it until it is too late. And I cannot affect anybody's decisions.

I bid you farewell and assure every one of you of the great presence of God dwelling in your hearts. May It protect you, guide you, and enlighten each one of you from now on.

The Great Being of Light has disappeared forever after had said that. After It had left, many people changed and broke free from apathy, though most of them delayed for some reasons. Some thought that they would manage to wake up later. Others called: „Help, help." Although the Beings with deeper knowledge would come to them and suggest how they could grow, overcome their limitations, and create another image of the world than the one coming from the external senses, those people seldom used their advice. They were getting more and more entangled in the chain of misery, hardships, fear, anger, and hatred.

It is similar now. One could ask what a man continuously asking for help gets since he doesn't follow suggestions concerning what is happening in his world and he doesn't draw any conclusions. I am not talking about every person that asks, of course.

There were also people among the inhabitants of the lost civilization that woke up at the last moment. The longer a person has been asleep, the more they suffer the deeper the shock their soul feels to once again anew awaken inside themselves a complete consciousness. Dear reader, as you will discover in the further part of the book, the shock turned out to be a truly hard experience to some. If they decided earlier, they would surely avoid such great distress.

More and more people have slowly forgotten that God could be expressed only through the love of Him. They didn't care enough to love Him with all their hearts, souls, thoughts, and feelings. They were growing apart from God, so they ceased to love themselves. They fell in to a vicious, self-driving circle. This in turn made them forget *Who They Were in Essence*.

They prospered at a very high spiritual level until they realized that the key to their former success was Love. They carried Light inside and showed direction, just like physical light. It indicated where to go, what happened somewhere else, how to get what they wanted, and how to make every desire come true.

Those who forgot this began to lose their spirituality and everything that concerned it. A perfect prosperity descended from God's plane to lower planes until it reached the earthly level it resides at today. The vibrations of those people's bodies began to lower and fade simultaneously.

A new belief commonly called the ego has filled them instead with the consciousness of God since then. They were persuaded that it is the source of it all, not God. This belief made them live in growing darkness and wander blindly. The reason for that was the lack of light and information that followed.

I will try to translate this phenomenon to physicality so

you can understand, how it works, dear reader. Imagine three roads. One is very well lit and it is as bright as if it was in the middle of the day. On the second road, the lanterns are located too far from each other, so it is half dark there. The third road doesn't have any source of light and there is complete darkness over it. When people were short of consciousness and feelings for God (inner Light), they didn't have any choice but to submit to their personal judgments and let a rampant ego dominate them.

This is how the Great Divine Law operates. Most people from the lost civilization relied on their reason. They ceased to understand that their former achievements had come from rising above the mind and physical concepts. They didn't realize that they let God act through them.

As you can see, dear reader, every soul has a choice. It can identify itself with a higher thing, such as God, or a lower thing, such as body, ego, or personality. The choice made by the soul determines the fundamental difference in the way of experiencing things.

When it identifies itself with its Higher Self, it dwells in the Light of Love and its road is well lit. It doesn't stumble on any obstacles. Even if obstacles show up, it can see them in advance and knows how to avoid them.

When it identifies itself with the body, it is walking the same road of life but in complete darkness. It stumbles every so often so it seems that it doesn't have any other choice. This creates the impression that it has to rely on the mercy of a cruel fate. It is a delusion, of course, because only in darkness does a very wide road seems to be narrow and bumpy.

This is why two people with different intensities of inner light, walking the same road of life, can perceive one situation in completely different ways.

The world fell apart for the people of the lost civilization that cease to love because Love is not only light, it is a basic building material. Without it, the entire existence began to break apart like a proverbial house of cards.

Until people knew that God wanted to express Himself through every desire, they joyously let it happen for the benefit of everyone. Since people took matters into their own hands, though, they forgot that God was the creator of everything and that a man cannot replace Him in any way. They blocked God's perfect manifestations when stopped allowing God to express Himself.

They were standing at the crossroads. They knew deep inside that only Divine Powers are solid, but they submitted to material powers and the delusion connected to them, which consequently led them astray. While descending deeper and deeper into matter, they let the material limitations of everyday life to dominate their entire existence.

They still loved but not what they should love. Their love concerned only material goods. They forgot what it truly meant to care for someone or something. They filled their lives with stimuli and actions that were not of God, so they lost spirituality of sight.

Giving priority to self-serving and material things, they grew inactive and egoistic. Instead of cooperating like they used to do, they tried to outdo their neighbors at all costs. This brought separation, greed, and discord to society. They wasted time they could use to create, serve, and progress on fights and quarrels.

They couldn't forgive themselves nor others as they once could, so they became more and more obstinate. They forgot about love, mutual understanding, and the Truth. They became mean, greedy, subservient, and insanely ambitious.

They didn't desire to hold on to God, their Source anymore, so they grew apart from Him even more, until everyone lost what was high and noble. They abandoned God, who provided them with care and safety over innumerable years. They were morally declining.

It is hard to say whether they were trudging unwittingly towards their own doom. One thing is certain though: it was getting worse and worse for them every moment but they couldn't or didn't want to break free from this lethargy. The situation eventually encompassed almost everybody. The time of the ultimate split came between the forces of so-called good and evil, consciousness and unconsciousness, Light and darkness.

Dear reader, it wasn't the first nor the last time. The history we don't know about contains many people that found their way and then regressed into ignorance again. It happens because God's energy can take any form a man wants to give it, as long as he is filled with Love.

And when he deals with a feeling that doesn't come from the Light, he can reach a point he is not able to go beyond. He feels then as if he has confronted a huge wall. The feeling that blocks the growth of any negative emotion can be: greed, hatred, jealousy, and all other Lightless emotions. A thought is a creator just like God created the entire Universe. People create their world with their own thoughts.

THE LOWER OCTAVES

The walls I mentioned are octaves. I wrote about them in the chapter concerning the lost civilization. People living in this early period dwelled permanently in light and moved through only three octaves: Happiness, Love, and Tolerance. Depending on the octaves of thoughts they resided in, particular feelings dominated them and had particular manifestations.

The octaves began to change at the time of the fall and new, lower octaves began to show in the Earth's atmosphere. It was not God who constructed them but the thoughts of individual people. The fourth octave was made of thoughts tainted with criticism and condemnation. It became the dominating octave and has remained that way ever since. Most people move in it, often unwittingly.

The next, fifth octave, was built from anger and fear. It is much smaller than the previous one. The sixth octave is of a smaller range, built from hatred. The seventh octave is crime.

This one is the lowest and the thinnest octave, contrary to appearances. Although much time has passed since then, most people cannot break free from what they created then. Also, seven octaves operate now.

Dear reader, remember all the miracles that happened so effortlessly in the lost civilization. You could work them since you used the Powerful, Omnipresent, Cosmic Law on a daily basis. As long as you acknowledged the God inside you, you were aware of those Great Laws operating. You knew how to activate Them to receive all the manifestations you wished for. You acknowledged God and the leading force in your life was Love.

Since you ceased to love, you began to forget, too. You didn't remember that it was God who was the Source of all that is. You didn't realize that it was because of Him that you lived in welfare that He was the giver and author of everything you had achieved. You ceased to love and you immediately forgot *Who You Were in Essence*. You no longer knew how to manage His manifestations. This was caused by the lack of Love but you couldn't realize it. Your consciousness fell into a lower vibration level and you didn't have access to basic information anymore.

When there was no Love within you, you not only started to separate from God but your body vibration began to decline until you began to descend from the world of the fourth dimension to the third dimension as we know it today. Individual people were operating at different speeds.

In the process of lowering vibrations, the Completeness of God expressed as the unity of female and male characteristics contained within one body became separated into two.

Until you lived in God, your body was lucent because God is Light. Since you ceased to love, Light began to fade within you. The structure of your body became denser until it reached the level you currently live in, dear reader.

It was then that you began to take a female or male form, depending on the body you were incarnated in. It didn't happen in one day, of course; it progressed just like you turned back from the Great Plan of Creation remaining in the Light of God.

Initially, those who loved God with all their hearts and those who turned back from Him lived on one plane. The first group kept their inner light while the second lost it gradually or completely. The second group slowly lost sight of those that still lived in light since their bodies' vibrations declined to a lower, third dimension. The bodies of those who loved God, however, were independently holding on to high vibrations so they remained in the fourth dimension.

The inhabitants of the fourth dimension kept their complete Consciousness since they still lived in the Light of God. Those that descended from the third dimension, however, gradually lost complete consciousness to the point that they lost the Light within them. At the same time, evil began to sneak into their lives. The inhabitants of the fourth dimension didn't experience this because they didn't submit to that evil because they had mastery over themselves.

It was only human consciousness declining to the third dimension since a man was still functioning in the fourth dimension for the most part. With your consciousness gone, you weren't able to understand what was happening to you. When you tried to return to the previous condition, fear would come to you. The fear grew and you didn't know why. You didn't realize that only the Divine part of a man can enter the fourth dimension and that personality and ego cannot access it.

You deal with the same situation today, in your present life. A part of you still remains in the fourth dimension, but are you aware of it? You probably aren't or you are occasionally. This comes from your declined consciousness. Only those who are completely conscious can move between dimensions freely and what's more, they can keep the memory of this movement. Those whose consciousness has declined don't remember it, although they have still the ability to move to the higher level. This concerns people who seem to be absentminded.

In order for you to experience life in lower dimensions, Mother Earth had to diminish her vibrations, too. She put on a thick, heavy physical body and lived like the people that inhabit her.

Diminishing vibrations, as we already mentioned, made those with lower vibrations of the third level blind to those who still lived on the high vibrations of the fourth level. Do you wonder, dear reader, how this is possible? Haven't you ever been blinded by a light that is so bright that you couldn't look at it? It is a similar phenomenon, but on a larger scale.

Those whose vibrations declined only a bit could still see people with high vibrations, but their image was blurred. They knew when they were standing in front of a lucent human figure but they couldn't recognize who it was. They realized the presence rather than seeing it with their own eyes. This resembles the phenomenon of warm air undulating over a heated surface such as an asphalt road. This was the way they saw a figure or its blurred outline. They could hardly recognize the person since a bright light was emanating from it. They also got the impression that people of higher vibrations were standing higher as if they were not walking along the Earth but moving above it, which gave the wrong impression that they were rising towards Heaven. This phenomenon was caused by different vibration levels, though.

Scientists confirm it. The natural result of two elements

of different vibrations touching is their mutual growing apart, pushing one away from the other. The object of a higher vibration always places itself above the one of the lower vibration.

While this difference in vibration level increased, those of lower vibrations thought that those of higher vibrations were ascending to Heaven. This is how those with clouded consciousness perceive things. This is where the concept of ascension comes from. This false belief is still present today. The teachings of religions are nothing but the division and loss of the gift of true inner vision.

I am writing about this since people usually don't understand these facts. Also, the Church doesn't mention it, placing ascensions in the ancient times. This is wrong because the process of rising still happens today.

People of high vibrations could still see everything clearly. One can see everything from above but almost nothing from below. It is a natural phenomenon since a Divine human nature can move freely between the levels while the outer nature cannot.

THE SPLIT

People whose bodies were fading and falling down did not realize the seriousness of their position. They didn't know that they lost light and descended from to the third dimension when they entered low emotions.

The dimension itself is a domain of very intensive pulsations caused by negative emotions. It was them that made the previous immortal life end in time with physical death. How is this possible?

Well, the human body is like a house. If you expose a house to pulsations of varied intensity, it will eventually fall down. It is the same with the human body. Exposed to constant nervous discord, it finally cannot stand the changing intensity and dies.

You may now begin to understand why you could live eternally in the fourth dimension and leave your physical body in the third dimension. A body without Love is exposed to big pulsations and eventually breaks apart. Only Love and peace can raise the body to a higher level where there is no pulsation and it can live eternally.

How did it affect this once magnificent civilization? A split was growing within. The great, wonderful people loving God and actively expressing Him were still living there along with other people that didn't.

The first group still remembered *Who They Were in Essence*. They loved their Divine Self and knew how to activate the Great Laws of Life, while the second group slowly lost this ability. Both sides were living in completely different ways, which widened the chasm between them.

You may wonder if parents watched the fall of their children in peace or vice versa. Well, they reacted in different ways.

There were people who stood by their belief in the perfection of the Divine Self in man with infallible firmness, no matter what their personality was going through. They were right in thinking that what the personality constructed was just an illusion, so they never considered it. They considered the Divine Self only.

A man remaining at a high vibration level couldn't take his neighbor's experiences literally since he knew that each experience, no matter how bad it would seem, served the growth of the soul. He didn't worry about what his dear one was going through. Watching it from a higher perspective, he knew perfectly well that only good can come out of a distressing experience, namely Higher Good. He accepted the experiences of others because he respected the free will they received from God Himself. He could not oppose it, no matter how far a man close to him grew apart from the Truth and how bad he behaved. He knew that he could not help him nor do anything for him.

Even if he tried to do something for his loved one, he

knew that he would still deal with his own life, experiences, and health, and not of another person's. He knew that he could not feel bad that he wouldn't this way soften the suffering of someone else. On the contrary, he knew that the other one would suffer even more and that he would suffer together with him. All he could do was sympathize with the one who chose such a tough experience. If he would show mercy instead of sympathy, he would lower himself to the other's vibration, which would have serious consequences. By focusing on something he didn't want, he would attract it. He would have to go through the same distressing experience.

From the present human point of view, we would describe those people as hard and insensitive. There were merciful and helpful people then, too. This is why the fallen grew in number and the ones who remained at the high level of growth became scarcer. I hope, dear reader, that you are beginning to understand what this is all about.

The only people that stayed at the high level were those that looked towards God with infallible faith and trusted Him completely. They never focused on the personalities of their loved ones and always looked at their perfect Higher Selves. They didn't focus on experiencing evil, but rather on the good things that could come out of it. Instead of an apparent evil, they saw only Higher Good. They understood that a person close to them experienced some distress just because their soul wanted to learn something new from it. They knew that all was good and that we should let even our close loved ones go their own way. They understood that no matter how difficult an experience may seem, our loved one must go through it alone in order to get to know it thoroughly. There is no way to learn anything from someone else's experience. Wise people accepted the choices of their loved ones. They were not angry because they understood that each man learns from his own mistakes, even the ones with negative attitudes. The people in this ancient society didn't demand that their loved ones stop this wrong behavior even if it meant a temporary loss of spiritual clarity.

Those wise people didn't leave their close ones or those who turned their back on God. The wise people helped others understand Divine Law and how to use it. They helped one another by sending Love and Light since they knew it was present within all of them. They didn't care if a person deserved it. They sent love even if people didn't want to turn back from the chosen road. They didn't care about achieving results, regardless of the amount of work they put in.

They even sent Light to those that offended, cursed, or hated them. If they forgot themselves for a moment and reacted the same way, their vibrations would lower and they would find themselves in the same place as their tormentor. Wishing to remain at the high vibration level, they had to be wiser and behave in the proper way. This was the Mastery of the wise. Each man that wants to achieve it should behave the same way.

Jesus confirmed it on the cross. He didn't condemn his persecutors for the same reason the people from the fourth dimension didn't condemn anyone. If he did, he wouldn't achieve the Resurrection that he had planned earlier. He achieved the highest Mastery because he never cared for individual human personalities, he saw only the Divine Self in everything. This gave Him a complete Power. It also enabled Him to take a huge effort and forgive his persecutors instead of imprecating them during hard times. He raised them that way. If Jesus submitted to his own personality then, he would immediately lower his vibrations.

He had to watch his own good in order to disperse it to everyone around. If he forgot about it for even a short while, he would have lost his Mastery and descended to the same level as everyone else.

People that kept their vibrations in the fourth dimension acted in the same way. Those who were persistent in their Mastery of self-control became the teachers of all mankind. These teachings are preserved even today because of Them. It is Them that show people how to live better. The system of spiritual leadership was formed from their teachings, which manifested on our planet for thousands of years afterward. They were regarded as gods in myths and legends. The same was done to Jesus: He was made God instead of showing His Way to others so they could follow Him. This is why He was taken away from the people for whom He came to Earth.

His example showed us what Real Life should be like. He proved that when one consequently practices the Divine Law, he can work miracles (the same ones you once worked). He can even conquer death. A Christian, however, doesn't take this into account since he is told to believe something else. Instead of believing in God with his soul, body, mind, and heart, he is ordered to put his hand on his heart and say: „Lord, I do not deserve to have you come under my roof..." (Matthew 8:7) Jesus' suffering is the only thing that is important to the Church; they neglect the teachings that come from His experiences. Jesus lived much longer after His resurrection than he did before His crucifixion but the Church only recognizes that he suffered, died, and was resurrected not as a man and as God. His teachings are not emphasized, according to the following reasoning: „What shall you understand, little ones, of his teachings?" The devotees should be told many times: „Follow Jesus' example. If one man went through these experiences, others can, too. Be as excellent as He was. However, we hear from a pulpit: „Although Jesus behaved as a man, he was God and this was why he

worked miracles." It contradicts the words of Jesus himself:
„You will do the works I have been doing, and you will do even
greater things than these." (John 14: 12) In order to turn the
devotees' attention from His teachings, his poverty is glorified
and His suffering on the cross is remembered instead of his con-
quering of death. It is said: „Look. Your God was crucified."
The fact that thousands of people were crucified is forgotten. It
is also forgotten that suffering, poverty, and other miseries don't
come from God. Dear reader, when I write about religion, I am
not saying that it is wrong or unnecessary. Many people
wouldn't be able to live without it. I am just saying that a priest
who preaches of God doesn't have the access to His Light, and
lives in darkness. He is as uninformed as any other man who has
turned his back on God. He teaches only what he was taught in
the past and he wrongly believes that it was true. He doesn't
realize this because he didn't search for the truth and he doesn't
know that entire systems have been formed to keep humanity in
darkness. The Church has expanded but maintains its old systems and isn't aware that it is misinformed. The Church teaches
lies not because it desires your doom or that it wants to deceive
you. It is just not informed enough. How many priests have truly
considered the actions of Constantine, the founder of the
Church? Probably very few priests did. The Church thinks that it
acts right, which is how it leads people lacking the Light. A
priest who becomes enlightened immediately leaves his priesthood since there is no place for him there anymore. Nowadays
there are few priests that are called towards enlightenment and it
is a job just like any other job.

I will write a few words about people who helped those
that turned their back on Light without watching their own good
or the Higher Good of mercy. Some of them fell to the level of
those whom they were helping, while others managed to hold on

to their old level yet unwittingly passed to the dark side.

In both cases, the point was to help other people. Seeing a man who was going astray to evil side, his helper felt his heart breaking, which is now a common phenomenon. The helper ignored the fact that an experience his loved one is going through helps him learn *Who He Is in Essence*. He didn't let his loved one learn from their mistakes or see the good that can come from the experience by discerning evil in a particular experience.

The helper used to perceive the world from the perspective of the Higher Good. Later he began to wrongly think that others were getting hurt because they experienced some misery so he did everything he could to pull them out from this „negative" state. He wanted to help them so much that he began to do it no matter the cost he would have to pay later. The helper didn't want to realize that a falling man had the right to do whatever he wanted to do even if he caused suffering by his conduct. He didn't want to acknowledge the fact that God gave people free will so they could learn from their own mistakes. He didn't let him learn from his experiences by imposing improvement upon him.

The helper's intentions were pure at the beginning, although they came from being overprotective. Time passed, however, and since the helper achieved no results, he began to use all methods available to see them. He wanted to manage the falling one or rather should say manipulate him to change his behavior. This way, only the good, and not evil, would return to him in the future. (If this pattern seems familiar to you, dear reader, consider whether or not you should let your loved ones experience and learn on their own mistakes. The sooner they go through this, the quicker they work through their lessons).

Such conduct made the helper act against God's will and

fall or descend. He would fall into the same pit he was trying to save his loved one from. He had good intentions but it's just like the proverb says: „The road to hell is paved with good intentions."

Many such helpers began to wrongly think that they had a peculiar special mission to fulfil, carrying the Light to the lost ones. People that were prototypes of later priests began to appear gradually.

They may have had good intentions but were mistaken in the process. They didn't notice that the spiritual Ego was awake inside of them and that ego, not God, was leading them. Although they still remembered *Who They Were in Essence* and were partially helping in God's name, they contradicted Him trying to affect other people's free will. They forgot that it was God's Plan for everyone to love Him freely without the pressure of the other people.

They were helpful but falling people didn't want to accept their guidance. He didn't benefit from their help. They even helped in the midst of loss. They had good intentions but the results were bad. Both sides turned their backs on God. Each one experienced this differently, but the final result was the same. They were falling to the level of the third dimension.

Dark Forces

Dear reader, when I talk about dark forces I don't mean that they are evil. Each man living in the darkness is not informed and he organizes entire systems that are also uninformed. He wrongly believes that he is supposed to act this way.

This is why, while considering any dark forces, you should be understanding and refrain from judging them, which keeps them from reaching you. If you judge or condemn them, you unwittingly become their victim because you attract what you focus on. Remember, the Light is information and darkness is lack of information. Live in Light and you won't ever be hurt.

It is similar with so-called black magic. I am directing those words to the readers who fear it so much that it stops them from living in a natural way. Know, dear reader, that it is not black magic influencing you, it is your own thoughts filled with enormous fear. It is the thoughts that attract it to you. Stop thinking about it and their power will never reach you.

Since people turned their back on God's Light, the „dark forces" started to operate inside them. They still had the same powerful energy they had before but they were turning it the opposite direction than they had before. They often used their power and God's energy to impose their will on people who forgot *Who They Were in Essence*. It was extremely easy for them to gain this power because the Spiritual Ego was much stronger in its actions than the little ego of the person they were helping. This is where priests come from.

You may wonder, dear reader, if it was possible at all to turn one's back on God and to maintain access to His great Energy at the same time. It was possible at one point because It is neutral in its character and one can use it both for good (accordant to God's will) and evil purposes (contradictory to His will). When you use God's energy to do good things, more good things return to you. Analogically, evil comes to the one who does wrong. The will to manipulate another person and affect their free will is also evil. People who did it obviously had good intentions at the beginning but they were getting more and more misguided on their way since they were grown apart from the Knowledge. And so, the helpers turned their back on God as well as those they wanted to help so much. Without access to all Knowledge, they kept a tight hold on its little fragments and the lives they were creating by their conduct. It was lacking Love and was based on enormous fear. They feared much themselves and they sent their fears to others. They were trying to manipulate people in order to stifle their fear at all costs.

Many people were influenced by them but these were only the people who had forgotten *Who They Were in Essence*. They could not influence those great ones who still had the strong Light inside them enough to reject this influence.

These were those great ones who were the absolute Masters of themselves. They knew the Great Law of God that said: „Only a man who has Love inside him can use all of his potential." So they loved with their all hearts since they knew that Love is the only fundamental material welding everything together.

They never separated themselves from the true Knowledge including the Great Basic Truth, even for a second. If they lacked Love, their lives would break apart like a proverbial house of cards. They didn't change. They stood firm in their decision to keep the Light of God and respect for all Life present in their lives.

However, those that forgot Love (since its place was taken by things such as mercy) ceased to respect life. They destroyed themselves when they destroyed life because everything is tightly bonded.

Dear reader, I truly hope that you now understand that all of God's Power dwelled, and still dwells, within you and that it all depends on your consciousness. You could use It at will but you could also reject It. Each conscious path creates new opportunities and leads to a new way of life and existence. All paths were and are equally allowable. You had and you still have your free will. You always choose your way independently. You could do whatever you wanted with your life—you could listen to what God had to tell you and take Him into your heart or push Him away. You could open yourself to His gifts or rebel and reject Him; you could choose to be happy or unhappy and cry as much as you wanted. Notice that some paths led to growth and prosperity while some led to a fall.

Once, in the times of the great prosperity of human civilization, you did what you wanted according to what you perceived to be right. You remembered, however, that the Law of God was irrevocable. It always guards its Eternal Order, saying that Love is the Benefactor, Gift, and Ruler of All. And so, when you loved, you had access to everything. You then ceased to love and the Source of your Life dried up so the fall of your civilization became unavoidable on a global scale.

Many religions consider the separation of mankind from God a motive that happened in the ancient past. As you can see, the fall is nothing but the disintegration of human consciousness, the transition from spiritual consciousness to a pitiful material consciousness.

THE FALL OF THE CIVILIZATION

Dear reader, I want to show you, step by step, how the fall of the magnificent civilization described above happened. The process has repeated itself many times over the course of Earth's history. It doesn't really matter if particular civilizations fell the same way, it is important that after the time of prosperity a slow destruction process began, eventually resulting in doom.

I don't want you to feel guilty because of that, though, nor burden yourself with a crushing feeling of disappointment and failure since it could paralyze you and stop your progress. Take it with understanding and believe that what is done is done. Consider the conclusions you may draw from this to benefit from this newly acquired or remembered knowledge. Use it since you cannot do anything else.

NEW CONDITION MANIFESTING

Before, you acted as though everything you did was the highest, purest, and most excellent purpose. You acted as if everything depended on successful progress in every event you participated in. This began to change eventually, though.

Here and there lazy and lethargic people were born who would not engage in Life anymore. It doesn't matter if you were one of them or if someone else came before you. What matters is that this condition manifested itself and encompassed more and more people.

It happened because the Excellent Divine condition lasted for too long and supersaturation began to occur. The change also may have occurred because of a false belief that it was always going to be that way.

The point is not that you acknowledged these extraordinary conditions as something natural and obvious, something you had an absolute right to have. The problem was the false belief that you can acquire it without effort, just like that.

When you submitted to this delusion, you slowly began to forget that it is only Unity with God that enables you to experience the constant flow of thoughts, life, power, and wisdom from the Spirit to your mind and body. You no longer realized that nothing but Unity with God was the cause of everything you experienced.

You started to think, live, and act as if your entire being was made by you, your external little self. It was then that your external physical senses started to deny God's existence since they couldn't see Him, touch Him, nor feel Him.

Not being able to reach God with your external senses, you began to forget that He was all Power, Intelligence, and Life. At the same time, you ceased to realize that your life, strength, and wisdom weakened as your consciousness grew apart from God.

You knew that God was the Spirit and you could reach, recognize, and feel Him only through your own soul. Since you started to approach life only intellectually, you lost your way to God. You couldn't find Him by expanding your external, objective awareness without engaging your soul.

Your soul enables you to realize that you are made of the same substance He is made of, just like all of God's children. Nevertheless, you can think independently from Him or to live in a separate consciousness. This ability to think independently allows you to think erroneously at the same time. A man who has separated his consciousness from God often makes mistakes since he cannot see the whole Truth but only a small piece.

By entering the increasingly limited consciousness, you ceased to engage in Living according to your own Higher Self and you began to live according to what your external senses suggested. Such an attitude brought completely different results to your daily existence than before. First of all, you started to think that you were the author of your own reality and you didn't realize anymore that it was God himself creating it.

You no longer took into account that God's solutions were going far beyond what your external mind could create. You took everything into your own hands and didn't let God manifest through you. Then you began to compete with God in your imaginary world, the one cut off from reality.

With only partial Truth at your disposal, you began to erroneously assume that what people had acquired, discovered, or learned over the centuries was their success only and that their knowledge was their own forever.

This is why you thought that you didn't need to strive anymore because nobody could take these achievements from you. You would most willingly stop and do nothing since you falsely thought you had everything you needed in order to live.

No man can stay immobilized, no matter how much he wants it, since God, Nature, and Life (which are all the same) are constantly growing and naturally pushing him to go forward. The natural tendency of Life as a huge whole is Love, Peace, Beauty, Harmony, and Abundance. It is like a powerful Spring of a river that is constantly welling up to overflow more and more with its Excellence for all manifestation. It constantly flows to support everything and it doesn't care who uses Its Excellent Energy.

You are forced to wish to become better and better since Life as the whole contains only the process of ascension. There is no other option.

If it wasn't for this constant pressure on the part of Life, many people's existence would be stopped. They would become mindless creatures, walking aimlessly through time. The con-

stant stream of Life, however, flows and pushes them forward.
The one who doesn't flow with the stream of Life must be
thrown out to the bank. And Life as a river flows forward, not
caring for those who stayed at the bank.

You have fully realized the fact so far (and now you realize it only partially) that although you have an earthly existence
in a body, you remained the same Son of God—Christ—born
from the Love and Excellence of God.

You remained His Son while descending to the Earth but
this doesn't mean that you are God himself. God's Son is not
God and the Father is not a son. The Father is more magnificent
than a son since he is the Source, the Creator of his son's life.
The Son emerged from Him and comes from Him. Though you
are a son you are not the Source. You are not the Creator of your
life. You cannot live independently, though may have delusions
of doing so.

Until then you knew that although you descended to the
Earth, you were still living in the world of God or Spirit and that
you were still His beloved Son. The fact that you were externally residing somewhere different than before didn't change the
fact that God's Kingdom was and still is your true reality, your
true home. When you descended to the Earth, everything
changed externally but nothing changed inside.

Until you kept the consciousness of being a Son, you remained in God's state and it never changed. It lasted as long as
you were able to keep this fundamental fact in your mind.
Whenever you forgot God, your Father, you momentarily broke
contact with Him and the conditions of your existence radically
changed.

THE NEW BELIEF

Breaking contact by forgetting is not the same as separation. When you forgot about God, you turned your back on Him but only imagined that you were isolated from Him. You began to live in an imaginary state. You couldn't come back to the full consciousness. With a limited consciousness, you didn't recognize that forgetfulness was the only source of your imaginary separation and not an actual parting.

It was an imaginary separation because you can never separate from your Source that is God. You live in Him and you are totally dependent on Him. You cannot make a single step without Him; you can't even bend your finger. By imagining a delusion that it is possible to separate from God, you began to live in the state of declined consciousness commonly called delusion.

God gave you free will and you can experience anything you want because of it. It was the same then as it is now. It is free will that makes you have various desires. It enables you to create thought forms, which is the limit of your efficacy. None of your desires would come true without God's participation. Without Him your thought forms would remain empty like they were the moment you created it.

The Author and the Source of all desires realized is God Himself. He gives you anything you want with joy and love. You can have innumerable desires and He will fulfil them all.

You can use those gifts, however, only if you live in Oneness of Mind with Him. Only in total, unconditional Oneness with God, your Father, „I Am," you let Love flow through you and you open yourself to receive His gifts simultaneously.

Your life was a continual process of discovering the gifts God bestowed upon you and you were happy. You got this crazy idea, however, that since you can create like God, you are God. You didn't consider the fact that you lived in God and you benefitted from His Source. You wrongly assumed that you were the source of your being.

You imagined that you were the author of your reality, an independent, separate being. You imagined that you were the author of your life and that you created what was around you. You forgot that no man can be an independent organism since he is inseparably bonded to the whole.

Your erroneous thinking blocked the flow of Love through you, which made disharmony dominate your life. You were forced to live in it as long as you were blocking Its flow.

Everything you meet on your path is the Gift of Divine Love. This Love gives you all the good things you asked for. You open yourself to it always when you open yourself to God, your Father, the „I Am" Presence. When you are united with Him, nothing can draw you back from recognizing, acknowledging, and using the Powerful presence of God that you are. This enables the Source to flow freely through you.

You lost this connection every time you ceased to love and submitted yourself to negativity of any kind. When you closed yourself to Love, you began to think falsely that God ceased to bestow you with His gifts even though this was not the case.

You thought that you didn't get His gifts anymore but you just couldn't see them nor open yourself to them. His gifts are always sent to you but they are waiting for you to receive them.

God is Love and you are united with Him when you love with all your heart and soul. When you lack love you turn your back on God and you wrongly think that you separate yourself from Him. His gifts cannot reach you because your erroneous belief becomes a proverbial spigot that shuts any flow from Him.

Connection of this kind resembles modern optical fibers. When there is any distortion there, the Light (or Love and Excellence) has an extremely difficult time breaking through to you and it equally difficult for you to break back to the Light. These disturbances are often so strong that making a connection is impossible for some time.

An Excellent Divine Energy is still flowing towards you, just like it always has. When you lack Love, you distort the natural tendency of Life by your negative thoughts and feelings and you force It to pass by you in another direction. You are constructing a kind of a dam on a river. Energy is like water. It always finds an outlet and flows along a new bed but it doesn't always reach you. When you desire something, you create thought forms but without a connection with God, your Source, no one can fill your thought form. I hope that you understand now why your desires are not realized.

If you turned back to God and called on God's Love to set you free, you could be free of any disturbances. You didn't want it, however, and you didn't benefit from what He offered you.

You were careful to always be in Love and keeping disharmony away. You called on the Law of Forgiveness and demanded wisdom and strength when you made a mistake to keep you making that mistake again. Then you stopped doing it because you forgot how important and necessary it was.

You turned your back on God when you forgot that you must dwell in God in order to coming directly to Him. To dwell in God means to commune with Him daily and to think of Him continuously. You worship Him, bless Him, and activate this enormous Force serving to realize all your needs. When you don't realize this fundamental fact anymore, you stop thinking of God and automatically disconnect with this Force. It becomes static and inactive then, as if you unplugged a TV and deprived yourself of electricity.

The Life Force, like electricity, is everywhere. You can use It only when you contact It, though. Otherwise it is as if it didn't exist to you.

Dear reader, are you now beginning to understand why you need a permanent bond with God? You have everything when you're with him—strength, health, wisdom, abundance, and more. You can function when you're separated from Him, but only counter-productively. How long? Until everything you got from God at the beginning of your physical life dissipates. This is why you are getting weaker, older, and beginning to forget things. You no longer have the connection that recharged you.

When you were thinking the right way, you lived in Unity with God and it was your Higher Self that was guiding you.

You realized *Who You Were in Essence* and your Spirit as free, active, and unlimited. You operated in unity with the Creator. Only God and His Son, Christ existed to you, manifesting in all people, making a big and happy family dwelling in the Heavenly Kingdom.

ESTABLISHING PERSONALITY

The moment you began to believe that you were the author of your reality, you felt separated from God and you started to compete with Him. This new and strange condition made a fundamental difference in your consciousness and pushed you towards an incorrect, distorted mentality.

When you were in Unity with God, you benefited from His creative powers. The new condition deprived you of the powers you used to have and made you feel separated from Him. Without His powers, you began to accept external appearances and they limited you more and more. You not only believed that it was possible to be separate from God, you also established an entirely new system of thought.

You didn't understand your position. You didn't realize where you really were, not only in your beliefs. This false, delusional belief that it is possible to separate from God drew further consequences.

You established personality. You became a separate little *self* (minuscule) which not only thought it had separated from God, its Father, but also that it wasn't His Son anymore.

Although you were still living in God and moving in Him, your little *self* didn't identify itself with the true *Self* (capital letter) that it truly was. You rejected your Divinity and Holiness by thinking this way. It is not true that you were deprived of your Holiness, as some religions may try to convince you.

Since then you have falsely believed that you are this little self. You have believed that this is your true identity and that it is independent from your real Higher Self, the one of Christ and God.

While you were connected to God, your Father, you also had contact with His Spirit. You let Him penetrate you and this brought harmony to your life. This enabled you to experience a continuous flow of thoughts, life, power, and wisdom from the Spirit to your own mind and body.

You still reckoned yourself to be a spiritual being, just dressed in a physical body. Only what was spiritual was most important to you and only then you could benefit from infinite and unlimited potential of achieving. Unity with the Spirit gave you rational advantages.

Later, during the fall, you established a totally new system of thinking. It seemed to you that you were just a physical being that might have something of a spirit. You completely forgot about the Spirit and soul. You began to prioritize the physical world and you became entangled in various limitations.

Each of those systems of thinking gave you completely different results. In the older system, you relied on the Truth, while the new one caused you to become increasingly delusional. These were your external senses guiding you, leading you more and more astray.

All the problems you currently experience came from the belief that you were separated from God.

You are living in an imaginary isolation that is the only source of your imaginary separation. In reality, you are permanently united with God, your Source, because you live, move, and exist in Him.

Your new belief, commonly called ego, made you believe that God's Son can part with God, his Father. Religions call this belief the original sin. They persuade you that God is far away in heaven while you are here on Earth.

The more you believed it, the stronger you became entangled in delusion and the harder it became to break free. You were constantly fighting with yourself and losing since an undisciplined mind and unloving heart guided you in the wrong direction.

You directed God's energy before. Then you didn't realize It anymore. You fell into growing obliviousness and this meant to your external senses that you were growing apart from Him. You felt separated not only from God but from everybody and everything, even your Higher Self. This delusion absorbed you completely and you have been stuck in it until now.

You cannot break free from it because you still erroneously believe that impossible things can happen. Separation is practically infeasible. You cannot divide the indivisible. God is the Whole, Oneness, and you live, move, and exist in Him.

The Almighty God is Omnipresent. He is not only around you but inside you and He penetrates all. He is the same Love, Wisdom, Intelligence, and Power that rules the entire Universe. How can an individual be distinct from this enormous whole?

Until you lived in Unity with God, you were a powerful Self. Later, you thought that you were a poor, little, unworthy meaningless human because you were falling deeper into the ignorance of your little external self. You didn't realize anymore that you were wrong.

You don't want to believe, even in front of yourself, that you still are as Divine as you were at the very beginning. You don't realize that Divinity was given to you forever ago. You forgot that you were born of Excellence and that you exist in God's Mind as a perfect being. Don't you feel it? Your distorted mentality caused this.

It is because of this distortion that you couldn't realize your real position and the position your false delusional beliefs, commonly called the ego that persuaded you of.

If you would change your beliefs to true ones (or turned back to truth) your ego would disappear at once, because there wouldn't be a false belief within you. However, you let your ego weave a delusion of separation that serve as a prison for your true self.

THE EMERGENCE OF GUILT

Dear reader, you must know that along with the false belief that you can separate yourself from God, a huge guiltiness has been growing inside of you. You felt deep inside that you did something very wrong and unworthy and that you sinned by separating yourself from God. This feeling trapped you like a bird in a cage. This was a vicious cycle. The guiltier you felt, the more you grew apart from God, which made you feel even more guilty, sinful, and unworthy. And the guilt always calls for punishment. You couldn't feel guilty and hope at the same time that you would go unpunished because these two exclude each other.

This guiltiness caused an enormous, unconscious fear that God would let you go and that you would be punished by Him. You were filling with pain, despair, anxiety, and suffering—all those emotions were created by the ignorance and activity of your external little self. You believed that God would eventually kill you for your terrible deed. This is how you brought death to your life.

The most important source of your guiltiness until now has been the false belief that you sinned against God when you grew apart from Him. You persuaded yourself that you were an independent, separate individual and that all that you were was a personality and a physical body.

This is not true, of course, but you were dominated by the ego that kept the Truth from penetrating your consciousness. You delude yourself. If you dared to accept the Truth just for a while, you would see that separation is absolutely impossible. The delusion you live in is like a soap bubble—it disperses as soon as you turn towards the Truth.

And here's the Truth: you can direct God's energy at will when you fully realize His presence. Presently, when you don't realize His Presence or turn away from God, you fall into oblivion and cease to recognize this Divine Energy. You forgot that the Powerful God's Presence inside and around you is the same Love, Wisdom, Intelligence, and Power that governs the whole Universe.

When you live in delusion you no longer realize that the Energy you use every day, to even bend your finger or raise your hand, is God in Action. Nothing but God's presence makes your heart beat and your blood circulate in your body. If it wasn't for His Essence that charges and energizes or vitalizes your external body, you wouldn't be able to function. You exist because God acts through you every second.

When you breathe, it is God breathing through you; when you walk the street God moves your body and tells you were to go. Life in all Its Manifestations is „God in Action." Your body doesn't have anything that would give you life and keep you alive.

It is animated by the Powerful God's Energy that has the

Intelligence, Power, and Action manifesting through the „I Am"
Presence. You are using It every moment of your life. All people
are using It, no matter whether they realize it or not.

Dear reader, I hope that you now understand the allegory
contained in the Bible. Banning Adam and Eve from Paradise
only symbolically describes what happened in human consciousness. It wasn't God who banned them from Paradise, it
was their own limited consciousness.

Everything is a matter of consciousness. When you had
the absolute, infinite confidence that you live in God, move in
Him, and have your being in Him, you also had complete consciousness. Presently, you are using your consciousness in only
a tiny, limited range, although the Truth still resides inside you.
It is hidden deeply so you must dare to bring it to the surface
and realize it.

When you open yourself to the Truth, you will feel this
Powerful Living Presence of God—the Energy of Life flowing
through your mind and body. First, it is going to be a very subtle, almost unnoticeable feeling. But you will sense it more
clearly in time. It gives you Life. The Substance of All That Is is
made from it. What moves you, moves the whole Universe and
everything that is around you.

CREATIVE MIND

Everything is a matter of consciousness. While the primitive civilization was in a period of prosperity, the main, fundamental activity was the achievement of „I Am." You knew that every time you expressed „I Am," either vocally or in a silent thought and feeling, you activated your Own Victorious Divinity. You realized that every time you said and felt „I Am," you released the Eternal Spring of Life so it could flow freely towards you. Everything that has ever existed in your life came from Its Powerful Essence.

By neglecting to acknowledge this Powerful Truth, you unwittingly reassessed and charged it with limitations of all kinds. You used to say: „I Am not, which means I don't have, I can't, I am not able to, I don't own, I don't know, I don't understand." This stifled the Great Presence of God within you, either consciously or unconsciously.

You stopped the Perfect Essence of Life from flowing through you when you spoke, thought, and felt in this negative way. It flowed and existed everywhere. It would express its Natural Perfection within you if it wasn't blocked by your erroneous thoughts, feelings, and ego.

Since you began to live in delusion, you naively thought that you could use the bad and inadequate phrases mentioned above and get positive results in the future as it was before.

You forgot that your mind is creative. The mind creates every condition that surrounds your whole life. You forgot that how you feel and perceive reality depends on the way you react to it and how you will see it in the future.

And the state of mind, dear reader, depends entirely upon what you think. When you don't think the right way—using negative expressions—you don't get what you really want. You get the opposite instead.

Your way of thinking was wrong and you didn't get what you expected. Well, Negative things that you couldn't have prevented already happened. However, instead of stopping yourself in the moment and reflecting on what you did wrong, you went forward with your negative thinking.

It happened because you took external appearances too seriously and gave them power with your seriousness. You thought that the things that were happening to you were important because they were negative and unwanted.

What seemed so evil to you, though, seemed to be evil because you only knew it partially. If you had access to complete knowledge as you had had before, you would understand that there was no „evil." You would know that „evil" was the germ of good.

Chaos grew in your life since you were not aware of the Good anymore. If you could access the complete Truth, you would not experience evil, poverty, disease, or other miseries since you wouldn't give them your power. The consciousness of the Truth made all things possible to you. Knowing the Truth, you lived in the Light and it was all up to you because you lived in Its great Abundance.

Since you began to live in limited consciousness, you no longer considered the fact that the greatest 'good' can emerge from apparent „evil." Therefore, the apparent evil you experienced at the time could be the most desired thing in the world. You thought negatively, though, and completely closed yourself off to Good, which led you to evil.

In order to reach the Truth, you would have to stop and reflect on it all. You didn't want to, however, since you were too negligent and lazy. You didn't consider whether those beliefs were true or not. You submitted to them, accepting the situation absolutely since you were too lazy to think. It seemed to you that it would be the simplest and most comfortable way. If you thought for a while you would understand that if you didn't conceive evil and see it consciously, it could never express itself because it wouldn't have the power of its own. Only good would exist and you would still be excellent, exactly the way God had planned it at the moment of calling you to manifested existence. There would still be true heaven on the Earth that God held in His mind at the very beginning and that you would be able to experience anew in the future when you would be able to create Them yourself.

ESCAPE FROM THINKING

You couldn't stop thinking, though, because God formed you that way. That means that you cannot stop thinking altogether. You must think since this is the way you were created.

You escaped into activities that liberated you from thinking, which were activities that were pleasant to you. Pursuing pleasures is nothing but escaping thinking. People who consider thinking to be hard and exhausting work to just that.

Does it mean that your life with God and in God wasn't pleasant to you so far? It was actually very pleasant indeed. You lived daily in the Octave of Love, Joy, and Happiness and It gave you everything it had in great abundance. You fell into passivity, though, and were automatically lowered from the high Octave to a lower, less comfortable one.

In order to avoid suffering caused by the feeling of falling down to worse, unwanted conditions, you began to seek a poor substitute for the previous conditions. This is why you engaged in various activities that were to bring you pleasure and relief.

Notice, dear reader, that when you do something that is pleasant to you, you can do it for hours without getting tired at all. What's more is that you get so engaged in the activity that it is hard to stop you from doing it. If some activity is not pleasant to you, though, you immediately become tired and you take a break since work exhausts you. It was the same then. You couldn't find anything that would bring the previous conditions back.

In the beginning, almost everyone took their lives seriously. But gradually, more people lost the consciousness of God. It was as if one single rotten apple slowly caused an entire box of apples to become rotten.

So instead of holding onto and becoming more like your Source, God, you gradually became separated from Him. It happened to almost everyone, except for the few who didn't lose what was noble and high.

You had freedom before and you achieved it by loving yourself, sympathizing with yourself, and being able to show respect, love, and sympathy to all other souls. And then everything began to change in your life because a man living in God's Light is much more sensitive than a man that is less spiritual and he easily absorbs both wanted and unwanted things. When you let the image of low desire be formed inside you, it activated thoughts that started to lead you astray.

You began to waste your time on the world's temporal things. You still knew that they were here only temporarily and that they would eventually fade. And although they were not present in your life for a long time, their trace was still there in the form of some misery. You knew it residually but you behaved like a moth flying to the light of a candle. You trudged forward with growing devotion and engagement.

Living in a new, limited consciousness, you didn't quite understand the reasons for your new behavior. You judged and criticized but it seemed like you were doing nothing wrong because there was no wickedness in your actions. Rather, it looked like foolishness and brain-fade. You reckoned your new conduct to be fun; you wanted to use it to diversify your boring life.

You thought that you could go wild and enjoy yourself since your fun was noble. In order for you to understand it, dear reader, look closer at what children do today at school. Do their wicked jokes have any deeper meaning? It was the same with you then.

You sometimes reflected and turned back from the wrong course. Your new method of conduct eventually became a habit and was harder to break free from. A habit is like a rut you fall into every time you are inattentive.

You tried to forget the fact that you turned your back on God by behaving so strangely. You couldn't deal with the negative emotions that were growing and pressing you. You subconsciously felt guilty, sinful, and impure and you felt all the horror of what you did „wrong." However, you continued to deny the fact that you forgot God.

In order to be able to function, you fooled yourself into believing that you didn't have any distressing emotions. You wanted to deafen them, fight them over, and deny them at all costs. So you denied that you had them. Modern psychology calls it suppression.

Suppression is like a balloon pushed under the water. You push it down and it jumps to the surface. Your guilt became so heavy that you couldn't hide it anymore. And while you couldn't deny it since it would jump to the surface like a balloon, you had to deal with it another way.

You took it and threw outside so you didn't have to try so hard to persuade yourself that you didn't have it. You saw what tormented you in other people. This way you started to project what you had inside to other people.

Dear reader, I wrote about projections in the second volume and I suggest you find that fragment and read it again.

The most difficult part was dealing with the fact that you turned your back on God. You implicitly envied those who were still standing by God and you looked at them enviously, even though you consciously denied it. By superseding it outside, you began to treat them dismissively, which eventually transformed into an open concept. It didn't happen all at once. At first you judged, condemned, and implicitly criticized them. In time you started to openly mock their achievements, pointing out that their wish to experience *who they wanted to be* was a mistake.

You forgot that in the former state of complete consciousness, judging others was impossible. Someone who knows the right way doesn't need to judge anyone since there is no evil in him. Where there is no evil or mistakes, there are no judgments either. It is possible, however, only when you submit trustingly to the guidance of your Higher Self.

Since you started to act according to your ego, you submitted to it with the same absolute trust you previously had in your Higher Self. It evoked a completely different behavior since acting in accordance to God is based on an unusual simplicity while acting according to ego is more complicated.

Since you declined in your consciousness, you not only started to judge but to share your „observations" with others. You spread gossip, whether or not it was true. You judged and criticized, which was a serious mistake. This „epidemic" led to an enormous loss for yourself and others.

You didn't know then that you were hurting yourself and

others who had unfortunately heard the gossip from you and reflected on it. I hope you now understand how the egoism or selfishness of the external world of feelings of a single person created problems that touched other people the moment they stopped paying attention.

Know, however, that no man that was touched by such an unfortunate action was a victim of these events and that he was helpless. God gave free will to everyone so they could manage and control the way they think and feel. Dear reader, keep this Great Truth in your mind and it will protect you from making mistakes in the future.

Until you remembered it, nothing in the external world could hurt you. When you started to forget, you made more and more mistakes. You didn't know then that preventing evil demands much less energy than dealing with the effects of evil.

Negative actions didn't hurt people who could resist and reject destructive suggestions, no matter how attractive they seemed. Those who held onto the Powerful God's presence or their Higher Divine Self were not threatened by any disturbance since they were protected by Love.

Love prevents all that is evil and cleanses and protects all that is good. It maintains the energy in the world of feelings so that destructive forces can't possess it and bring disharmony. When you forgot God, you didn't have enough love to protect yourself against disharmony.

Pursuing pleasures became the only sense of your life. You wasted all your time on it, which caused you to forget God, your Father. You replaced life in blissfulness, joy, and love with pleasures of lower senses. You were extraordinarily excited by your stupid jokes, tricks, and laughs, but you didn't realize that you would eventually experience suffering and pain if you continued to act against the rules.

THE EMERGENCE OF TECHNOLOGY

Everything is a matter of a complement. When your life was harmonious, you attracted harmonious people and harmonious situations. You were filled with inner power and it gave you all the good things. You could benefit from them since you lived in Abundance, which came from the consciousness of Its completeness.

When you started to turn your back on God's Light, you began to feel more disharmony. Your inner power faded along with your inner light, which made it harder for you to create the things you desired.

Until then, you knew that you were made in the image and likeness of God Himself, so you concluded you had everything you needed for a satisfactory life. You knew you didn't need anything since you had everything inside you. You didn't have to do or attain anything else. Because of this fundamental knowledge, you never lost contact with God, your Father.

Later, instead of relying on God like you had before, you began to take everything into your own hands. Doing so, you deprived yourself of God's Power and help. You couldn't open yourself to everything waiting for you for reasons you couldn't understand. You started to think that you had to work hard to get anything.

The law of complement worked here, too. Since you lacked light and power, you attracted many other people that lacked Light as well. It was them that brought technology to your common life.

You greeted it with a great enthusiasm but you felt deep inside that it wasn't a good solution for you. You ignored this premonition because of reasons you didn't understand because you thought the technology would bring new possibilities to your life.

By descending into a declining consciousness, you didn't understand that your fascination with technology would bring much devastation to your life. It happened because you no longer realized that you submitted to the delusion of your smart ego by taking everything into your own hands. Your ego persuaded you continuously that you were the author of everything in your life.

You didn't pay attention to the fact that you were depriving yourself of your own power on behalf of other people and things by living under the dictation of your ego. You forgot that the natural aim of every man was to expand his or her independence and refrain from rejecting it because of external matters, such as new technology. However, you were enchanted by new technologies and you took the easy way out. You rejected your creative powers on behalf of various gadgets and trumpery the strange technology gave you. This was the reason that you be-

gan to rely on the talents and abilities of others instead of cultivating and developing your own faculties.

You stopped supporting your own creative powers. They
are like muscles. If you don't train them, they become frail or
fade. You were straying from the Path without realizing it.

Technologies developed quickly. They created the delusion that they could create miracles that were bigger than you
could create yourself. You didn't realize then that you had taken
the easy way out. You gave your energy to the people that offered you those inventions by giving them your interest. In return for this, you gave them your power through your interest
and fascination. A cycle of mutual admiration and dependency
was created this way.

Instead of defending yourself with all your might, you
became more and more fascinated by the new situation. You
were filled with pride. You perpetually thought that the biggest
event in the history of the world was taking place. You didn't
realize that you were becoming more and more deluded. You
didn't know then that you would eventually be unable to live
without technology.

It happened soon. You made yourself so dependent on
technology and the whims of people who provided you with
technology that you were surprised to see you could create almost nothing yourself. You were suffering but you didn't know
how to go back to earlier conditions. You broke down because
you saw that the people creating these technologies were not
spiritually advanced. They denied the existence of spiritual laws.
Although they developed wonderful rules and created technologies on the foundation of so-called science, they were all un-
dermining spiritual laws.

Your eyes opened a bit, but with no effect. You couldn't
find the way to the principles that were fundamental to you be-

fore and which you squandered so much. This is how you gave your creative powers and authority over to strange hands. You suffered more because you didn't understand how someone could be a master of shaping material reality without understanding their spiritual dependencies. You didn't understand how someone could be a master of manipulation and delusion while striving for evil and the delusion of truth.

Eventually you stopped attempting to discern whether a man offering you a wonderful technology came from Light or darkness. You couldn't find yourself in that new reality nor recognize whether you received true information. You were unable to tell if someone was depriving you of information.

You were dependent on other people's mercy or disfavor since you were deprived of God's Light and forced to function on the basis of limited data. No wonder it was so easy to manipulate you. You lacked intuition.

When you were connected to God, the Source of all Power, you feared nothing. You knew that It was fearless, that it could do anything you could imagine, and manage all coincidences. You were convinced there was nothing that all Power couldn't do.

Life in a state of delusion of the ego made you think that you could live without God. You began to feel that you lacked everything and that there was not enough for everybody. Your life changed into a constant struggle. You thought that if you didn't fight, you wouldn't get what you desired. You didn't know that it was your ego manipulating you.

You obviously had the right to submit to it, take everything into your own hands, and fight for every single thing. God gave you free will and you could use it as you wished. However, you changed your life into hell by relying only on yourself.

You knew so far that nothing happens that is not in accordance with your will. Later you felt captive, as if you didn't have the will at all. You lived in the state of separated consciousness and you feared terribly. You felt separated from the Source of your Power, which enabled various doubts to haunt you. You worried about everything—what you were going to eat, how you were going to live with your family, and even what you were going to wear. You forgot that God, our Father, took care of all the sustenance we needed to live. Additionally, He gave you a thousand times more than you could use. All you needed was given to you in excess so there was no sense in worrying. But you were not able to realize it anymore. Maybe it was because you were so busy acquiring material goods. You were not interested in your growth so you stopped it altogether. In the end, you totally forgot about your soul. You let it fall since you thought that you stood on the threshold of the new „golden age," just like everyone else around you.

THE CHANGES

Your life began to change since you forgot that you needed a firm decision to constantly reflect on your knowledge about God and your Source in order to live in the most ideal way.

You had previously only listened to your Higher Self so the results of your actions were always perfect. The results of your actions became increasingly miserable since you couldn't control your life anymore once you let your external parts guide you.

When your Higher Self only existed to you, you didn't consider what was external. Since you began to reckon your numerous personalities to be you, you submitted to the growing delusion.

Until that time, the attention of your mental and emotional world rested on the I Am Presence only and It created Harmony, Excellence, and Happiness for you. Forgetting the I

Am Presence, you turned your back on It and directed yourself to the outer world, drawing things that you thought would make you happy. However, you never got what you expected. The things that happened instead dispelled your delusions.

You no longer understood that everything that came from the I Am Presence had its beginning and end in the physical world. Obtaining external things made you happy only at the beginning, since you became unhappy when you lost them. Everything that didn't come from your Higher Self, or the I Am Presence, was only temporary. You couldn't keep it forever, even if you submitted to the powerful delusion that it made you very happy.

You wanted to keep external matters that made you happy at all costs. You no longer realized that there are no such methods or measures on this world that can create external things you desire and then keep them to provide you with Permanent Happiness. It was different with the things coming from your own I Am Presence. Your Happiness had a chance of becoming Eternal and it still does.

And so this new, so-called happiness didn't last long. New pleasures gave you joy but only at the very beginning. After some time, instead of the expected even greater joy, sadness and even tears came to you. For the first time in your life, you felt fear and anger that you had experienced such disappointment. You didn't know the cause of it. You wondered where the grief that transformed into despair had come from. You eventually realized that it came because you had destroyed and lost everything so carelessly.

When you united your consciousness with the Spirit, you were healthy, rich, and strong and your life was at peace. It all happened naturally so you didn't have to ask for it. When you separated your consciousness from the Spirit, your life began to fall and you began to lack everything.

Your health got worse and you lacked the strength and mental energy to do anything. Chaos and discord surrounded you since, as you know, it all depends on the state of your consciousness. When you were conscious of your unity with God, your Father, you were also conscious of everything else since all is contained in that consciousness.

God doesn't know disease, poverty, or any other misery. The consciousness of disease is false since it is formed as an effect of shallow judgment and only when you are in the state of separated consciousness.

When you were conscious of God, you were also conscious of Life and perfect health. It is normal and obvious since God is an Excellent, Pure Life and full of Health itself. It is inconceivable that the flow of the Pure Life could create anything but perfect health. God is a living substance that you are also made of—you are as perfect and healthy as He is.

You cannot be conscious of Life and disease at the same time. It is impossible. By achieving a complete consciousness of Life, you also lose the consciousness of disease. This is why consciousness of disease is possible only when you are in the state of separated consciousness and it doesn't come from anything but your shallow judgment. You were guided by Love in everything so far. You saw God in everything. You knew that every woman and every man, no matter their present condition, is as excellent as God is. It couldn't be otherwise. You lived in a perfectly good world and there was not a person or a thing that wouldn't be absolutely adequate there.

Since everything is God and there is nothing but God, you turned to other people as god turns to other gods. It was possible since you saw good in everything that happened around you. Because of this, your mind emanated light and was constantly expanding. You were absolutely aware of your divine condition. You lived like a god and you saw gods in others.

You once appreciated and admired everyone. You treated even a beggar or wanderer with the highest respect. You knew that a man that doesn't appear proper at a certain moment is just as good as a man that does. Things changed when you drifted away from God. You couldn't appreciate the value of any man you accidentally met. You treated people with aversion or even contempt since you couldn't see God in them anymore. No wonder you lacked Love. Your mind gradually shrunk and you started looking for evil in everything.

Dear reader, realize that a mind that experiences evil cannot recognize good. It knows only evil and nothing more. And the mind that recognizes evil has a limited consciousness. It cannot understand that life operates according to the rule of complementing and reacts to its own needs. It has a limited consciousness and is extremely surprised by everything it meets every day. It cannot understand that it is itself that attracts certain things into its life.

The proverbial executioner will never show up in your life if you consciously choose not to be a victim. You would attract destruction if you ceased fearing it.

It is similar with diseases. If you didn't reflect on ailments, you would never become ill. It doesn't matter if you reflect consciously or unconsciously and if you reflect on yourself or others. Even if you did, you would get better as soon as possible. I hope you understand better now what it is all about.

Dear reader, you and only you are the only one that has ever been responsible for any disturbances in your life. Since you let negative conditions guide you and control you, nobody could help you, even God himself.

You have free will so that you can choose what want to

experience for yourself—health or disease, happiness or misery, excellence or imperfection. Don't blame God for what you chose for yourself or created unwittingly.

Realize that nobody but you blocked yourself on the way to the Source. You deny yourself access to the Source if you desire to hurt others or your intentions are unjust or threatening. It doesn't matter if you send negative emotions towards yourself or someone else. No, you didn't hear me wrong. You cannot negate nor depreciate your value since you are as important as everyone else. If you condescend, know that you do it in vain. Nobody is better or worse than their neighbor since everyone is equally important in the school of life.

Dear reader, you will never receive Love, Wisdom, or Power from the Highest One if you have mean intentions regarding yourself or other people. No one is more or less important to God because we are all his Children. You can benefit from the Source only when your goals are noble, perfect, and of the highest value.

At the beginning of the ancient civilization, you never paid attention to appearances, no matter how big or serious they seemed to be. You accepted only God and His Excellence. You later let yourself accept false appearances of the physical world that you had seen or heard. This is how you sowed evil since you classified certain things as wrong, even if they weren't wrong.

If you didn't conceive evil and see it in your consciousness, it could never show itself since it wouldn't have a power of its own. Only good would exist in your world, and you would be as perfect as you were at the moment you were called into your manifested existence. The moment you saw any evil, you began to act like an activated magnet. You attracted it to yourself and it began to permeate all of your experiences. As you can see, a so-called evil appeared in your life just because it was drawn to your thoughts. This happened even though you had free will and complete authority to choose what you think about at any given moment.

When you experienced what you attracted in this unfortunate way, you often chose to feel sorry for yourself instead of reflecting on how it happened. You didn't want to acknowledge that nothing but your thoughts and feelings built or created disharmony in the past and you had to experience it.

You called it evil. But what you perceived as evil was only partly apparent to you because you could only recognize it partially. If you had the access to complete knowledge, you would understand that there is no evil since every evil is the germ of Good. You couldn't see the Good, however, since you lacked consciousness of It.

There was chaos in your life. If you got access to the Truth back, you wouldn't believe in evil, poverty, disease, or any other misery anymore. You would know that everything you experience in your life was created or attracted by you. If you knew the Truth, you would know that when your mind accepts and consents to a thing or condition, it immediately attracts it to its world.

You would not be a victim of a situation anymore and you would become its master. Since you were able to attract the „evil" you presently experience, you could begin to create the Good the same way. You would enjoy it and savor it and it would make you happy. Your fate was (and still is) in your own hands since it is up to you how you manage your own mind.

You would gain complete consciousness then that there are only two kinds of activities in Life—Internal and external. You can let your Internal activity govern you according to the Excellence Plan and you will experience all the Good in your life. You will experience the opposite if you let external activity govern your life. It will rule according to the imperfection of the senses but it will also give you much „evil."

You united your Stream of Life with what was disharmonious by focusing your attention on it. The Flame of Life releases the Energy of Life onto everything you focus your attention on. The moment you let your attention rest on anything, you begin to agree to something and accept it since you allow your mind to unite with that thing.

By the way, isn't it worth considering what you attract, dear reader, when you continuously contemplate bad or unwanted conditions? Do you attract success or failure this way?

When you acquire the complete consciousness of those dependencies, nothing will be impossible. You will discover that you live in Divine Abundance you can choose from at your will.

HABITS

In the beginning, when you started to go astray you were able at any moment to turn back. You didn't want turn back, though since you thought what you were doing was fun, even fantastic.

Eventually you realized that it was not as wonderful as you had thought it was at the very beginning. You stayed in this situation even though things got worse and worse. You didn't yet know how to break free from these conditions so you didn't do anything. You got lost in time and couldn't come back to the perfect condition you had existed in previously.

Your fall was caused by foolish thoughts expressed with much easiness. Each thought created a successive thought, which continued until you created so many that you couldn't control them anymore and you totally lost it.

You got lost in this new state of consciousness and no longer realized that it was enough to send love, peace, and good

will to everyone instead of judging and criticizing and everything would start to change for the better. It would be this way
even if the criticism was directed towards yourself. Love and
compassion would be the best answer.

One way brings harmony and the other perpetuates disharmony. But you couldn't recognize it anymore. You reacted
with anger, behaving like the one who criticized you. Each disharmonious feeling would eventually destroy what you desired
so strongly.

Remember how many times your soul sent a warning to
your personality, telling you that the thing you were doing
would bring you trouble. But it was not just your soul warning
you.

Think about how many times your personal spirit guides
and guardian angels whispered suggestions to you but you ignored them because you were too busy. How many times they
reminded you of *Who You Were in Essence!* You ignored and
distorted their words every time. You didn't want to listen, even
though you were used to listening.

The „Great Presence" of Life has reminded your eternal
self over the course of innumerable ages that the Cosmic Law of
Excellence and Authority was the Law of Love. Sometimes you
don't listen because you forgot long ago that you have an inner
counselor with you, which is the key to your freedom and joy.

This new, negative state of mind was embedded within
you until it became an ordinary habit. The results it brought
were the complete opposite of those you had known.

The external self or personality is nothing but a collection
of habits. Each one of them is like a print of an automatic stamp
that prints the same image all the time. In order to get a new print,
you would have to change the matrix or re-examine, find, and
change the habit that became this automatic stamp to you.

You were obedient to your soul until this point. You believed in God and that you get what you ask for. You began to doubt it more often till one day you lost your trust altogether.

You couldn't ask with the absolute faith you had possessed previously. You stopped believing that you could get anything you asked for. Since you didn't trust, you didn't receive, even though you were constantly praying with a particular intention. You lacked faith. A vicious circle was formed this way. And Jesus emphasized: „Whatever you ask for in prayer, believe that you have received it, and it will be yours." (Mark 11:24)

Until then, you used to bless everything you had come in contact with. That's why you never experienced disharmony and if it did appear, it was replaced by the Holy Flame of God's Love, which is inviolable.

When you ceased to bless and started to criticize, judge, and condemn everything, disharmony snuck into your life. You had your free will and a right to use it the way you wanted. You didn't yet know that by letting yourself fall into a habit of criticizing and judging, you were mostly hurting yourself.

You are not able to hurt the one that dwells in the state of love for all people and things. Why? It is because love is a Protective Armor that nobody can pierce from outside. God, who is Love, does it. This is how He protects His children who are with Him and in Him.

It is different when you turn your back on God and you lack Love. You don't have enough strength to defend yourself against the outer world and you don't have the protection of the Love Circle. This is how Universal Laws operate. According to them, Love is the only master Strength. It is Cosmic Law since Love is God.

These laws operate against those who forget them with severity and bring certain perfect advantage to those who follow them. This is why the condition you used to live in before gave you wealth, faculties, health, and happiness while the new state of your mind deprived you of it all since it operated beyond the Law.

One of the great Life Laws says that similarities attract (I will wrote more of the Laws in the fourth volume). When you were good in your character, you acted right and wished only good things for yourself and others; you thought right and received or attracted goodness of all kinds.

You automatically became evil without realizing it when you thought contrary to God's character. It doesn't matter if you forgot yourself for a while or didn't pay attention to your way of thinking in general. The way you think now creates your reality in the future.

If a certain thought dwells in your mind for a short time, a manifestation will result. It will remain until opposing thoughts annihilate it. It is different when you think varying things constantly. The results expand in circles and consolidate. The repeating thoughts become habits and you become what you continuously think about.

Dear reader, you are exactly what you think about since your soul participates in everything that you do. You are a living record of your own history. Your body contains your biography and all the information concerning every event and interaction you've experienced so far.

Additionally, all your decisions reflect the state of your spirit and affect your health. Your body has become a living manifestation of your strengths, weaknesses, hopes, and concerns. Are you satisfied with what it manifests? You can change it anytime by changing your habitual thinking.

Remind yourself of a time when you were connected to your inner Being. Your body was beautiful and magnificent and your step was light as if you were flowing in air above the earth. Since you separated from It, your body has become increasingly heavy and ugly. You shambled. Look at children and you will understand what I am talking about. They are playful and careless until they become like us by adopting our way of thinking.

NEGATIVITY

When you opened yourself to a negative force or a dark side of life, it was as if you became trapped in a spider's web. You became more and more entangled. This resulted from the vibrating work of your life's energy. The vibrating energy transfers all qualities residing inside you to the atmosphere outside you. You relive them when you breathe them in.

A thought's vibrations move eternally with enormous speed. Whenever you think of something, the object of your thought gets immediately created. It actually has existed before you thought of it because a conscious thought is just a reflection of your original thought matrix.

Once negative energy was activated, it began to swirl on your path and create discord wherever you went. It grew because you attuned yourself to receive disturbances created by like-minded people. An enormous force ran towards you.

You can compare this phenomenon to a small snowball

hurtling off a mountain top that will eventually make an ava-lanche. The snowball is small and innocent but it grows enor-mously on the way, gathering everything it meets on its path. It is identical to the energy of thoughts. When it comes back to us, it strikes us with a great impetus and we think we cannot defend ourselves against it.

Many people suffer a lot, although they don't realize that it comes from the violent vibrations they attracted because they focused on negative things. This explains why fear, pain, and similar feelings leave such a deep imprint and they take a long time to be shaken off.

Until you focused on a conscious unity with God, you could read His thoughts and that made you wise and trusting. You felt free and safe. It all changed then. You became anxious and feared that you were unable to reach the Truth.

Your mind showed you distorted things and knocked you out of the right relations. In this new state of mind, you thought you couldn't reach God, which made you become more lost. This negative condition grew deeper and consolidated, leading you into deeper delusion.

If you effort into it and began to think in a positive way, you would easily rid yourself of these delusions. You didn't try to do it, though, since you thought that a negative force soaked you up more and more. It seemed to be too hard to break free from its claws. I hope that you understand better why living in harmony and preventing evil demands less energy that correct-ing what evil managed to create already.

As you can see, negative thoughts are the cause of the majority of distressful things happening in your life. The short moments of joy can happen to you, but true joy attained by reaching Truth and Light is not yet possible.

THE TRANSFORMATION

Dear reader, as you saw only a small quantity of thoughts on a certain subject was enough to bring a total transformation to your life. It obviously didn't happen all at once. This was a slow process that was transforming your successes into increasingly bigger failures. Negative thoughts made you replace thoughts of courage, power, inspiration, and harmony by thoughts of failure, despair, lack, limitations, and discord.

Such uncontrolled, unmanaged thoughts brought all kinds of discord, diseases, and suffering to your life. You may ask how it was possible. It's simple. When your new thoughts became rooted deep inside of you, physical tissues of your body also submitted themselves to change.

You began to see life from a totally new perspective. The old issues gradually faded and a new, worse reality formed within you. You even felt as if you were born anew, physically this time, and not of the Spirit, as had happened before.

Your life was taking a completely new meaning, quite different from the old one. You knew before that there was only One Presence, One Intelligence, and One Power operating in your mind and body, and that it was God. You were constantly looking towards your Divine Self, which is the Author of your Individualization, so you were filled with joy, confidence, hope, and energy. Then you forgot about Him completely, so you could see only your helplessness.

You didn't see a chance of success or fortune, which had previously been very important to you. It was as if you had suddenly become blind. You could think only about failure, doom, and setbacks. The thoughts you were saturated with began to emanate to those surrounding you.

The law of complements began to operate here. You had previously thought positive thoughts and were surrounded by positive people. Since you started to think negatively, you attracted new companions that also thought negatively.

You weren't the only one that stopped growing. You pulled others down with you. You affected the change in your environment, circumstances, and life's conditions.

NEGATIVE WORDS

There was not a negative word in your vocabulary before because you let your Higher, Divine Self guide you. When you let yourself be guided by your external, human, little self, it started to form negative phrases such as „I am not," I can't," „I don't have," „I don't know," and „I'm unable."

Your little self was trying to make excuses for having closed the Door to God and His Light by creating these phrases. It tried to convince itself that it is helpless and passive. Since it once formed a negative word, it repeated it constantly. These negative words grew in number, of course, which led to a cycle of negative actions and negative results.

First, your health failed, which had never happened before. Additionally, your loved ones turned their backs on you for reasons that were incomprehensible to you. You were left alone.

You didn't know yet that it was a totally normal and natural phenomenon. When people don't love strongly enough or don't love at all, they push everybody away and naturally every-body avoids them.

As for diseases, you didn't develop them consciously, of course. Your ailments resulted from your old behaviors and negative attitudes. However, you could not associate those facts. You didn't think they could affect your health.

Time passed and even when the pain grew so strong you couldn't bear it, you were not able to force yourself to reflect on your life. Observing yourself and others was enough. By associ-ating various facts, you would have a chance of understanding where your ailments came from.

You might have noticed then that not everyone around you reacted to various events in the same negative way that you did. And since not everybody was affected by negative emo-tions, you had a chance of recognizing that there were other pos-sibilities, too.

You would understand then that nothing but your thoughts, filled with fear and bitterness, were this poisonous substance that caused your disease. You would realize that a negative emotion dominated you and this was the reason that your disease developed.

You would also realize that you have hated yourself and others for a very long time. You would discover that you knew deep inside that you should let things go and forgive. You pre-ferred not to do this, though, because anger seemed like an easi-er option.

You maintained a terrible pain for a long time, which creat-ed an opportunity to soften and improve yourself. Who knows? Maybe you could have started to forgive yourself and others. Even if you didn't know what to forgive, you could forgive everyone and everything that had ever made you suffered. You would have the opportunity to forgive yourself above everything else.

Forgiving oneself is one of the most difficult things there is. You would have the chance to understand that it was you making yourself sick. You would refrain from submitting to the delusion that your disease was attacking you for some external reasons. If you forgave truly, you would notice the pain beginning to recede. The moment you would forgive absolutely, you would become absolutely healthy and your disease would be forgotten. You would love yourself and others anew, and wonderful people would gather around you again.

The Returning Wave

Dear reader, you have often been unwise enough to believe you could bring negativity into your life and create disharmony without there being harmful consequences.

Each criticism, reprimand, aspersion, and judgment issued by you would return to your life like a boomerang. These oppressed you with double force and wickedness, since they grew stronger on their way. These forces attacked you when you least expected it.

When they reached you, it was difficult for you to recognize your own responsibility. This is why you complained about feeling sorry for yourself all the time. You felt that you didn't deserve this treatment. You had already forgotten that Higher Laws operate in the Universe and that whatever you send must come back to you because this is how the Law of a Circle operates.

You couldn't understand that you are what you send.

You criticized others so you attracted people who criticized you. They somehow submitted to the pressure you placed on them to return what you had sent them.

You gossiped and mocked the others and they did exactly the same to you. Instead of getting better, you became worse since many negative emotions were growing inside of you. The same Law was operating here: you attracted more and more of the bad feeling.

Thought vibrations are much stronger than matter vibrations. Physical attacks can leave visible damage but thought attacks hurt much more deeply. A thought is much stronger than matter. A violent attack of the thought vibration is stronger than a physical strike and lasts much longer.

Each thought, whether it's yours or someone else's, flows through your body and causes physiological reactions. Some thoughts are like deep shocks, causing changes in the entire body. Take fear as an example. You will notice how strongly it affects all the organs in your body. An ordinary fear you have experienced many times makes your stomach shrink and your heart beat very quickly, flooding you with a cold sweat.

Now try comparing this condition to the feeling that accompanies your thoughts when they're filled with love. Remember your relaxed body, joyous heart, and weightless feeling. It is a great difference, isn't it?

Not all thoughts evoke such deep states and reactions of the body, of course. Much of it is shallow because many thoughts are unconscious. Many thoughts are unimportant to us, which is why they flow through us without leaving a trace. However, all conscious and unconscious thoughts evoke big biological changes within us.

Not everyone behaving the way you do suffers from the same effects, of course. One person may react to a returning wave with irritation, another with strong anxiety, and yet another with weakened health. No matter the reactions, the cause is always the same. There are strong relationships between the psyche, emotions, and particular ailments.

Whenever I had to deal with people suffering from a coronary disease, they all denied having love and closeness in their lives. People suffering from lower back pain had chronic financial problems or feared for their survival, while people with cancer could not forgive, let go of, or break free from past issues. People with blood diseases had deep family conflicts.

You could list them endlessly. Dear reader, realize that although each mental problem shows in various parts of the body, a particular problem will cause the same physical ailment for everybody since we are all the same. We differ in the color of our eyes, hair, and skin but we're all the same when it comes to our body and spirit.

You were once healthy and you prospered when you blessed everyone and sent them love. You didn't consider whether a particular man deserved the good you were sending him. Goodness would return to you in various forms.

You then became unfriendly towards people. You cursed them instead of loving and blessing them. You sent them thoughts filled with judgment, criticism, and condemnation. You either forgot or ignored the fact that everything you send must eventually return to you. This is the Law and it is unswerving.

When you sent good things, good things got sent back to you and you were very pleased with this fact. When you sent evil, evil had to come back to you and gave you less and less reasons to enjoy your life. You despaired and lost hope for a better life because of these deteriorating circumstances.

It would not come to that if you had immediately recognized a negative thought or feeling and reacted to it in time. You would acquire a chance to regain balance.

You forgot already that the best and most efficient way to learn is from your own mistakes. Even if you judged things, criticized people, and generated discord, you would not have to worry about it. You wouldn't see any problem because you would have a complete Consciousness of the fact that Love was your protection.

When you lived in God's Light honestly and out of your absolute free will, you were aware of when you acted wrong but also realized that you still had the power to reevaluate the energy you received. You received goodness because you sent it out.

You didn't despair when you had to go through distressing experiences. You understood that no matter how painful they seemed, they were here for you to learn something from them. Learning from experiences gives true knowledge that comes from practice and not just the shadow that comes from observation. You cannot learn much from someone else's experience simply because you start to forget it after a while. If you experience something yourself, however, the lessons are recorded in your subconscious and can never be forgotten. This creates a simple conclusion. In order to learn fully and not just fragments, each man should experience everything so it becomes imprinted permanently. This is what the process of excelling and growing is about. The True Life is constant growth and moving forward is Excellent Divine Order.

Learning through experience is about getting to know a negative thing and not to moil yourself with it. We are supposed to overcome ourselves so that negativity can't control or absorb us. We don't get stuck in negativity in our present lives or lives to come.

Dear reader, I will try to explain this with the example of present habits. Let us assume that you don't know what stimulants are and you don't realize what they do to people. It is not enough for you to observe others, such as drunk people. Deep inside, you will desire to go through this experience yourself to see what it's like to be stunned. It doesn't matter if you smoke your first cigarette, drink alcohol, or take drugs. It doesn't matter if you do it one or many times. The point is that you experience what it's like to be in a certain state. You may learn what alcohol or other stimulants are and you will feel the unpleasant effects of a hangover or some other unpleasantness from drinking. Our experiences are about the lessons we learn from them. It is good to get to know something but one should not „moil" their energy while experiencing. This is why you cannot experience any negative thing for too long because the longer you do it, the harder it is to break free from this energy. Your body gets used to lower energies and pulls you down into addiction. I wrote about involution in the second volume. It is worth coming back to it.

You may have not enough strength to oppose the addiction. It is you who must break free from it since your body won't help you. On the contrary, it will encourage you to stay in a state of addiction. The Art of Living is about learning some negative experience and overcoming yourself so that you can break free from it as quickly as possible. If you don't, you will let your Life Stream join with this negative energy during the negative experience. And the negative energy is like a tornado, which with a powerful spiral force pulling you in like a whirlpool. You never enter a negative state because it is difficult for you to stay on its surface without moiling in its content. If you are too weak to oppose it, you unwittingly let the negative side absorb you all the more. It is like a moor, pulling you into it until you lose yourself in it completely.

As you can see once again, preventing evil demands far

less energy than correcting what evil managed to do already. If you commit to remembering what God is, though, you can break free from the negativity at any moment. Instead of despairing and losing hope because of various outer negative circumstances, you can use the Energy and Power of God to overcome the negative situation.

You did nothing with it in the ancient civilization. You behaved like you didn't take it into account at all and forgot that it was possible long ago.

LOWERING OF VIBRATIONS

Your oblivion or ignorance came from the fact that you let yourself be stuck in negativity for too long. You agreed that your body's vibrations descended towards denser activity where the light was lacking. Light is Information and Its lack is lack of information.

In the past, you gave everything you did to God. Later, you started to take your fate into your own hands. This is how you grew apart from Him and began to lack the information to keep yourself from forgetting about Him. You forgot that God's plan was so much better since it went far beyond everything that your external, little self could create.

And it was extremely difficult to ascend from there to a previous, excellent level. It was a question of Consciousness itself. You no longer realized that living in God and with God was possible, which would mean that you would forget Him entirely.

As you can see, dear reader, your problem was not testing an experience that was taking you away from God. Your problem was allowing it to gain the momentum that caused you to forget and lose yourself. You then thought (wrongly of course) that you were not able to stop this process. You could turn back but you didn't want to. Your laziness suggested that you go with the flow and not oppose it.

The main cause of you enormous problems and challenges was your fear and hatred of particular situations. Hatred and fear. You should have withdrawn your maintaining energy to prevent yourself from feeding the problem with your fear and hatred.

If you had withdrawn your energy, you would have gained a chance to guess how you made your mistake and you could try to repair it and recognize how to avoid it in future. However, instead of enjoying the option of repairing your mistakes, you criticized yourself even more and condemned yourself for making them. Such an attitude made you confront even more mistakes. You wanted to forget that each experience, no matter how tragic or evil it was, gave you an opportunity to learn about your experience, which could be turned into knowledge. Knowledge coming from practice is true knowledge that one cannot forget since it is strongly imprinted in the subconscious. A shallow and casual image coming only from observations eventually dissipates in memory. This is why you opposed your wrongdoings instead of rising above them as soon as you noticed them. It didn't matter whether you struggled with an internal or external problem since you were entering negativity with your behavior. Instead of repairing the situation, you brought more chaos and discord upon yourself. And when you were struggling with your problems, they grew in number until you collapsed under their weight. This is how a vicious circle was formed. It all happened because you let discord, judgment, and criticism invade your thoughts.

You could return to your prior conditions if you became aware of your mistakes and repaired them.

You had never fought before, even in your thoughts. You knew that you could attract a real fight by just thinking about a fight. Then you started to fight with everything you met in life. You once knew that one cannot master destructive conditions by struggling against them. You no longer realized that everything you wrestled, rebelled, opposed, and fought against with your thoughts immediately showed inside you and was eventually transferred to the outside world.

I will try to explain it to you. When you observe anything outside you that makes you anxious, an image of it forms inside of you. Your feelings start to fight against the unwanted picture and join the disturbed feeling of other people living in the same situation. Every time you start to fight destructive conditions that surround you or were imposed on you, you open yourself to every other destructive condition of the physical world and the destructive tendencies of mankind. This is what has always been and there is no exception to this rule.

Instead of fighting something you don't want, rely on God totally. Send Him love and this will bring you a relief from all anxiety.

Dear reader, I hope you better understand the reasons that you were unable to realize your intentions as easily as before. You either didn't understand the rules or simply didn't follow them.

You once focused only on your positive visions. They always manifested themselves. Whatever you did, you never feared that your desire would not manifest itself or that it would be taken away from you. You realized that everyone can stand in Light and attract everything he possesses already anyway. Since you had the same opportunity as everyone else to fulfill your desires, you never wanted to take away anybody's desire. You didn't need to.

Your success was due to a proper way of thinking. You controlled your substance intake and clearly demanded what you wanted. This conduct brought you everything you needed and accelerated your growth.

You focused on a positive vision but sent negative thoughts that often blocked or neutralized your positive visions because you operated on declining vibrations.

You were unable to see the results of your positive visions immediately since your consciousness had diminished, as you had had before. Therefore, you were forced to wait until they became manifested. You didn't know that the visions have a harder, longer way to manifest according to the difference in their vibrations. And when the realization was delayed, you started to lack faith, so you let yourself have doubts.

You could still realize your desires since you had the same possibilities. You needed a true faith, a confidence that God existed as a vast Abundance. Jesus said: „According to your faith, it will be given to you.". You once prospered only because you were open to God. Later you began to lack faith and doubt everything, which led you to true doom. These doubts made you see your failure instead of successes. You forgot that you create everything you focus on since the thing that your thoughts gather around always takes a material shape. If you focused on your success, you would inevitably achieve it. When you focused on your failure, you created its image in your mind, which made it become materialized. The more energy you engaged to create a dark picture of doom, the quicker and more assuredly it would come.

FEELINGS

At the beginning of the ancient civilization, you remained immovable no matter what was happening around you. You approached your feelings with due respect, understanding, and care. You knew that they stimulated your progress and activated your growth and that they helped you understand yourself and others.

Such an approach came from a deep knowledge because your feelings were necessary to give color to your life. The source of feelings is perception of the outer world and their intensity and color depend on the way that you experience them. If you didn't have feelings, you wouldn't have a chance to see the world around you. You knew that your world would be dark, bland, and grayish without them.

You respected your feelings and were careful not to 'moil' with them. You carefully guarded them so that they were always pure and neutral. This is why you never submitted your feelings to judgment, no matter what they were. You could only judge what you did but not what you felt. You didn't do it, though, because you believed everything to be good and you saw only good everywhere.

You couldn't even become angry nor see evil since you focused only on the thoughts that your Inner Being agreed with. You immediately experienced positive emotions or unconditional love then, meaning that you united with God and there is no evil in God.

You then ceased to understand your feelings since you started to perceive them differently. You began to divide them into positive and negative, pleasant and unpleasant, comfortable and uncomfortable. You absorbed each suggestion like a proverbial sponge as it multiplied around you.

As long as you saw only higher good in everything, you were absolutely sure that even the greatest amount of judgment, hatred, gossip, criticism, or condemnation could not hurt you or reach you in any way. You were protected by the Love that you were filled with.

When you started to see evil, you began to feel that it was hurting you since it reached you also. This is why you built walls every time you felt emotionally threatened. The walls you built around you were made of fear. You built them since you feared that you would be hurt, rejected, and criticized.

So it was not the external world threatening you, but your own sensitivity. You surrounded yourself with walls so you didn't feel the negative. You didn't know that you suppressed your own emotions by doing this. However, you were not able to perceive the world around the right way. You rejected people who seemed to be threatening you before they managed to reject you. You didn't know that the walls you built hurt you much more than the people you feared letting in. They blocked you completely, closed your heart, and deteriorated the weak condition of your spirit.

When you separated yourself from your emotions and feelings, you were not able to reach the source of your suffering, weakness, and fears lying at its foundation. You couldn't heal yourself and become the whole you used to be.

OPPOSING FORCES

You realized that there are positive and negative forces present in all of creation. You never feared nor condemned negative forces since you knew that you needed them. They served you as a measure to become stronger and more aware of your Victorious, Positive Strength. You always turned towards positive forces and you knew even though negative forces existed, they couldn't reach you if you were mindful of them. Even if you contacted negative energy, you knew that you still could break free from it on your own.

You then started to perceive only the negative side of life. You became more entangled in it since you couldn't see a positive side. You opened yourself to negative forces when negative emotions were stirred up inside of you. If you immediately recognized the negative thoughts and feelings that evoked them, you wouldn't go further and you would change them into positive. They would bring you positive results, as it had been before.

But you feared negative forces too much to oppose them. You forgot that there is a Consciousness Balance resembling a clock pendulum inside of you. Each time you changed your thinking from negative to positive, you instantaneously returned to your positive pole, where you were safe.

You committed to always acting within the Perfect Balance before. You lived in Love, Wisdom, and Power and moved along the Middle Path before. You then started to sway from one extreme to another: from great joy to great despair or depression and from trust to doubt.

You knew before that you had free will, which enabled you to always feel free. You then ceased to use it and felt like a captive, even though you still had the freedom to choose your own thoughts.

Captivity came from losing the awareness that it was you who decided whether or not you still wanted to think about things that made you feel bad. You forgot that you have the power to decide whether or not you want to change the thought to a more positive one that can make you feel much better.

You didn't guard your thoughts and you often didn't know what they concerned. This state of mind made you involuntarily catch strange, negative thoughts that filled the atmosphere. You felt more and more oppressed, but how could you feel otherwise if your thoughts were running around like a wandering dog, bringing the garbage they met on their way against your own good? Life became a real trouble to you since you used your free will in the wrong way.

You no longer realized that you create every moment of what you experience. It was usually done by your thoughts, and sometimes by strange suggestions that you would involuntarily take. You sowed or created them each time you thought of something. Depending on a slurry or seed, you harvested huge crops in the form of „good" or „evil." This is how you material-ized a proverbial heaven or hell for yourself and others.

You created your small world the same way that the thought of God created universes. Everything that existed around you manifested through the operation of your own thoughts. Positive thoughts created what you called good. Nega-tive thoughts created what you were not pleased with.

Nothing lasts forever. If you were mindful and changed the subject of your thoughts, you would soon obtain different results. Rejecting negative thoughts and emotions would let you discover not only internal peace, joy, and happiness, but would enable you to find the true purpose of your life again.

Remember the old time. You wanted to experience, and kept the fact that you were the only manager of your life and activity in your consciousness. This made you responsible for choosing what you wanted to manifest. You focused your vision on the chosen goal and held to it with firm, joyous determination to achieve what you intended and you immediately received it.

You never took what others wanted from you into ac-count. It was your fate, not theirs. They had their life. You knew that every man had the same opportunity to realize his desires.

This attitude quelled your fear of creation. You knew that you had the power to neutralize all erroneous creations, no matter if you created them unwittingly or deliberately. It was very simple. If you didn't like the experiences you were going through, you changed your thoughts in order to experience dif-ferent things in the future.

You never paid attention to external events, no matter how bad they seemed to you. You didn't feel despair or lose hope because of unfavorable circumstances either. You always knew that you could always invoke the Only Power, Energy, or Activity that you could use: God.

You then forgot this simple rule. Although you still could control everything, you didn't do it since you didn't want to put any effort. You submitted to the feeling of helplessness and captivity. You started to think that the unpleasant events formed themselves and you felt like their victim. You didn't realize that it was you who unwittingly created them.

NEW FEELINGS

You were in the process of changes. They were small at the beginning, almost unnoticeable to your surroundings. However, you felt them quite intensely. You got to know new feelings all the time. Emotions you had never experienced before and that you didn't understand tormented you.

This may be hard to understand for contemporary people that are torn by various emotions every day. For a man whose feelings were the source of his continuous bliss and ecstasy, however, this was a tragedy of an unimaginable range, especially since he didn't know anything else before.

At the beginning of the ancient civilization, you knew only love, happiness, joy, bliss, admiration, peace, and satisfaction. Then you got to know negative feelings and the list became increasingly long. You first felt fear and anger, and then shame, disappointment, and helplessness. You despaired, raged, felt guilty, sad, angry, sympathetic, uncertain, anxious, irritated, and grievous.

You learned hatred, envy, and jealousy not only when you turned them towards others, but also when they came back to you. It is cyclical. What you sent eventually came back to you. The later it returned, the more it pressed, since it grew in strength on the way, gathering thoughts and feelings similar to yours.

The worst of all feelings was doubt, which continuously rose within you. You didn't know the emotion until then and you didn't realize that each time you listened to its suggestions, you cut the roots of goodness deep inside you. You didn't yet know that you slowly killed yourself each time you experienced doubt. Your spirit was committing a kind of a small, unnoticeable external suicide.

Doubt was born in your own mind. At first it was as a silent whisper but it grew stronger and louder until it became a deafening negation of everything you contacted. It transferred to a desire to leave all the good behind. This is how you totally rejected God, your Creator.

When doubt touched you or someone close to you, it's contagious character affected the lives of everybody around. People touched by it were being pushed deeper and deeper until they reached the abysses of pain and suffering, where nothing received what is good and true.

You couldn't accept the new condition in any way and you didn't know how to return to the previous one. The more these negative feelings tormented you, the worse you felt and the harder it was for you to regain balance, harmony, and the middle course. You hampered your growth more and more, which increased your doubt.

Dear reader, as you will discover in a later part of the book, doubt is a substitute for hell, a place with no hope and peace. It is an internal human enemy. It eventually reached almost all of mankind. Isn't it the same nowadays?

Descending

Your problem was not the fact that experiences led you to turn your back on God, but that you allowed the dynamics of the process to gain impetus, in which you lost yourself.

You began to persuade yourself that you were not able to neither stop nor reverse this dynamic. This state of mind led to a constant decline of your vibrations, so your body began to lose its glow. It turned towards the dense activity. This process lasted as long as the material physicality that we know today was formed.

It didn't happen all at once, in one day. Emotions slowly and unnoticeably began to sneak into your Self, like the snake in the paradise garden. It happened slowly enough for you not to recognize or associate the cause and effect.

You lived in the Light before, so the manifestation of your activity was instantaneous. Since your light was fading slowly, the manifestation was delayed. This is not surprising because it had more difficulties to overcome.

Besides, your mind was going through a process of slowly blacking out. While new, negative results manifested in your life, you didn't realize that they were caused by your false thinking.

A different perception of reality formed within you, followed by a new way of experiencing things. This began a cycle of bad emotions causing even worse ones—vibrations were set into motion and constantly pressed you to think negative thoughts.

Thoughts are vibrations. Your thoughts caused bigger negative emotions to grow from small ones. You fell into an invisible spiral that pulled you down with a great force.

You refrained from doing wrong before but this wasn't because you were unable to. You just realized that it was not advantageous. You knew that good attracts more good and that even the smallest evil attracts more evil. You forgot about it later because your consciousness had declined. You acted contrary to your former knowledge. You thought falsely, which created bad experiences and you criticized them. The effect was that they grew in number. So it all started from a single, unobtrusive, meaningless, negative thought. A whole avalanche came from it.

DOUBLE VISION

You begin to see everything double. Instead of seeing and feeling only the good in everything (as you had been doing until this point), you began to classify your experiences by the amount of evil in them. You saw good rarely, and I mean a so-called „higher good," of course.

I would like to turn the reader's attention to an important issue here. The point is that it didn't matter how you behaved in a certain situation, if you were going through an unwanted experience personally, or saw others going through it. The only thing that was important was how you interpreted what you saw, heard, and felt—whether you classified it as a higher good or evil. It was a very important issue that you didn't take into account.

You no longer realized that you attract what you focus your attention on, especially the intense emotions. It can be easily concluded that every experience you classified as good, created more good of itself, while evil brought more unpleasant experiences. This is how earlier traits and experiences came back to you.

The same feelings were still inside you but the difference was the way that you experience them. If you classified something as positive, positive emotions awoke in you, which created positive results such as joy, youth, strength, and good. If you classified something as negative, you experienced negative emotions that created unpleasant experiences you couldn't deal with. If you looked at it from a distance, you would realize that it was ironic or paradoxical. It would be difficult for you to believe that your own consciousness can create a proverbial heaven or hell as the result of the same event.

Emotional reactions to certain events had nothing to do with the events themselves because it was always you that decided whether or not something was good or bad when it happened. More importantly, you taught yourself how to classify those occurrences.

THOUGHTS

All evil comes from a single negative thought. If you, whether you are its author or recipient, ignored it and didn't think about it anymore, it wouldn't affect you even if it was highly negative.

However, you couldn't resist a temptation and reflected on negative thoughts in various forms, which activated your negative emotions. Thoughts like this are easily strengthened by emotions and attract the thoughts of other people in similar situations. Circling wider, it became more dangerous since it affected other people, making them think the same way.

These thoughts or energy forms accumulated. You charged them with your energy and they charged you. This is how a negatively charged energy field was formed. The difference was that you gained when you drew from one field while you lost when you drew from the other.

Dear reader, do you realize how many thought forms

are sent deliberately just to make you think a certain way? Some are created to affect your decisions, tempting you to buy something, while others are intended to make you angry, afraid, or dominate you. Don't ever be afraid of this influence, though, because none of these thoughts can affect you if you refuse to accept them. You accept it only when you show interest in it and reflect on it.

Each thought returns to you as the sender like a boomerang. Some thoughts fade independently because of lack of interest in them, while others grow in strength continuously. They become charged when you reflect on them and then they automatically get sent forth. When they return, they are much stronger than before and press with greater strength. It is more difficult to oppose them then, so it is easier to encourage a man to think about them further. The process goes on as long as the subject of certain thoughts becomes materialized.

If the content of a thought was once based on the Truth, it created good. If you thought about something that you had earlier classified as evil, it created a negative reality. You received the same kind of evil in its physical tangible form that you had earlier seen and contemplated. Every thought operates according to the same mechanism, even the most unobtrusive one that has the power to become extremely powerful. It created a spiral of positive and negative situations. As I mentioned before, it didn't concern you only. When it reached more people, it activated the irresistible wish to think about and discuss them. It was often the cause of quarrels, conflicts, or big fights.

There was not a moment, though, that you or anybody else was the victim of such a situation. It all depended on the level of your consciousness. It was easy to think negatively about something without realizing it. You usually became self-aware only when you received results that you hadn't expected at all. You didn't repair them even then, however. Instead of reflecting on how you attracted such a negative event, you would start complaining about your fate. Reflection could help you in the future and keep you from making the same mistake twice. You would attract what you really wanted.

You didn't control the flow of your thoughts because your consciousness had declined and you wanted to take the easy way out. You forgot that once you let some thoughts come to you, you have to be very strong to be able to break free from them and their undesired results. It is very difficult to deal with.

There is no sense in being angry with the past, though. This is a negative emotion also. What is done is done. You can, however, decide your future. In order to avoid a useless internal fight, one must remember not to let a negative thought form next time. It needs to be quelled at the very beginning, the moment it arises, since it is often too late then. It becomes so intrusive that we cannot deal with it.

MANIFESTATION

While your consciousness was declining, everything went inside you to some point, which means that the effects of the process were visible only at the level of your feelings and emotions. After some time, negative thoughts dressed as feelings began to bring abundant fruits in a form of physical manifestations. They were completely different from the old ones.

Slowly but consequently, you began to experience failures and lose what you had previously achieved miraculously. Greed, jealousy, and hatred began to sneak into your feelings like a snake in the grass, which pressed you to take revenge.

You were fighting with the alleged enemies because you were blaming someone else for the distressing things happening to you. You didn't see that responsibility was on your side, while others just mirrored you. Only you were responsible for distressing experiences because you had created them through your negative thoughts. If you didn't like this life, you could begin to choose different thoughts in order to experience something else in the future.

You didn't want to accept nor understand the reason for you failures, so you were constantly fighting. And the more you opposed the things you didn't want, the more unwanted things you attracted. You didn't know that you attract what you oppose all the more. And your inner sense of the struggle became materialized as a struggle on the physical plane.

You experienced losses in every domain of your life, without realizing the cause of it. That was double visioning. Instead of seeing and feeling only the higher good, you began to classify your experiences as evil.

You became ill, poor, and hungry as a result. You felt like a victim of what had happened, not the direct author. It was then that you began to blame God as the main author of your misery. God didn't have anything to do with it, however. He is Excellence and Abundance, so He doesn't know poverty, disease, or hunger.

Dear reader, think about what God would do to you if you turned your back on Him. Would He deprive you of a chance to understand your mistake and make it impossible for you to correct your actions? He saw your life from a broad perspective and you saw it from the perspective of your momentary experiences. You defined them as failures, misery, tragedies, or punishment for your wrong deeds. He saw a chance to learn new lessons from your difficult experiences. You forgot already that you had come to the Earth to learn more about love and devotion. And where did your love and devotion go?

If God or some other Great Being of Light tried to suggest what you should do, He could block the chance. And it was of a great value, providing you understood it yourself. The fact that They know better didn't give them the right to take away our precious opportunities to learn those difficult lessons.

It's true that you were poor, ill, and conflicted with much trouble. It was all happening, however, because of your limited consciousness, which was suffering from deteriorating vibrations. You could only work on yourself by working on yourself and recognizing God as the basic Source of All that Is. You used to request things from Him with childish innocence since you trusted Him infinitely. You asked Him as a child asking its parent, knowing it will certainly get what it asks for. And you got the fulfilment of your every desire from Him in return.

During the fall, you turned to God to ask Him for some things but you couldn't rely on Him exclusively anymore. You wanted to keep everything in your own hands at all costs, which meant that you took it from God's hands as if you no longer realized that the infinite abundance resides there. How could you expect to receive any good if you didn't use the Source? You behaved like a fisherman who, instead of throwing down his fishing rod to the pool brimming with fish, throws it into a puddle because he foolishly thinks that he knows better about where the fish are. No wonder certain doubts snuck up on you. You couldn't doubt and expect something at the same time. When you doubted, you didn't expect, but whoever expected couldn't let themselves submit to the slightest doubt. It would ruin the entire manifestation. The Holy Scripture confirms it by saying: „According to your faith it will be given to you."

You were poor and ill but your lesson gave you the opportunity to remember that you could ask for anything, provided that you do it with an absolute faith and that you believe with all your heart that you will get what you ask for. You were not able to do it, though, since you didn't love. In order to receive, you would have to raise love above all, but you couldn't or didn't want to love like you once did.

You didn't receive the good things that God would have given to you with great joy since you lacked faith and love. You thought they were out of your reach. The truth, however, was that you didn't want to reach for them. And so, you stopped asking Him. There were many reasons for that. You falsely thought that God wouldn't give you anything. You thought that you were not worthy of Him and you forgot that in order to receive, one must first ask and believe that he would receive.

Dear reader, please realize that free will is a gift. This seems to be a trouble not only to you, but to the whole Earth. You were responsive and open to God at the beginning and then you began to doubt. This was miserable for not only you but most people.

Please realize another important fact, dear reader. You often said with fear in your voice: „God, heal my disease and take the misery, poverty, and unhappiness away from me." And you got more of what you asked for with great fear. You felt ill and you became more ill, you felt poor and you became poorer. It happened when you didn't control your thoughts and didn't manage to use them. Such „carelessness" brought all kind of discord and suffering into your life. You forgot that your thoughts were continuously creating your world. They were creating your world not only occasionally but constantly.

You used to say with trust and faith in your voice: „God, give me this." And you got it. You didn't even have to ask much. You were healthy since you felt healthy and more of God's energy would flow to you, which brought even more health. It was the same with wealth, happiness, or any other thing. You were rich because you felt rich, you were happy because you felt happy. There was no reason then for you to feel different than you had before. You received everything only through conscious control of your thoughts. I hope that you understand the following words better: „For whoever has will be given more, and they will have an abundance. Whoever does not have, even what they have will be taken from them." (Matthew 25:29)

Dear reader, realize that the knowledge concerning creativity of thoughts has been always dwelling in your internal world. You once got what you desired and were conscious of this knowledge. Since you started to forget about your inner world, you began to believe in only what the outer world offered you. You didn't look at the results of your doings anymore. You involuntarily trudged forward, constantly creating chaos in your own world. It was so because your consciousness was fading. You let uncontrolled thoughts and desires form within you. It all depends on a proper way of thinking.

Realize that when you controlled your being and clearly demanded what you wanted, it brought you the fulfilment of your needs and accelerated your growth. When you ceased to control it, however, you received what your good or bad fortune brought you. You behaved like a proverbial cork in the water, at the mercy of wind and waves. Don't be surprised that life was lashing you and throwing you around. Since you didn't want or didn't know what to demand from Life, you couldn't expect that it would be successful.

This is how the Great Principle Of Life operates, or in other words, the Universal Laws. You always get what you ask for. Remember that when you were aware of your thoughts, you lived in excellence, since you deliberately attracted the manifestation of your desires. Without realizing your thoughts, you also got some things from life but these were expressions of your carelessness, laziness, and inattention. You always received something. In order for you to enjoy the gift, you had to be absolutely conscious of what you asked for. Otherwise, you created unconsciously and inattentively.

If you had an opportunity to look at your former life from an outsider's perspective, you would easily see that you were protected and supported when you were living „godlike." You wouldn't receive anything, however, if you didn't control your thoughts and feelings. Love was your protection and support. To reach and liberate it, however, you had to invite It into your life through deep devotion and love.

God gives you His Love so your external self can act according to the Cosmic Law. Only when it operates in Love does it become the Directing Intelligence that protects you from disharmony because of constructive activity. When your thoughts and feelings are expressed in a discordant way, the Excellence that you desire so much cannot arise in you. You could gain it any moment, but only because of Love.

CONSEQUENCES

Dear reader, as you can see, your new ancient reality came from the fact that you wanted to be this way. One could say that you worked this position out and that you deserved it because of your negative thinking. Instead of loving freedom, you chose the chains of poverty, disease, and failures. Nobody could wean you away from it since this fate served the right purpose that the higher good was.

You took a dense physical body in order to bear everything you so carelessly attracted. Your constant false thinking caused you to not only stop growing but to recede. You descended from your magnificent fourth dimension to the third dimension.

This was caused by your negative feelings as a reaction to thoughts vibrating much lower than the vibrations of Love. The descending wasn't permanent, though. If you reflected in time, you could have come back to the old glory, and your body would brighten up with the same glow as before. It was possible since you descended to the third dimension only with your consciousness. The rest of you was still residing in the fourth dimension. However, you didn't realize it anymore because your consciousness had declined and you were unable to understand what was actually happening to you. If you raised your consciousness a bit, you could move freely between dimensions.

The connection between a physical body in the third dimension and the more magnificent, lucent body in the fourth dimension is a question demanding a decision out of one's own free will. Nobody will do it for you. Unfortunately, your personality was prone to constantly wander, so it couldn't or didn't want to make this spiritual connection anymore.

Not everybody submitted to moving into the third dimension. There were people who still lived in the Light of God. They never lost Love, Wisdom, or Power, so they still had the predisposition to operate freely in the fourth dimension. Their bodies were brimming with as much light as they had before. Although negative conditions filled with fear, anger, and hatred surrounded them, their Inner Wisdom kept them from moiling with themselves. If you followed them, you would easily come back Home to the fourth dimension.

THE THIRD DIMENSION

Until you lived on high vibrations of the fourth dimension, your body was filled with light and you saw God in everything that Is. You had a complete consciousness and you knew God as the Highest Intelligence, being and manifesting in all.

You understood then that you could have access to His Source, Wisdom, Love, and Power harmonizing with everything. This bond with everything was fundamental to your existence. You saw only Good in everything since you directed your energy only towards God. You were so tightly united with Him that you had all His powers and attributes.

You began to lose them when you ceased to love. A curtain between Him and you was formed. The Magnificent Beauty of God was slowly forgotten. You were submerged in a feeling of being lost and helpless.

Without access to Wisdom, you couldn't embrace God

with your mind nor understand Him since He dwelled beyond your intellect.

You used to live with God and in God. You saw Him in All that Is, and you reckoned all people to be your brothers and sisters. You felt separated from them and this made you see only the negative side of life.

When people talk of Wisdom, they usually think of the knowledge gained and abilities concerning an efficient approach to life. To me, Wisdom is the Power to see the Truth. You can choose a goal that seems right to you and measures its realization the best when you know the Truth.

Wisdom is the most desired gift one can receive since it is the only thing that leads a person to behaving in a proper way. Wisdom, however, is not the only value you can get from the Highest Intelligence. You can also get physical energy, vitality, or life's force.

Without Wisdom you lacked balance, the power of right thinking, and control and direction of your thoughts. You couldn't avoid difficulties coming from wrong thinking nor choose a right way to satisfy specific needs.

Were you stuck in the new condition for good? You certainly were not. You would have to consciously and constantly commune with God again, though. Only constant contact with Him gave you access to His Power and enabled you to use It. Remember: unity with God made all material factors submit automatically to spirituality. If you returned to Unity with God, your mind would rise to the old horizons and improve your desires so that they shed their bad habits. It would get completed automatically like your childish fascinations. They just left you when you matured. You probably don't remember the time it passed as a specific moment. It is similar with the mind. A mind submerged in God returns to the Higher

Level, where there are not lost tendencies or impure passions anymore. They are not attractive anymore and they are replaced by more attractive sensations.

You didn't want it, however, and you persuaded yourself that you could not benefit from Wisdom. Since you let yourself be guided by ego, you fell down. You submitted to the delusion that you were not strong enough to raise yourself to the old level. It was a false impression caused by intense emotions tormenting you, of course. And it would be enough if you turned your attention to your thoughts and feelings. It is like the light of a torch. Such a tiny gleam of the Light of Wisdom would sharpen your sight and prevent the situation from getting worse. It would clean your consciousness of the chaos you constantly found yourself in. If you watched your emotions, they would immediately calm down, and their grip would become looser. However, you didn't want to watch or heal them since you thought they were evil, wrong, and out of place.

The third dimension, in which you came to live, became a zone of intensive pulsations. The cause was the rampant emotions of you and other people. Life must end with death in this space. No matter can bear constant shocks and remain untouched. It is exactly the same with a physical body. Submitted to constant pressure of various amplitude of pulsations (a different scale of negative emotions), it must break apart sooner or later.

You remained untouched until that time, regardless of what happened to you. You thought of yourself exclusively in the context of eternal Life. Then you began to rage with emotions. No wonder you began to see yourself as a being breaking apart, getting old and dying. As you can see, dear reader, you let yourself have negative emotions and this is how death came into your life.

False thinking of this kind came from the condition of separated consciousness. Since you started to create fearful thoughts, brimming with suffering and worry, they created disease or ugliness, known as senility. Your soul participated in everything and was present for every moment of those changes. Your decisions reflected the state of your spirit and affected your health. And so, each declaration based on fear concerning your age, the process of getting old, and death led you inevitably towards it.

A certain number of positive thoughts would be enough to completely change your life and bring the old order back. This simple process could change your failures into successes. You would have to replace your old thoughts of failure, despair, lack, limitation, and discord with new thoughts of courage, power, inspiration, and harmony. Instead of thinking of ailments, senility, and death, you would have to call on the thoughts of enthusiasm, youth, and eternal life.

New thoughts are similar to young plants. If only they rooted inside you deeply, your physical tissues would change also. You would begin to perceive life in a completely new light. Old issues would be forgotten. Everything would become new, as if you were born twice—not physically but spiritually. You would become renewed and filled with joy, confidence, hope, and energy. You would recognize new opportunities for success which had previously not made sense to you because of your negative state of mind. It is possible since a soul is the essence of your life and all decisions, contacts, and events get reflected in it. Isn't life simple?

You wouldn't be the only person benefitting from it. You would state to emanate thoughts of success to everyone around you. They would help you go higher and further in return. You would attract new successful people.

As you can see, dear reader, everyone had the opportunity to transform themselves, the environment, and personal circumstances because of a change in their method of thinking. Thoughts can positively impact Forces of Nature and Mother Earth.

You didn't want to change, however, since your carelessness caused you to trust in the guidance of your ego too much.

Generations passed and more people died. They commonly thought that death wasn't a man's choice, but an inevitable, natural phenomenon. Eventually, almost everybody decided to die. The Earthly School was founded for them to give them a second chance to learn their lessons. I suggest you come back to the second volume and read about it one more time. With the knowledge you presently have, you will understand these excerpts in a completely new way.

Death wouldn't reach people of the fourth dimension, though. They have remained in the Light of God, where there is no death or other limitations. There were never old people at this level, only elders that had unexplored layers of Love and Wisdom. Love is something more than kindness towards Life and people.

Those great ones live eternally since they realize that there is only one powerful, evolutionary process in the Universe, which is consciously, generated Love. If they didn't use it consciously, they wouldn't have received love or sympathy for themselves and they wouldn't be able to show respect, love, or sympathy to other people.

They achieved freedom for themselves and others when they lived in Love. They neutralized negativity sent to them by others with their great love.

At the time of the ancient civilization, the elders were

not only wise, but strong and filled with energy. They achieved this perfect condition because of joyous, loving, and pure thoughts about the image of beauty and expression of their eternal youth. This enabled them to maintain their life energy and live eternally.

As you can see, dear reader, Love is much more than being kind. It is a Master Power of Life, splendid in its operation. When you lacked a complete consciousness, however, your mind wasn't able to understand It. You forgot that only Love maintains Life, expresses Excellence, and creates and protects manifestations.

As you can see, dear reader, God has never taken anything from you. It was you who turned your back on Him. You apart from Him by letting the wrong thoughts come to you.

CHILDREN

Children born to families in the third dimension were told that they were as loved and safe as the children that came before them. They nevertheless felt insecure and lost. They heard one thing from their parents and sensed something else. They could feel the constantly flowing fear from grown-ups, so they began to fear, too.

Children learn by imitating and nothing works better with them than a good example. Once, by watching the elders and parents that were a good example to them, they automatically became happy. They grew up feeling safe and there was neither fear nor egoism inside them.

Then there were no elders anymore. They were replaced by old people who were completely lost and didn't know what to do with their lives, who needed care themselves. The duty to bring up children was transferred to juvenile, unprepared, and overworked parents. How could they give a good example and teach anything if they were lost, helpless, and emotionally tormented themselves?

Children that imitated their frustrated parents grew up in a wild and egoistic way. With each generation, the society became more and more primitive. Primitiveness didn't come from the fact that other, worse children were coming to the world since each child is good and perfect, coming from God. There are no evil children. Each one is born of light and universal love. The problem was that grown-ups lost their power to shape a child as the most wonderful, perfect being. If children were brought up the old way, they would grow quickly and see only perfection around. Since they were not guided at all or in the wrong way, their inner light didn't have the opportunity to kindle with bright flame and began to fade gradually. Eventually, children became as deprived of light as their parents.

One time, every child knew only Eternal Life. It was confirmed since it was a ubiquitous belief. Later, just after it was born, it almost immediately learned that it would have to die one day. Nobody had to explain this to a child. It subconsciously sensed what people around thought of it and it encoded it in its subconscious, too. It wasn't important whether it saw death with its own eye or heard people talking about it. This knowledge only confirmed what it had subconsciously sensed before.

Children were rejecting this frightening thought from their consciousness. The older they were, the more they were able to escape it. However, the thought pushed into the subconscious was like a balloon pushed under the water. You press it, but it easily finds a way to come to the surface. It is exactly the same with a stifled thought—it affects your every choice anyway.

And since you must die, most young people decided life was too short to treat it seriously. They didn't want to reflect on anything. They would come to the conclusion that they should take life as if they lived only once. They learned to enjoy life and take as much from it as possible.

They wasted their energy doing unimportant things by thinking this way. Their energy dispersed and they began to grow old and decrepit and die.

Centuries passed and many people gave many different characteristics of death and limitations to the Universal Substance of God. This is why human bodies began to show these characteristics. This is why senility is presently so awful, decrepit, soulless, and mortal.

People who had kept their inner Light co-existed on the same plane as people who had lost it. Although they lived in the same space, they stopped seeing each other. It came from the inner Light that glowed at different levels of vibration. Life in the Light of God was invisible to those who were deprived of Him. No man is able to recognize what he doesn't have inside him. People living in Light, however, didn't have a problem with seeing those who were deprived of It. You can see everything from above and almost nothing from below.

A thread connecting this once magnificent community was eventually naturally broken. It happened because of a large difference between the levels of Light and Energy vibrations. This happened to friends, families, and strangers.

Few managed to maintain their high condition since none of the Great Ones wasted time or energy caring about the consequences of other humans' actions. He understood perfectly well that each man is one way and not another, because he wants to be this way. If he tried to help the other in any way, he would decline to the level of the fallen ones and could not stay at his high level. Those Great Ones maintained complete consciousness of the presence of themselves and everyone else.

People of low vibrations, however, didn't realize the presence of the Great Ones, although they were still living next to Them. To those who didn't have enough energy, people of a high energy level, became permanently invisible.

This is how there came to be a natural, automatic parting between those who loved and those who didn't want to or who persuaded themselves that they couldn't love.

THE CHANGE OF CLIMATE

Instead of holding on to God, the Source, and striving to be like Him in every way, individual people began to gradually grow apart from Him. Almost everyone lost what was high and noble about God.

The majority rejected what provided them with care and safety, which caused intense negative emotions to torment them. Mother Nature answered to that, too. Winds and storms tormented the Earth the same way negative emotions tormented individual people.

It is quite a natural process since everything is one big whole. Together with the change of human attitude to Life, the Earth's climate began to change, too. It grew unfriendly to everyone.

Strange, unusual phenomena began to occur in nature. It became more dangerous as more people turned their backs on God. Plants died because of lack of rain, which caused people to starve.

When rain would come after a long draught, it was so violent and abundant that instead of moistening the Earth as it had before, it caused floods. The Earth would shake and volcanoes would erupt.

Considering how the Earth once had a soft climate, these phenomena were exceptionally frightening. People had never experienced such raw, ruthless activities on Earth before. They were used to sunny days, warmth, and a light pleasant breeze. Light warm rain would occasionally fall just to moisten plants. Storms, hurricanes, and earthquakes never happened.

Dear reader, I think you can guess why the climate on Earth changed so radically. Mankind neglected its rays of Love and Wisdom for too long and was using its free will the wrong way. This is why the need came to cleanse the Earth from the effects of the negative use of Divine Energy. Much hatred, anger, vindictiveness, and other negative feelings arose in people. Thoughts filled with anger and violence affected not only individual people but also lands, soil, and all of Life.

The Great Ocean of Universal Substance of the Universe records and absorbs negative traits sent by people with a negative attitude. When it gets overdone, It throws them away, giving them back to the source or people who are their authors in the form of various natural cataclysms.

This is how it brings everything towards Perfection, which liberates the Earth from the works of human creation. It operates with the help of the four elements of Nature: Air, Fire, Water, and Earth.

Nature elements are a mirror of human activity since almost every man experiences his own cataclysms. They show in different forms. It can be thoughts and feelings, such as anger with oneself, others, places, and even objects. This is how people send, consciously or unwittingly, the feelings of re-venge, hatred, despair, etc. Emotions once sent out never fade away.

This is why the elements of Nature are forced to register those negative human traits. They absorb human distresses and when they get oversaturated with their content, they give them back to the sender in the form of storms and tempests.

Activity of this kind obviously hurts Mother Earth and causes abnormal climate conditions but this is the only way the Forces of Nature can cleanse Life from pollution that was caused by mankind. This is how they take everything out of the shadow and bring it to the Light.

Bad weather and cataclysms are nothing but Nature's way of shaking the human pollution, discordant thoughts, and feelings. This is how Nature returns to its unspoiled state of Divine Flawlessness.

Try to observe such a condition after an ordinary storm or big tempest. You will see that nature gets renewed in spite of great losses. You may feel that something wonderful and refreshing flows in the air. It will be a sign of Nature's return to the state of purity, balance, and Divinity. This is the state you lived in every day.

Dear reader, you may be surprised by the fact that cata-clysms didn't reach everyone. They widely circumvented those who didn't turn their backs on God. Havens of peace, calm, harmony, and beauty were forming around them, protecting them from any threats. This phenomenon can be compared to an oasis in a desert, a small island in the middle of the great ocean, or the eye of the cyclone. Unfriendly conditions circle around such havens but calm, peace, and safety reign inside of them. Although there is not enough water and food in a desert, there is plenty of it in an oasis. The island is also self-contained.

Cataclysms are exclusively due to a destructive human influence. When there is no cause in the form of negative thoughts and emotions, there is no effect in the form of a cataclysm, either.

You may now better understand the meaning of the following words: „Live in this world but don't be of this world." When you find yourself under God's protection, you cannot be hurt even if others are hurt. You have free will and you can turn back to God at any moment to get help.

But first you must fill yourself with His Love because only Love can protect you from all negativity. If there is no negativity inside you, you won't experience any cataclysms. Unneeded tragedies and sufferings will repeatedly occur in your life until you decide to fill yourself with Love.

You suffered much at the time of the fall and cursed God by saying: „God is blind if He lets all of this happen." You reacted like this because you felt like a victim of unfortunate events and not their direct author. You didn't understand that God Almighty let this situation be, according to His Law. He did this for your own good and the good of the whole world. His vision is infinitely more reasonable, attentive, and keen than the vision of your eyes. Besides, you didn't take into account that the earthly atmosphere cannot be infinitely moiled with negativity coming from you or other people. And God knows that when you pollute it once, you cannot remove the pollution, but to make the negativity burn out inside you, fade, and causing „harm" to you at the same time (I used a quotation mark since you are to learn from it so this is not a real harm).

Nature went wild because people were submitting to growing destruction and regress. They didn't see their part in it since fear snuck into them and was eventually transformed into superstition. They blamed God for everything; though; He didn't have anything to do with that.

NEW STRUCTURES

Losing the ability to perceive the world in higher ranges of vibration was very troublesome. Since you ceased to see the Light, your consciousness diminished, which caused you to turn your attention to solely the physical aspects of things. You were no longer able to understand that matter is the final result of higher forces having effect on it.

Since you ceased to see with your inner eye, you thought that matter was the beginning of everything, your true reality. Your limited perception in the third dimension caused you forget all the truths you could ever need living inside of you.

You became passive and egoistic as you fell into lower vibrations. A previous creator turned into a reproducer. A creator is his own master while a reproducer is dependent on others.

You felt addicted and did your best to outperform others in your achievements and insisted to dominate. This brought increasing divisiveness and greed upon you, which caused discord. The time you spent on fights and quarrels could have been spent being creative.

You became more and more submerged in the dark range of evil. You sabotaged yourself and others. You forgot that constructive results can be achieved only through the creative multiplication of energy.

You also lost consciousness of the fact that you only benefit when everyone else benefits. When everyone else loses, you're the first one to suffer loss. These were not always material things, money, or wealth because you could always lose your health, luck, happiness, loved ones, or the things you valued most.

You were growing weak because you didn't follow the rule mentioned above. In order to strengthen your position, you began to form alliances. Leaders and masters emerged from these alliances. Lines were eventually formed to keep authority in the hands of a small group of people.

Along with the masters, warriors appeared to defend the people with authority. They have been fighting for power and domination ever since. People have been trapped in their desire for violence, hatred, and war for ages now. Their leaders fell into the delusion that such conduct will make people obey them. They forgot that true authority comes from knowledge, and that wisdom is about using knowledge with care and charity. The right leader would know that people can always change when they are properly guided, even if it seemed that the nation was completely ignorant. A wise leader knows that no man is innately stupid. He needs to remember the self that he has been through various incarnations.

As you can see, dear reader, I am writing about the culture of a prehistoric society yet the techniques of control and political games surrounding authority have remained the same. It seems that some people's ambitions never change.

Instead of helping each other like they had before, people began to confront each other. It doesn't matter whether those fights were among family members, friends, or entire nations.

It eventually became impossible to oppose them since they often deliberately turned their negative thoughts towards others. This caused great destruction, devastation, and suffering. Where did it come from? Well, besides forming a destructive force with their own power, they also used a destructive force generated by mankind, bringing destruction to entire races or continents.

There was no chance for such fight to ever come to an end because these people couldn't forgive themselves or others. They spread hatred, which germinated into more hatred in the future. It was impossible for them to ever obtain Peace. They didn't want to change their conduct; they didn't even know it was possible.

TYRANNY

I would like to return to the topic of the fascination you felt when new technologies arrived during the fall of civilization. Until then, you could have created anything just as well as the new technology could. At first you were interested in it out of pure curiosity but later it began to pull you down more and more until you lost yourself in it completely. Eventually technology became necessary for your growth. You could compare it to the contemporary fascination with the newest models of mobiles, tablets, computer games, etc.

You were caught by bitter surprise when you realized that you couldn't live without it. You discovered that what you thought had been growth was actually a great delusion. You had been self-sufficient until this point. You had created all that you needed but then technology replaced it. You were disappointed to see that you were losing your creative powers in an incomprehensible way. When you look at it from a different perspective, the cause becomes quite clear. You had sought the Source of Power in God before and then you began to ascribe It to people. It was coming solely from the consciousness of being United with the Spirit but you had forgotten about it. If you remembered this, you would know that you received all the Goods through your intuition and spiritual understanding. You could consciously affect the course of matters in the fourth dimension only when your heart and mind were open to the living God. You could maintain this unity only through passionate Love of your Source. You became interested in something else, though, and the Source became unimportant to you. When you ceased to love Him, you automatically ceased to be aware of His Presence. You let yourself think wrongly that it was God who took away the powers that were given to you earlier. You fell into delusion because your unconsciousness had been fed with anger, which spread to others. The power of God was still inside you and you could benefit from it any moment but you were not aware of this fundamental fact anymore. You used your free will in a careless way. Almost everyone in this previously lucent civilization began to lose their Divine Gift.

Time passed and technology developed. You noticed with sadness that it caused Love to fade within people. The people that were the most deprived of Love were the ones that provided technology. They were using it for the wrong purpose. Dabbling in the matters of science and technology was dangerous without proper understanding of the subject of love. Mechanization anticipated your spirit consciousness.

Power is constructive only when one uses it wisely. When it is deprived of Love, it is like a raging bull attacking everybody around.

People still created things but they sensed they were doing it wrong because of the remnants of their universal consciousness. They feared their Creator and their hearts lacked this magnificent love that could soften the negative influence of a creative genius. And what was the effect of it? Designers of machinery raised it above God. Machines took control over their constructors and didn't let them quell.

It is not inventions themselves. Both then and now, each one of them was perfect. For each could serve people in the right way and even help them in spiritual growth. In order for the last case to come true, a man would have to come back to the point in which spiritual learning is more important to him than controlling others or having money, as it is now.

And so, most inventions got into the wrong hands. Those splendid ideas and inventions were used by people isolated in their fear, thinking they had to manipulate human growth personally. They used those wonderful technical achievements to gain control over other people. They controlled everything and everybody, manipulating every situation. Governments, financial elites, and military powers traded threats and fear. They lacked love and they sowed seeds of suffering by their evil thoughts, feelings, and deeds in all earthly beings.

A group of maniacal people eventually created a weapon that could destroy not only many people but an entire section of the universe.

Their thinking, unusually fertile concerning inventions but cut off from love's influence, brought them to make military use of their projects. Evil leaders deliberately instigated war, leading millions of people to their doom, while individuals did nothing to prevent it.

Love itself would be enough for one person to give to another. It would conquer the disbelief and aggression of human thoughts once and for all. As you can see, even a single man, including you, can bring peace at any time.

Dear reader, technology on Earth can only develop to a certain point. They could go further with it, but they need Love to do it. Unfortunately, people forget Love in places where technology develops quickly. Those people want to rule the world in their arrogant belief that their creativity makes them like gods. They are like armed time bombs ready to explode on a sudden impulse or great negative thought. Most of those people abandoned both love and their responsibility.

They were at war and although they didn't fight themselves because they had machines to do it for them, they turned the planet into a pile of debris, devastated beyond words. The sides of various conflicts murdered each other. It concerned everyone: not just men but also women and children.

They treated Mother Earth in the same inhuman way. I don't want to write about it since you wouldn't be able to imagine their cruelty anyway. They did so because they focused almost exclusively on the intellectual aspects of life, nothing else. They thought they could do what they wanted and if the Earth was inadvertently hurt, they planned to colonize other planets and move there.

The culture of this society developed much more quickly than other cultures. Its mental potential overgrew ours, as well as our science and technology.

People of the falling civilization didn't see how much their perception was changing. When they had resided in the fourth dimension, they knew unusual facts about things such as Earth and other planets. They considered them to be gigantic, living creatures formed from light and wisdom, just as alive as humans. When they fell into the third dimension, this knowledge wasn't accessible to them anymore.

Scientists no longer understood that there were entire

civilizations in space created by other beings. It could have been due to the fact that they were not able to see them with their physical senses anymore. Although they occasionally observed UFOs (formerly known as spaceships) they didn't see physical life on other planets. Their problem was that they didn't recognize the civilization of immaterial beings, invisible to the physical eye. It was much harder to strengthen one's vibration than to destroy it. It all is a question of consciousness.

They didn't consider the fact that life could exist in space where they used their cruel weapons. So they contravened the intricately woven and delicate elements, both physical and immaterial, of the Earth and other planets.

They believed they were wise and provident so they didn't care for other people, the Earth, or Life in general. Only the people of the third dimension could act in such a mindless way, of course. No man with a healthy mind would irritate, or hurt own Mother. No man would destroy the life giving Source that feeds him and keeps him alive.

Their ignorance caused them to destroy It ruthlessly. They thought they didn't need the Earth at all. They fell into the delusion that they were self-sufficient that they could feed themselves and manage without the Earth's help. They didn't consider the fact, however, that the Earth draws energy from the Sun and feeds all life with it. When they followed the Earth out of their own free will, they expressed love and wisdom. When they forgot about it, they began to destroy all life.

Nobody cared that forests were being cut and destroyed. Nobody planted new trees since they didn't consider what people were going to breathe with when all the sources of oxygen would be destroyed. People polluted and modified food and water and nobody cared what they were going to eat in the future. They didn't reflect on how a man can survive in an open

dead space. They destroyed Nature but they destroyed themselves more than anything else. God doesn't make nor manifest
the world in this way. Only a man can do that. Nature must be
harmonized. Nature is Life, Energy, and Renewal.

People destroyed everything around them in those
times since they lacked Love. Care for life on Earth faded
away. Instead of caring for their own nest, they destroyed it.
They were killing themselves and their planet that had been
feeding them in such a perfect way.

THE DOOM OF THE CIVILIZATION

Dear reader, can you imagine what happens when a great number of people gets killed at the same time? Can you imagine crowds of souls liberated from their physical bodies crowding around the Earth? They are frightened and cannot go on. They are in great pain and they don't know where to go or how to continue their growth.

This is what happened then. Deprived of their physical covering, the souls blocked the movement of spherical forces around the Earth. They blocked the atmosphere so efficiently that the Light meant for the Earth couldn't reach the planet. Lack of light meant lack of information.

Most of these souls didn't want to return to the Light since pain, anger, and hatred kept them captive and close to the Earth. They struggled like they had been and refused to let go.

There were many of them and they increased in number since war continued on the Earth. The souls crowded in irregular groups, causing powerful whirls to form. The whirls pulled the population of suffering souls like tornadoes, throwing negativity towards the Earth that was the basis for future wars. Shrouded souls not only evoked powerful negative emotions and fear of the living, they also caused many new wars and cataclysms. The problem eventually escalated and brought fatal consequences.

A vicious circle was formed. More and more people were getting killed at war, and their souls were suddenly liberated of the physical covering, which caused even more fierce fights. People still living on Earth didn't realize what the real reason for their hatred was. Each side thought it fought for the right cause, not realizing that they were attracting more negative emotions all along.

When the whirls were filled to the brim and negative energy gathered within them became even stronger, they would explode and suffering souls thrown out with an enormous strength would flood the entire solar system. They broke free from the whirls but their movement was chaotic, making the problem bigger for the Earth's inhabitants. Exploding whirls caused volcanic eruptions, earthquakes, and hurricanes on the material plane.

The natural phenomena became more powerful every second. How could it be otherwise while thoughts filled with anger and violence affected not only people, but Mother Earth, seas, lands, and all of life? The Elements of Nature were forced to record all this.

Over the years of wars, ignorance, and misunderstanding, humanity degraded morally and filled the atmosphere around it with falsehood and unreality. The Forces of Nature were filled with the same elements. This was a huge problem for the Earth and its inhabitants. No wonder it evoked huge fear—the Forces of Nature only responded to what they were getting from the living and from the souls deprived of physical bodies.

A whirl slowly formed around this previously magnificent civilization, which eventually made a physical manifestation. The Earth was flooded with negative gravity and constantly losing its balance. It eventually completely lost its balance and shook up the ocean's water. Nobody could stop the doom, even God, since there was no vision of a better future for the Earth. It had to be destroyed in order to become rebuilt in the future.

You may complain and say: ,,This is awful. How could it happen? How could the entire civilization die in a single moment?" Know that you suffer because you don't really realize the processes that were going on at that time. Each time a cataclysm takes place, whether it's big or small a solution comes; which is the best thing on the world for everybody participating in the experience.

Think of what God could do with people who didn't give themselves the smallest chance of learning through any means other than suffering. They killed not only themselves with their thoughts and unworthy deeds but also their planet. They destroyed everything until they destroyed themselves. They had no plan for their futures because they didn't understand how important balance was for their lives. Even animals live in harmony yet those people couldn't. They declined to a level lower than an animal's.

Remind yourself of the old times. You once lived in freedom and wandered across the Earth that was a powerful and magnificent seat of infinite beauty and love. You benefited from its Sources with handfuls. Now compare It to the Earth at the moment before doom struck. Didn't It look rather like a frightening dark cave where the darkness of Spirit lurked, wars raged, and hatred spread. It became a place where people let their own fear manifest in their leaders' decisions. The leaders hurt It with their own fear, ignorance, and evil; they hurt cosmic space and the beings who lived like you did, even though they didn't see them. Ultimately, all creation is Oneness.

You can say that people irritated the Earth and hurt It for so long, that they generated Its desire to get rid of them. Tired and tormented by violence, the Earth got rid of the people hurting It in exactly the same way an animal tries to get rid of fleas. It threw them down to the vast abyss of the ocean.

Suddenly, all of the inhabitants of the Earth submerged underwater over the course of one day. This was the end of an earthly experience for people who had once lived in such excellence.

The doom came suddenly, but remember that the Great Space Master manifested himself a few years prior and predicted a disaster that would happen if people didn't change their ways. It was the same Great Being of Light that drew the Light that was the cause of the formation and maintenance of this great civilization. Right before the doom, the Great Beings of Light reached out to each man individually to tell them that they would be protected if they let themselves be guided only by Love. It was declared that the ultimate destruction would follow and that it was going to be sudden and total. Although these words reached everybody, only few people were persuaded for good.

The humans that were warned believed that the doom wouldn't come since the Greater Life wouldn't allow hatred, violence, and war to reach cosmic space where there were more forms of life than anyone could imagine. It was said that if governments and military forces would use the killing weapon against nations and Mother Earth, they would attract disaster to themselves. It was explained that this was not a punishment nor God's revenge, but the Universal Principle operating. The entire Universe is based upon this Principle, including the law of cause and effect. I will write more about this in the fourth volume.

People were alarmed by this prophecy at first, but not for long. They reflected on what could happen and what they could change in order to prevent it. But the memory of the Great Being's Presence faded in less than a year and people started to doubt that the prophesy would ever be fulfilled. The Great Beings still tried to clean the doubts from people's minds with all their might, of course, but they often failed.

Most people were too „provident" to worry about such „silly things" they heard from everyone around them. They were too busy thinking about their everyday lives and securing a future for themselves, their children, and their grandchildren. Things such as schools and securing resources for old age were more important to them than the act of reflecting on their souls. The more advanced in growth or close to God they were, however, the louder they heard the prophecy, which led them to safety when the disaster finally came. The lost people were those that had grown apart from God long ago. They were too skeptical to believe the presence warning them. They could not be saved since they didn't want to listen.

Dear reader, many people ask God how he could let tragedy happen. I say He could. Didn't He give man his free will to use it the way he wanted? A man may attract some unpleasant, even tragic experiences, but he learns many valuable things from them. God treats His children like an earthly parent teaching their child to walk. A child falls down and gets a small injury. It stands up just to fall down again but it eventually understands how to walk and no longer falls down. We are students in the earthly school. Our experiences are nothing but learning how to walk, serving the purpose of reminding you of your Unity with God. We are all immortal, Divine, and indestructible. If you deeply believe in immortality, you will understand that we never really die—we are constantly reborn and we live eternally.

Dear reader, you may now thoroughly understand that every disaster, whether big or small, is not the spontaneous whim of God but the answer to incorrect human choices. Everyone has been warned. Only those that could fully hear, understand, and appreciate the information used it. Many heard it but never reacted to it. Some didn't react out of fear and disbelief while others didn't react out of pure carelessness and laziness. They didn't want to believe that it was possible for doom to come or that society had gone astray long before and had been slowly disintegrating. Their discord quickly grew bigger instead of getting smaller. And since they didn't want to follow the Fundamental Laws of Balance and Purity, they were removed from the opportunity for a new beginning.

All cataclysms, not just doom, serve a purpose. Their range depends on whether or not an escalation of negative emotions and deeds concerns an individual or many people. It is only when a range of the phenomena encompasses almost the whole population and reaches a critical point that a cataclysm occurs on a large scale.

An entire civilization can disappear from the Earth's surface in different ways. This is how the laws of nature operate. The results are the same regardless of whether the disaster concerns a human, state, or all humanity. It always happens when something is oversaturated with greed or desire. Such a situation can happen when prime and prosperity begin to fade and the devastation and doom of the organism becomes visible.

Over the eons of time in the history of the Earth, many splendid civilizations were lost in the same way. Some of them are still remembered while other are not. Atlantis and Lemuria are still known.

But let us get back to the time of doom. All the magnificence of the civilization and most of its inhabitants were swept from the Earth' surface. Only a few „miraculously" saved survivors remained. They preceded later civilizations, including ours, but I will write about that in the fourth volume.

It needs to be emphasized here that the doom concerned only people from the third dimension, while in the fourth dimension everybody lived as perfectly as they had before. They didn't forget their Divine background and heritage and still followed the basic Laws of Balance and Purity. Unfortunately, only a few people could maintain this high level of enlightenment even though everyone used to have it. Nothing changed in the life of the Great Ones since Love protected Them. It kept their bodies in good condition so that the doom couldn't reach them.

Although cataclysms ruthlessly affected the third dimension, it missed the wonderful people from the fourth dimension since they didn't experience the cataclysms of feelings.

They resided in the emanations of the spiritual zone like everybody once had. This level is located above the third dimension. Although we commonly call it heaven, it is not the same zone that human souls go to after their death. It is the zone of living people and discarnate ghosts cannot access it. People reside somewhere else after they die, which I wrote about in detail in the second volume.

In summary: the people that resided in the fourth dimension were those that focused their vision on a goal and held onto it with strong and joyous determination. They never worried about others, even when a person going astray was someone dear and close to them. This was an act of true, deep wisdom, not indifference. This is how they could focus their vision and be completely aware of the fact that every person is the manager of their life and activity.

This wisdom suggested that a man going astray chooses himself, no matter how much good advice he gets. Taking care of him while he stubbornly stands by his choice is a waste of energy. Besides, such a man not only attracted his suffering by making a „bad" choice, he also spread it to other people. A man of a high vibration shouldn't worry about other people since he wouldn't gain anything and would be burdened with a low, impure vibration. He would be stopped in his growth and fall along with the people he was trying to help.

Remember how many great souls stubbornly and persistently helped others without caring about their own good. They fell down to the third dimension with those they wanted to help. Did the Great Ones from the fourth dimension turn their backs on the fallen and leave them on their own? Absolutely not!

Over innumerable millennia, they have showed the disoriented and struggling world what one could achieve in the state of Unity with the Spirit. In order to encourage them to achieve Unity, they demonstrated how one could control the Forces of Nature. They modeled how to materialize food directly from the universal substance. They revealed Wisdom that the limited human consciousness didn't have the access to. They manifested inner and outer wealth and strength which helped them overcome death.

Isn't it strange that people in a state of delusion forgot

what was good so quickly? They all lived in the same excellent way that they had before. The Great Ones reminded and returned consciousness to those who had lost it. They repeated that the „miracles" they worked were nothing special and that everyone could perform them.

Nothing could reach the fallen, though. They thought that they had been banned for their sins. They didn't feel worthy enough to solicit for what they had lost. They didn't understand the reasons why they found themselves at a lower consciousness level. Additionally, they looked at those of a higher vibration with fear because They were exceptionally Wise and Bright. Instead of looking at Them as brothers, people made Them Gods and Goddesses. Even in dreams, they couldn't imagine that they could equal them.

As you can see, dear reader, everything is a matter of consciousness. Consciousness is Light, Love, Information, Power, and Wisdom. The fallen ones closed themselves off to all that.

Wonderful, Great People lived and still live in the Heavenly Kingdom. They live in the same emanations we all lived in once. They kept their identity since they didn't lose their ideals. We presently call them Masters. They are the root of humanity and preserve all of its cultural goods. It is often Them that establish the beginnings of a new civilization based on Great Knowledge and Experience.

Dear reader, I hope you can see that it is humanity, not God that sends destruction to the Earth. It can be proven by the fact that it was only the third dimension submitting to doom, while the fourth remained as intact as it was at the very beginning.

PROPHECIES

There were more causes of the first civilization's doom besides the causes I mentioned above. After humanity descended to the third dimension, it was predicted that a great war called „Armageddon" would eventually come. Nobody noticed that this prophesy originally concerned only the mental plane. People almost summoned it to the physical plane by constantly thinking about it. This idea was maintained and stoked up in human minds for so long that it became inevitable. Mankind accepted it and therefore expected it and was determined to live through the experience. This explains why people loved war so much. They thought that it was human destiny and that they could not change it.

The civilization described here ended with a cataclysm, which was much more effective than „Armageddon," which would release a large amount of hatred. This is why a cataclysm or doom in which many people get killed is much more advantageous than any war. A cataclysm liberates many things so they can pursue growth.

I would like to talk about prophesies in general now. Each prophecy, though ominous, is nothing but the ability of the prophet's consciousness to describe the future. It is based on the realization of the consequences of what happens to our energy now.

Although a prophet makes a kind of a map while talking about their destiny, they never declare it as final since there is always room for change.

The danger of each prophecy is that most people consider it to be a forecast of an event, not a probability. This is why all forecasts and prophesies concerning cataclysms on Earth evoke so much anxiety in people.

Dear reader, take these prophecies as options, not facts. All prophecies tell of probabilities of events. They present an understanding of something that may happen in the future if events don't change. In order for you to understand it, I will give you an example.

If you are sitting on a proverbial branch and sawing it off of the tree, it is easy to predict that you will fall with the branch. If you took this prophesy as a warning and changed what you were doing, you would move to the other side of the branch and avoid falling. If you consider the prophecy as a fact that cannot be avoided, however, you will continue sawing. When you fall down, you can say that the prophecy was fulfilled and that a fall was meant to be. You acknowledged this to be your destiny, fate, and death that you would believe because you didn't think you had any effect on the outcome. You could affect but didn't take this into account since you blindly believed in the prophecy.

Dear reader, never ever fear any prophesy. You shouldn't think about cataclysms so that you don't attract what you don't want to experience. Remember that you attract what you focus on. Even if a small cataclysm was to come, remember that nothing wrong or contrary to your higher good can happen to you. Trust and realize that God never sends destruction to the Earth. It is mankind that does it for itself. When you live in Love, with God and in God, no cataclysm will ever reach you. Love will lift you up high enough to keep you from experiencing any failure or a cataclysm. This also means that you can avoid the state known as death. Ultimately, those who once chose life in Love have never experienced that, remaining in the fourth dimension.

Even if your soul's choice is the transformation called death, you probably understand by now that it is not the end. You would just move from one classroom to the next after death. There is nothing to fear because only good will come to both you and your loved ones, no matter what happens.

You don't have to live in fear since nothing ever happens suddenly, within a day. You are always warned in time. A true part of prophesy is warning people about things that can happen to them or confront them in the future if they don't change their conduct. A Prophet forecasting the future just says: „This is where we are going." He simultaneously warns and suggests that we should consider whether or not we want to follow this path. That is when we can reflect on our mistakes and change our direction. A prophecy is a suggestion, not a command. It's a recommendation on how to correct our course and direct it to safer waters.

Remember! A true prophesy (false ones should simply be ignored) is never about presenting a future vision that leaves people without options. A choice is always there but people may not always want to take this opportunity. They do nothing with their lives and pigeonhole things.

You could ask yourself whether or not it was possible to rescue people from the ancient magnificent civilization. It definitely was. It would have been enough for them to listen to and follow the Truth. It was announced everywhere, day and night, but only few accepted It enough to change their lives.

The rest dropped out since their faith and determination wasn't strong enough. This huge number of people suffered because they believed they were helpless. They forgot long ago that their everyday matters in the external world were reflections of their inner reality and what they carried within their souls. It wasn't enough to hear the Truth; It needed to be accepted and followed. It was human ignorance concerning the essence of life that made them go astray. They agreed to live in the delusion and suffering that followed. I am writing about it in detail since a similar phenomenon is currently taking place. Many people announce imminent disasters. One prophecy tells of the end of the world. The „world" of this prophecy, however, is not the Earth, but the ruling order and organization of society. The Earth, our world, is a living, sensitive being, full of both love and hate. The „world" from this prophesy concerns the system of human relations.

This prophesy doesn't tell us about the end of the world in a total disaster. It tells us about a man becoming awakened. This is how people will benefit from their heritage in a new way.

When a man wakes up, his „world" will come to an end. The „world" of the Heavenly Kingdom, the one you once lived in, in the lost civilization will come. From the perspective of Masters and their understanding, nothing is determined concerning the Earth because everything depends on the changes that will follow in human consciousness and the consciousness of the Earth. They think that the Universe wouldn't benefit if the Earth was destroyed because of thoughtless actions of its inhabitants, unaware and deprived of love.

Many sapient people claim that we are coming to the end of the world. We are approaching enlightenment, however, not doom. They tell of the end of the human „world" and the beginning of God's „world," transgressing from the third dimension to the fourth. The process began at the beginning of the last century.

Dear reader, haven't you noticed that we started a process of acceleration long ago and it's becoming more and more intense? We are entering the increasing Light and obtaining more and more information. What it took to learn almost a lifetime, let's say in the eighteen century, you presently absorb only in a few years. The acceleration explains why so many people cannot bear the growing intensity of vibration or Light and die and why so many people become so severely ill. This process serves to transform your body, mind, and soul as quickly as possible and lift it up to the Light.

We must know that each time a change happens in the history of the Earth, the Earth itself evolves, too. It operates similarly to humans. At the time of our present transformation, we receive great opportunities but are also exposed to great dangers. One can evolve along with the Earth into the fourth dimension or close oneself to the process, drop out, and begin everything anew, as it happened in the case of the lost civilization.

You will read details about the doom in the fourth volume. Such processes follow cyclically around every 26,800 years. This is how long it takes the Milky Way to make a full circle. This process is known as reallocation or translocation since the Earth's axis moves.

In order to find oneself in the fourth dimension or in Heavenly Kingdom, one doesn't need to go through death, as some religions teach. You need to raise your consciousness enough for it to touch Heaven. Heaven is a state of consciousness and not a place where we go after death.

Other rules govern the Heavenly Kingdom more than our world. In order to get there, you must become attuned to them early. When you vibrate at lower frequencies, you can't enter places that vibrate more quickly. You should not only acquire the knowledge passed in this elaboration but follow it. People in our world fight but they cooperate in the Kingdom. Everybody there works for the common good and they work together to multiply energy. One man strives for domination over the other. He does it just to get an advantage and the highest position in the world. Dear reader, don't delude yourself into thinking that you're better and that you shouldn't play the game. Almost everybody does. The only difference is the intensity of pressure, ranging from minimal and almost unnoticeable to overt manipulation and violence.

Relationships in this world are like that of a master and servant but everyone is equal in the Kingdom. They are friends, not foes. Life there is based on love and gratitude, while here it is dominated by anger, aggression, and jealousy. This world is based on conflict and competition—many people hurt each other while everyone is brothers in the world of God and they help each other.

Many people destroy the Earth in order to gain some benefits from it. In the Kingdom, however, the Highest Good is the most important thing for everyone. People are mean and short-sighted here while the soul's growth is the only thing that matters in the Kingdom. People are unable to love here yet everyone in the Kingdom benefits from the magnificent energies of Love. Conscious creativity is encouraged there while we rely on blind fate here. It is no wonder that everything creates itself here. There is no hunger nor suffering in God's Kingdom because there is no evil there. Our world is totally submerged in it, though.

In His Kingdom, nobody needs benefactions, donators, or charity institutions because there is an abundance of everything for everyone. In our world, you are almost expected to be generous, give alms, disown yourself, fulfill your obligations participating in masses or Sabbath (as your religion persuades you) and such a conduct is considered to be a virtue. In God's Kingdom, however, you are only expected to be self-conscious because it enables your consciousness to freely reach the Abundance of God's Goods that will satisfy all your needs. When a man lives in the consciousness of those Goods, Excellence is the only that that exists in his life. Analogically, we lack Them in our world since there is no complete consciousness in it.

Dear reader, you can pass to the side of the Heavenly Kingdom now. You don't have to wait until after death, as your religion teaches you. You would have to love God though your own free will and not because you were forced to by fear but because 'love' remains an empty cliché to you. When you love your Creator above all, your pure heart can join the Spirit and peace comes to you and the Earth. Then you will enter the Kingdom.

You will then discover that your main desire is to achieve permanent happiness. You will cease to pursue fading happiness that comes as the result of your external senses. Faith, hope, and love will dwell in your heart forever. Showing compassion to your neighbors and being kind will become your second nature. You will achieve permanent harmony and balance and you will feel as if you were born anew. It will mean that you have broken free from the past completely.

You won't enter any new, unfamiliar world, but you will summon the heavenly Kingdom you used to live in. If this state of spirit was established, the problem of hunger, poverty, disease, and misery would fade for you and everyone else.

Unfortunately, people in our times have become so disconnected from their spirit and discordant with their nature. They won't emanate love, mercy, and simplicity until it changes. They won't be pure enough to rid themselves of their omnipresent fear and rise above themselves. No matter what others do, it is their problem, not yours. You create your life and they create theirs.

It is true that there are great changes happening on the Earth right now. They are due to the evolution of both the Earth and you, personally. They don't have to be fatal changes, though, as many people claim, but they can bring fatal results to some people.

THE CONCLUSION

I remind all doubtful readers of the Akashic Records. Everything that has ever happened on Earth is recorded in It. It is like an enormous library and one can find information about not only single lives but entire nations, civilizations, and planets. It records the history of the Earth and the whole Universe from the dawn of time to the present day. Everyone can use this as a resource to find out more about what interests them.

There are many people in the world that can read from It. This does not include clairvoyants and fortune tellers, whom look into the astral world and see low vibration levels. Besides, the astral world has seven main levels divided into many sublevels. This is why everyone has a different interpretation of it. This is because people can only look at the level they find themselves on and one level higher. This explains why everyone that tells fortunes receives different answers on one issue. It comes from the level of his vibration and the vibration of his client.

The knowledge coming from the Akashic Records, however, definitely goes beyond the astral world. It is solid and dependable. Everybody who has a proper predisposition can look into it and see the same thing. It is not enough to simply have a predisposition and receive information from it, though. There are some limitations connected to the vibration level awaiting you. You will receive as much as your vibration level is capable of. You cannot receive more since you are unable to accept it. Even if you could, you wouldn't be able to use the information because you wouldn't understand it. You need to „grow up" to everything. God will not allow a phenomenon you aren't prepared for to decompose you. Instead of promoting growth, it would make you fall and would shake your senses to the state of insanity. This was the fate of many people who wanted to get to know something they were not ready for yet.

This book was written according to similar principles. While reading it the first time, you will understand it in a different way than when you read it a second time. You will absorb and understand as much you are able to at the level you presently dwell in. As soon as you assimilate the knowledge or transform it in your mind, you will become more open and will easily absorb more information. Every time you reach for this book, you will recognize new aspects that you weren't able to realize before. You will start to remember more and more since the level of your consciousness will rise. You will become increasingly enlightened and allow more light to flow to you, which will raise your vibrations. It will come naturally. A great number of my readers confirm it, so I dare to claim that my books are not meant to be read but studied page by page. Here is my message: read it slowly and try to comprehend every sentence.

Continue to re-read it until you internalize the

knowledge and get rid of your pervasive fear. I trust that you will remember everything then since all of the knowledge is already contained within you. When you are ready to reach it, you will be able to say: „God, return my lost memory to me."

You will start to benefit from your Divine character that was given to you for you to enjoy forever. This priceless gift is a true heritage for yourself and all of mankind. You should appreciate its worth, while reading about your history in the lost civilization. You can come back to this state at any moment since everything is a matter of consciousness— everything you did once you can have now because you decide what experiences you will have. In order to do that, you must first get rid of your habits that brought you to the present unwanted condition.

Getting rid of habits is like weeding a garden. It is difficult to weed, even if you do it with great carefulness. You have to be watchful so weeds don't grow back. It is arduous yet rewarding work. Just take a look at a clean, well-groomed garden and you will understand what I am talking about.

Don't ever compare yourself to others. No matter what they do, you must make a decision that you will start working on yourself. Nobody will do it for you. I know that it would be easier to work in a team and it would be more wonderful if your loved ones could grow with you. You cannot wait forever, though. It may be that it will never happen. You will waste your chance the same way they wasted their chance. Don't press them or expect them to follow you because it is useless for everyone. You will waste your energy and they will do what they want to do anyway.

Most people don't change anything in their lives because they feel all right with what they have. When everything falls apart around them, they cry: „God, help me." God always

386 IN THE WHEEL OF LIFE, VOLUME III

helps, but these are just empty callings in most cases. Once they improve even a little bit, they forget everything they learned and fall back into their old habits. Think about whether it is like that with you, too, and if it is, decide that you want something more for yourself from this day on and start to act differently.

Dear reader, I wrote this book for you to reflect and notice if what happened in the past is happening now. Aren't we, as the whole of mankind, going the same direction that people of the falling ancient civilization were going? Haven't the same people that want to control everything and everybody using cameras, satellites, and electronic devices appeared among us? Should we let a few madmen destroy this wonderful planet like it has been done many times before? We must care for the planet, which exists just to help you become spiritually fulfilled, learn love, and understand everything that is alive.

You may downplay what I am writing about because you don't realize that you can greatly influence all living things as one individual. I know that you stopped believing in the power and abundance of God long ago. With your free will you have embezzled Divine Energy for a long time and you don't know now how to return to the Source.

Please realize, though, that there is only one mighty and invincible evolutionary process in the Universe. This is the Power of Love, which is consciously generated. Nothing but Love created this world and it is only Love that keeps it going and providing Blessings and Natural Forces. Everything is energy but Love is the most primal and omnipresent of all energies in existence. It is the essence of our being and our universe. It is the basic „building material" that bonds and unites everything and everybody. Love is more than a goal, fuel, or ideal. Love's energy is more powerful than any bomb and more delicate than pollen.

Since Love controls and maintains every system in the world, only Love can save you and this world of the claws of each negative, destructive force that is capable of destroying or perverting any of Life's elements.

Until you reach Love, absolutely useless tragedy and suffering will continue to appear in your life. When you finally understand that Love is the all-encompassing energy that has a healing influence upon your body, mind, and soul, you will immediately reject all diseases and chronic pain. You will understand that Love is the most powerful healer. You will experience its healing work if you open yourself to it.

You suffer because you haven't learned to master this basic and pure force yet. When you do, the healing may appear at all levels, both individual and global.

I truly hope that this book will teach you recognize, grow within, and expand because of love, especially concerning yourself. It is only when you are filled with self-love that you are able to express it and direct it at other people. It is never the other way round. Love will prompt you to experience more joy, health, and happiness in your life.

Over the eons, the Earth has been pulled into this destructive current of technical and mechanical influences by its inhabitants many times. This happened because they lacked Love, the „basic building material". Each civilization had a few controllers trying to use machines to empower the energy in order to chase and control other people's thoughts. Such problems usually ended with wars but they also supported mass destruction, as I've described above. Mankind had to start from the beginning each time.

I am not writing this to evoke fear in you nor trammel you with guiltiness. Such emotions never bring any good. They would just stop your growth and evoke mental resistance, depression, and discouragement. I am sharing my observations with you so you can immediately start solving your problems and make honest commitments concerning your future.

Firstly, realize that there are many people nowadays who „feed themselves" and use the energy of fear in many ways. They deliberately instigate it within people and they invent new ways to strengthen it. They even design various devices in order to send and strengthen emotional anxiety and make fear grow. They will do it as long as they don't alter their vibrations to match that of love. Until then, they will strive to limit the freedom of choice for average, unaware people.

They affect people in many ways but the most frequent and obvious is through advertisements. They use subliminal sounds and add pictures and videos that no one can see. The human subconscious detects them perfectly, however. Such manipulation is legally forbidden but they do it anyway because profits are more important than acting responsibly. What do they get from this? Besides financial profits, they rob the mental energy of you and everybody else, giving you a distorted image of reality. It is easy for them then to take control over you. They know that when you take the bait, you will be „theirs" until the end of your incarnation. Many people in the world do it, including pharmaceutical companies, insurers, banks, television, and other institutions.

Dear reader, I am not claiming that advertisers are evil. I just want to show you how clever they operate in order to get what they want from you and make you passive so that you'll buy and do whatever they demand. You may not realize how many matters of this world are determined to make you think or feel a certain way and vibrate on a lower level of consciousness. Entire teams of people work on it. They obviously don't impose anything on you since everything goes according to your will. It is you who decides what to watch, listen, believe in, and rebel against.

I don't want to judge who is right and who isn't here. I just want to disperse your delusions concerning what you are told to believe. I don't claim that it is wrong, either. Dear reader, I would like you to look at it from a broader perspective and to start thinking on your own, not according to what they tell you to think.

You know by now that your thoughts have creative power. What will your creativity be like if you think in a way that was imposed on you by someone else? Do people want you to be healthy, happy, and rich? Well, they certainly don't, because they wouldn't be able to manipulate or control you like they used to. Think about the power of seven billion incorrect thoughts. What does the power of thoughts of people cheated everyday create for everyone? Can you expect any good from it? I think you can do nothing but learn to discern the energies and choose only those that are best for you.

I'm going to say something very important, dear reader. Never, ever condemn manipulators. Always remember that God gave people their free will. Everyone has an undisputed right to live in this world, exist, and do whatever they want to do. You can do nothing about it, even when you don't like what other people do. If some energy tries to frighten, manipulate, or control you, isn't it your business to ignore it? You have free will and you can decide who you want to cooperate with.

Remember that even if someone has developed fantastic faculties, it doesn't necessarily mean that they are advanced spiritually. Remember the situation the lost civilization found itself in. Learn to distinguish these issues.

Never fear what you are going through. You have the potential to create your own reality, even when other people want to create a different reality for you. You have free will and it is up to you if you accept something or reject it. Free will means creating reality your own way.

Dare to be you. You don't have to be like other people. It doesn't matter that they let others create a strange reality for them. You may be in that situation yourself and let others direct you through different types of manipulation and control. It is this way because you seek the answers outside and not inside yourself. However, God gave you your free will that enables you to fulfil all of your desires. You are free in every situation, including the one you find yourself in right now. You just have to understand, in the deepest levels of your consciousness, that you are the only author of your daily experiences. Even if you were a prisoner or slave, you are still free. When you recognize that your thoughts of guilt, fear, hatred, jealousy, and greed created your present experiences, you will immediately feel free. You might have undertaken things in this incarnation that help you learn to appreciate freedom. You wouldn't learn the subject if you were not captive in some way.

You mostly submit to the creativity of thoughts coming from your present life, but it happens, and not infrequently, that they may have their source in your former incarnation. It is of not much importance, though. Be sure that when you start to reflect on it, you will discover the following dependency – since you can create something you are not satisfied with for yourself, you can as easily create different results. You will become a master of your situation and if you start thinking in the right way, you will experience things that will lift you up in the future.

Dear reader, only you can discover and create the most proper reality for yourself. Nobody will do it for you since it dwells within you, deep inside your heart. Turn your attention this way and you will discover a true gift. Regardless of what happens around you, always listen to yourself.

Never condemn anything that happens to you, your family members, or distant strangers. Don't complain or take pity on others, either. If you condemn or take pity on them, know that you strengthen the thing you take pity on. When you condemn anything, you help it grow instead of destroying it. When you take pity on someone, you make their misery worse instead of helping them. If you send love to people instead, you help them rise to a higher vibration level and you neutralize the negative force that they are stuck in. It may be easier for you to do this when you realize that all people live in the zone of the free will, where duality is inevitable. This is why pairs of opposites exist—good and bad, confidence and doubt, wealth and poverty, freedom and tyranny, peace and fear, health and disease, etc. There are so many options that a man has an infinite number of accessible paths from which he can choose something for himself.

Realize that individual human souls are not equally perfect when it comes to using the power of mind and that some of them must experience distress, pain, and humiliation since this is how they learn important things. When you understand it thoroughly, you automatically stop suffering when you hear about their apparent „misery." You will understand that nothing „wrong" happens to them and that this is necessary for their soul to get a chance to grow, strengthen itself, and strive for excellence.

Let people experience everything that you may deem 'evil' or 'unjust.' Ultimately, a man decides what he chooses for himself to experience. He is the only person responsible for his choice, not you. Nobody ever, in any circumstances, is dependent on another, though it may seem so.

Knowing all of that, don't look at a less spiritually developed person with contempt or negligence. Treat everyone with respect and don't take someone else's experience too lightly. What is understandable for some can be unbearable for others that are working through a problem at the moment. People are usually unable to comprehend anything until it reaches them by the thoughts that attracted a distressful experience.

Take care of yourself. You have free will so you can create and follow innumerable choices, no matter what others choose. Create your new reality. Break free from improving the world and start to improve you. First of all, accept *Who You really Are* and never acknowledge transitory identities. Remember how you used to do it when you loved God first and then you loved yourself as a magnificent soul full of beautiful light created in an ancient time. This is the reason that you can create your internal peace and love. The external world will ultimately return all of this to you since it will become like a reflection of your inner world.

The only reason for you to see the difference between people is that individuals are not equally self-conscious. Forgive them because you are not fully self-conscious, either. All differences come exclusively from the consciousness level that people manifest in their lives.

It all depends on the state of mind. The way an individual feels and perceives reality determines his reaction to it and this is how it presents itself to him in the future.

Therefore, you must recognize your responsibility in everything that you meet in life. It is only when you accept the Laws presented in this elaboration and assimilate them that you will be able to anchor yourself in Light. You will become increasingly enlightened.

As you can see, dear reader, you have no choice but to

begin to change yourself and hope that others will follow. It is time for peace and love to come to dwell within you.

The time has come for you to learn to share them because by creatively multiplying your energy and its common use, you can remove a dark zone of evil from the spiritual body of Mother Earth and become truly happy.

I want to say that I ultimately planned on closing this elaboration, „In the Wheel of Life" in three volumes. While I was writing these books, however, I received many questions from readers that indicated that not many people understood the content of the book. Also, many people suggested expanding particular subjects. I wanted to live up to this task so I had to add the fourth volume.

In the fourth volume, I will record the castaway's lives from the moment of doom until now, including chapters about the universal laws, karma, and so on. And so I bid you farewell, dear reader, until next time.

THE END OF THE THIRD VOLUME

HELP

Dear reader, if you are in a situation where you cannot cope you may turn to me and ask me to help at the following address:

IN POLAND:

Wanda Pratnicka
P.O. Box 257
81-963 Gdynia 1 / Poland

IN THE UNITED STATES:

Wanda Pratnicka
46-02 21st Street, PO BOX 1544
Long Island City, NY 11109 / USA

E-mail: info@WandaPratnicka.com
Web: www.WandaPratnicka.com

You may also phone my office at:

Phone in **Poland**: +48 58 555 9815
Fax in Poland: +48 58 550 6812

Phone in the **United States**: 631 402 1254
Phone in the **United Kingdom**: 02032 984727
Please take a look at our website ("Contact") for current phone numbers in the country of your residence.

I will need to have the following information:

    1) Forenames and surname
    2) Date of birth
    3) Place of permanent stay

For the help to be effective I will most often need to have the details of all the people residing in the house/apartment because in the majority of cases the whole family is in need of help.

If you are a public person or for any reason you are unwilling / unable to pass to me your personal data (which I fully under-stand and respect) you still can use my services (checking and cleansing of you and your near ones) without passing to me or to my associates any of your personal information.
That option is certainly making it more difficult for me and I am willing to grant that option only in rare, justified cases and for a higher fee. Please call to receive more information on that matter.

Please note that I am also giving private consultations for problems not connected to the presence of ghosts. Ask my staff to receive more information about that option.

If the subject of this book has aroused your interest then I will be happy to hear your opinion of it.

BOOK ORDERING

You can order this book at the following address:

IN POLAND:

Centrum Publishers
P.O. Box 257
81-963 Gdynia 1 / Poland

IN THE UNITED STATES:

Wanda Pratnicka
46-02 21st Street, PO BOX 1544
Long Island City, NY 11109 / USA

e-mail: info@WandaPratnicka.com
www.WandaPratnicka.com

You may also phone my office at:

Phone in **Poland**: +48 58 555 9815
Fax in Poland: +48 58 550 6812

Phone in the **United States**: 631 402 1254
Phone in the **United Kingdom**: 02032 984727

Please take a look at our website ("Contact") for current phone numbers in the country of your residence.

All books can be ordered from Amazon.com for the US and Amazon.co.uk for the United Kingdom. The books are also available for purchase from Ebay.

WANDA PRATNICKA
*Possessed by Ghosts –
Exorcisms in XXI
century*

This book is
aimed at all readers, not
just those who are
interested in the esoteric
arts. It presents in an
accessible and surpris-
ingly clear way the
causes of the toxic
associations that arise
between people and
ghosts. It contains a
large dose of the psy-

chology of soul. Ghosts are the souls of people who, for various reasons, overlooked their own death, did not have the courage to depart for the other world or were detained, or even dragged from the road, by their dear ones weeping for those souls. When they remain in the world of the living they possess people and this can be the cause of very unfortunate, and sometimes even tragic, experiences. The presence of ghosts within a person causes powerful mood swings from strong negative emotional outbursts to profound depression. They evoke powerful anxiety attacks, persuade those who are possessed to commit suicide, have strong influences on the psyche and are the cause of mental illnesses. Additionally, the physical illnesses of the person who died are very often transferred by the ghost to the person possessed.

The subject of this book could be a panacea for very many of our world's misfortunes. From various states of mental disturbance, deviations, dependencies, severe psychiatric illnesses including those requiring isolation, through to chronic diseases or those that are considered to be incurable.

The question of ghosts also applies to various everyday situations like the demanding behavior of a family member, difficulties with learning, with people close to one, work colleagues or business associates. They often lead to helplessness, loneliness, isolation, or to difficult financial, health and social situations.

What is a frequent cause of various diseases, misfortunes, lesser or greater failures? How can one deal with them, how can one guard against them in the future? That's what this book is about. It is also a reply to the endless questions asked by people turning to Wanda Pratnicka for help. They often believe that the things that have happened to them are unique, they happened only to them. They wonder why they are suffering so much. They think that maybe they did something bad and that now they're being punished. Or maybe it's the work of some curse or black magic.

Possessed by Ghosts is a very exceptional work. Nobody before has described the dependencies that exist between the world of ghosts and that of people in such an extensive, comprehensible and profound way. It allows you to understand the causes of these dependencies and shows how to free yourself from them. It is a guide that leads to a life of peace, satisfaction, enthusiasm and wealth.

It is a handbook for anyone who is pursuing personal and spiritual development. It shows the universal laws that govern our world and is a testament to the author's spiritual maturity.

WANDA PRATNICKA about *Possessed by Ghosts – Exorcisms in XXI century*:

"For many years I really wanted to read a good book about exorcisms, but I never found one. Unfortunately, till now nobody had written one. So I had to do it myself. In it there are answers to questions asked every day by my patients, but also answers to questions I asked myself.

In it, I address those who have tried everything, every method, every remedy to ease their problems or those of their near ones. Unfortunately, none of them worked or if they did work they did so for only a short time. I wrote it also for those who are only at the beginning, they sense that something bad is happening to them or their families, or that not everything is as it should be. I wrote it for those who are healthy and happy, too, those who have nothing wrong with them or their nearest. They are the very ones who could help in many tragedies which are taking place inside their neighbors' homes, or to an unhappy family nearby, or to some hooligan or drug addict in the street where they live. Sometimes one can help simply with a piece of advice about what can be done in a given situation or with the information that something can be done at all.

Usually, the fact is that the person who is possessed is unaware of his or her state. By helping such a person we are really helping ourselves since we no longer hear the fights the other side of the wall, or our neighborhood becomes quieter. In extreme cases we may even prevent a suicide, a rape or even worse. It affects, therefore, not just the individual but most often all of us."

WANDA PRATNICKA
In the Wheel of Life
Volumes I-IV

Wanda Pratnicka presents the Universal Laws ruling our Universe over the span of approximately **two thousand pages** in her new book **consisting of four volumes.** These laws have the same impact on our daily lives as they do on our overarching concepts of spiritual development. The author often raises extremely complicated and deep questions, presenting them in an exceptionally simple way. Her work is easily comprehended by experts in the esoteric field and novices alike. An expert will find the correct way to interpret the studies of the greatest Teachers of humanity, and the beginner will find explanations full of truth, peace, and light concerning all areas of daily life. The book discusses the entire range of what human experiences consist of. It raises questions corresponding to physical space, as well as higher worlds including the etheric, astral, mental, causal, and higher. This work is intended for people interested in spiritual development, as well as people who constantly work on improving their situation, whether it be emotional, material, interpersonal, etc.

Volume I and II contain further explanation of all phenomena mentioned in the author's previous book, *Possessed by Ghosts: Exorcisms in the 21st Century.*

A note from the author regarding **Volumes I-IV** of *In the Wheel of Life*:

"This knowledge will help you discover meaning in your experiences and what the purpose of your life and the lives of those close to you is. You will find out how the distant past influences your present life and what will happen with you when you are separated from your physical body. These are very essential matters because this knowledge has an influence not only on your journey here on Earth, but on the entire range of experiences each human shares while going through the transition commonly known as death of the physical body.

Information contained in this book will allow you to look at life from a completely different perspective, free of fear and the illusions you have accepted as the truth until this point."

WANDA PRATNICKA
In the Wheel
of Life
Volume I

Wanda Pratnicka
about **Volume I:**

In this Volume I would like to present to you, dear reader, Life from a broader perspective and guide you step by step through all its stages. I discuss your soul, illuminate *Who You Are in Essence*, and explain what caused you to come to Earth. Consequently, you will come to understand the goal of your own and other people's lives.

By learning about your energetic bodies, you will come to understand how significant they are not only in this life, but also after the death of the physical body. Then you will come to understand your role here on Earth and you will find it easier to take responsibility for your life.

I explain specific chakras in detail and outline their functions in our daily lives. By learning about each individual chakra, you will realize that each one presents a given situation from a completely different angle.

Furthermore, you will find out how the distant past influences your current life, which will help you look at your life from a new, fearless perspective and free yourself from the illusions that you have accepted as the truth until now. You will also stop postponing your growth for later because you will understand that avoiding taking responsibility for your life will disturb your energy. Consequently, this will manifest in your life as troubles, difficulties, and even tragedies with serious illnesses included. Thanks to the knowledge contained in here, you will recognize what functions in your life incorrectly and why you have certain experiences. As a result you will be able to exchange them for more satisfying ones.

You already know everything I present here in the deepest levels of Your Being. Hence, my role is to only remind you of what you already know.

WANDA PRATNICKA
In the Wheel
of Life
Volume II

Wanda Pratnicka about **Volume II**:
"In Volume II, I present Life from an even broader perspective. I wrote Volume I assuming that you lived on Earth only once. In this book, I describe your Life from the perspective of many incarnations and gently

lead you step-by-step from life here on Earth, through so-called death and all levels of existence that follow, and into the next life in physicality.

Essentially, it will help you realize what we commonly call death is not the end of life, but a transition from one state to another. This will lead you to the conclusion that you never die, you only exchange bodies like clothes, and as a soul you exist eternally.

This knowledge will spontaneously and completely change your view on Life and free you from both fear of death and life. It will also free you from the fear of a dangerous, vengeful, unjust God.

Taking a look at one's own life from the perspective of many lives answers a very essential question about ostensible injustice.

Who knows? Perhaps you will stop blaming God for injustice when you will realize why He, who ultimately is only Love, put people on earth in such extreme diverse conditions.

By accepting this broadened perspective you will come to understand why some people are happy, healthy, beautiful, and wealthy, while others lack everything. People in the latter group struggle greatly every day and deceive themselves into believing that there is no chance for a better future.

You will become convinced that you are not a victim of your life, but your life's creator. This will allow you to take responsibility for your life. The knowledge contained in my book gives you this responsibility, but also the tools to introduce your psyche to changes that will lead to a better, happier, more secure and wealthy life on all fronts. I wish you this from the bottom of my heart."

WANDA PRATNICKA
In the Wheel
of Life
Volume III

Wanda Pratnicka about
Volume III:
In Volume III I describe the existence of the human soul from the perspective of all of Earth's prior civilizations. The book begins with my description of the time that humans came to Earth due to their own free will to join with other souls and create a wonderful, Light civilization.

The main building material of this civilization was True Love and Faith in God. Because of true Love and deep Faith, this civilization worked out the Eternal Higher Laws of Life, which remain in each human being today. This civilization created a great power which became the impetus behind all mental activity. This inborn Divinity was passed over without a slightest change from generation to generation. Peace and complete satisfaction emerged from this great activity of the Higher Mind for millions of years.

Dear reader, looking at Life from this perspective will help you understand what life is truly about, which will allow you to correct your own life. I will narrate each stage of the downfall of this great civilization, which will give you the opportunity to not only recognize own mistakes, but also avoid them in the future.

The Laws of Life that were worked out in the First Civilization are still present in each human being but are almost completely forgotten by most people. The Laws of Life will enable you to free yourself once and for all from compulsive thinking about the lack of Good in which you live in on a daily basis and locate your true being.

You will become convinced that the control that your compulsive, mistaken pretensions have over you is only an illusion. In reality, you have power over them but you don't use it because you don't realize you have it. The knowledge contained in this book will lead you to Power and Wisdom. You cannot be serene, strong, persistent, and secure without them.

WANDA PRATNICKA
Know the Truth
And Be Free

A note from the author:

I am addressing this book to everyone irrespective of race or religion because one day we will all deal with our own or someone else's death. We should adequately prepare for this event, especially when we are sick, elderly or

have someone in our family who is rapidly approaching the transition we call "death". If you have lost a loved one and have been grieving then this book is perfect for you. The wisdom contained here will also help you to heal from past traumatic experiences that followed the passing of loved ones.

Most people fear death. Do you realize that the fear of death is the cause for most, if not all, misfortunes in this world? It is not caused by death itself, but rather from a lack of information on this subject. Therefore, knowledge about death while you are alive is as important as the air that you breathe.

By familiarizing yourself with this text you will stop living your life with constant frustration. If on a deep level of your being you adapt to guidance from this book, you will get rid of your fear of death once and for all. And having rid yourself of this fear you will begin to make different, more conscious choices. Then it's not out of the question that you will become amazingly wise and happy.

From the chapter "Preface":

"Do you realize that the fear of death is the primary cause of most, if not all of our internal adversities? The fear of death is like the interior of a simmering volcano. It is that hidden, constant fear that no amount of money or superficial effort can neutralize. This fear is the essence of all things. It is a fear that emanates not only from death itself, but also from a lack of understanding of this very emotional subject. Traditional media is not making it any easier to understand death. Death is either not shown or, for example in movies and video games it is presented in a banal or unrealistic way.

Therefore most people leave things up to chance, not

knowing how to control their life on Earth as well as after death. When you familiarize yourself with the information introduced in this book you will no longer waste your life. You will begin to make different, more conscious choices. Who knows, maybe you will become amazingly wise and happy. Once and for all you will get rid of your fears and stop living in constant frustration. You will understand that what you fear the most (most often unconsciously) doesn't even exist, because what you call death is just taking off your body in the same way that you take off and throw away the old clothes that you don't need anymore. Meanwhile you, the essence of you, moves forward. Where? Well, to understand this is extraordinarily important because what you know about death, what you think about it during your life and what you expect from it, will determine what you will experience in the future. Therefore, the knowledge you acquire about death in your lifetime is as important as the air that you breathe because your future depends on it. I hope that you will come to understand that everything that happens to you depends only and solely of you. You must take your life into your own hands because nobody else will help you with it.

Nobody can get by in life without the knowledge provided in this book. It is especially important when you are sick, aged or you have someone in your family who is quickly approaching the transition commonly known as "death". If you have lost someone close to you and you are mourning then this book is appropriate for you. This book will explain every tragedy and it will help you heal any wounds in your heart caused by the loss of someone dear to you."

From the chapter "Introduction":

"Dear reader, we are living in times of great change. We should be very happy about this, but many people are constantly worrying about impending doom. It is causing people great, unconscious fear. I took on this task to not only mitigate this fear, but to permanently remove it. It is not possible for us to live with such a burden and function normally. It will negatively affect not only your life, but life in general.

No matter what you are afraid of right now, with this fear there is a fundamental, overarching fear associated with your death and non-existence. You are not even conscious of this fact. This is the reason why many people object to closely looking at this subject. These people are thinking naively deluding themselves into thinking that if they don't touch this subject, death will pass them by. In reality, it is the other way around. Only when you get to know the phenomenon commonly known as "death", when you understand and accept it then you will have a chance that this so-called "death" won't return to haunt you."

Perhaps, like many other people you are afraid to think about death. This is because you know nothing or very little about it. Therefore, you don't understand what happens in the moment of "death" and as a result a great fear paralyses you about this occurrence.

The word "death" should be written in quotes because in reality there is no death. You never die. Only your physical body dies. During so-called "death" you take off your body in the same way you take off old, used, unneeded clothing and you - as the essence of you - still exists, and this is the eternal life. The transformation called death is in reality a movement from one state of consciousness into another one. It is as if you were moving from one classroom to another.

WANDA PRATNICKA is a psychologist M.A., parapsychologist, psychic, spiritual teacher and exorcist. During her 45 years of practice she has helped tens of thousands of people around the world. Her first book *Possessed by Ghosts – Exorcisms in XXI century* became a bestseller in Poland shortly after publication of its first edition. The book was translated to English, German, Spanish, Russian, Japanese and currently other translations are being prepared.

Wanda Pratnicka's next literary work *In the Wheel of Life* consists of four volumes and around 2,000 pages. Her books are aimed to all readers, not just those who are interested in the esoteric arts.

These books present, in an accessible and surprisingly clear way, the universal laws of the Universe, a soul's psychology, deep matters in regards to true human origin and the causes of toxic associations that arise between people and ghosts. Ghosts are the souls of people who, for various reasons, overlooked their own death, did not have the courage to depart for the other world or were detained by their dear ones weeping for those souls. When they remain in the world of the living, they possess people and this can be the cause of very unfortunate and sometimes even tragic experiences. Starting from the mildest symptoms, the presence of ghosts within a person causes powerful mood swings from strong negative emotional outbursts to profound depression. They evoke powerful anxiety attacks, persuade those who are possessed to commit suicide, have strong influence on psyche and are the cause of mental illnesses. Additionally, the physical illnesses of the person who died are often transferred by the ghost to the person possessed.

Wanda Pratnicka's newest book is *Know the Truth and Be Free* which cures such problems as fear of death/life or traumatic experiences that result from loved ones' loss/death.